Fighting Their Own War

Fighting Their Own War

South African Blacks and the First World War

Albert Grundlingh

RAVAN PRESS JOHANNESBURG

Published by Ravan Press (Pty) Ltd
P O Box 31134, Braamfontein,
Johannesburg, 2017
South Africa

First published 1987

ISBN 0 86975 321 5

Cover design: Jeff Lok
Cover photograph: Courtesy of the Cape Archives
Typeset by: Opus 61

Printed by Galvin and Sales, Cape Town

To Mauritz Sr., Mauritz Jr., and Annamari

Contents

Abbreviations

A.G.	Archives of the Adjudant-General
A.P.S.	Aborigines Protection Society Papers
B.L.	Archives of the Magistrate Bethal
C.A.B.	Cabinet Papers (Britain)
C.G.	Archives of the Commandant-General
C.M.T.	Chief Magistrate Transkei
C.N.C.	Chief Native Commissioner (Natal)
C.O.	Colonial Office Records
C.S.O.	Chief Staff Officer
D.C.	Archives of the Secretary for the Department of Defence
1/E.L.N.	Archives of the Magistrate East London
G.G.	Archives of the Governor-General
G.N.L.B.	Government Native Labour Bureau
J.	Archives of the Secretary for the Department of Justice
K.1.	Archives of the Rebellion Losses Commission
1/L.S.M.	Archives of the Magistrate Ladysmith
M.N.I.	Archives of the Secretary for the Department of Mines and Industries
MUN.	Ministry of Munitions
N.A.	Archives of the Secretary for the Department of Native Affairs (Union)
O.C. Records	Archives of the Officer Commanding Records
P.M.	Archives of the Secretary for the Department of the Prime Minister
P.V.M.	Archives of the Provost Marshal
S.	Archives of the Secretary to the Government (Basutoland)
S.A.N.L.C.	South African Native Labour Contingent

S.A.N.N.C.	South African Native National Congress
S.A.P.	Archives of the South African Police
S.C.	Select Committee
S.N.A.	Archives of the Secretary for Native Affairs (Natal)
1/T.B.U.	Archives of the Magistrate Tabankulu
1/U.T.A.	Archives of the Magistrate Umtata
U.G.	Union Government
U.W.H.	Union War Histories
T.	Board of Trade Records
W.W.I. 1914/1918	W.W.I. 1914/1918 Group
W.W.I. G.S.W.A.	W.W.I. German South West Africa Group, 1914/1918
W.W.I. I.S.D.	W.W.I. Imperial Service Details, 1914/1918
W.O.	War Office Records

Preface

This book deals with the impact of the First World War on South African blacks. It analyzes their responses to and participation in the war, and also evaluates the wider ramifications of the war as these affected black people in South Africa.

The problem of terminology is and will probably remain a vexed issue in South African society. Although it has become common practice in recent works to use 'blacks' as a collective term for Africans, Indians and 'coloureds', in this study the term 'black' is used interchangeably with 'African' to indicate a specific population group. It does not, however, imply some kind of 'intellectual apartheid', or that race is the only or overriding factor in social relations.

The book is based on a D.Litt et Phil. thesis submitted in Afrikaans in December 1981 to the University of South Africa under the title, 'Die Suid-Afrikaanse Gekleurdes en die Eerste Wêreldoorlog'. The thesis included 'coloureds' and Indians, but to cut back on publication costs and also to sharpen the focus of the work, these 'groups' are not discussed here. The multi-faceted experience of 'coloureds' and Indians during the war will hopefully form the subject of a future article. The topic is further confined to blacks of the Union of South Africa, and there are only occasional references to recruits from the High Commission territories of the time.

In translating and preparing the relevant aspects of the thesis for publication, I have found it necessary to revise and condense the original text substantially, and at times to include new material. The book therefore differs from the thesis not only in language, but also in manner of presentation.

A number of institutions and individuals assisted me in the course of this work. The staffs of the various libraries and archival depots were unfailingly helpful during my period of research. Prof. S.B. Spies acted as supervisor for the original thesis and I benefited not only from his incisive and constructive criticism, but also from his on-going interest in this project. I am also indebted to Maurice Boucher, Jane Carruthers, Greg Cuthbertson, Bob Edgar, Louis Grundlingh, Peter Warwick and Brian Willan for the assistance they have given and the professional interest they have shown. In particular, I am grateful to my friend and colleague Peter Colenbrander, who willingly and cheerfully checked translations and made many penetrating suggestions on points of style and substance. I was, moreover, privileged in having the support and encouragement of Mauritz and Beatie Grundlingh.

My greatest debt is to my wife, Annamari, who, with remarkable resilience, coped with this book, her own work and our children. In many ways she made it possible for me to complete a task that stretched over several years.

Albert Grundlingh
Pretoria
July 1985

Introduction

The transformation of South African historiography over the past fifteen years has opened up several new and interrelated fields of enquiry. Invaluable work has been done on, *inter alia*, the South African political economy, marginalized groups in society, working class organizations and culture, gender and, to a slightly lesser extent, the nature of rural change and changing social relationships in the countryside. However, war-related processes and military affairs in general have been largely by-passed. With a few notable exceptions,[1] military scholarship, whether in history or in other disciplines, is still firmly in the hands of narrow traditionalists.

In view of the increasingly pervasive influence of the military in contemporary South Africa and the mounting concern of those in the broadly defined extra-parliamentary 'progressive democratic' movement over the role of the military in society, it is perhaps somewhat surprising that 'revisionist' scholarship has yet to move into this field. On the one hand, military matters and wars as such, as opposed to their causes, are probably considered an inappropriate context for the examination of those larger issues of race and class, social structure, consciousness and capitalism which have come to constitute the general areas of historical investigation. It is, however, instructive to note the remarks of E.J. Hobsbawm on the various dimensions of violent upheavals:

> I think the profitability of the studies of social conflict requires more careful assessment . . . . That they always dramatize crucial aspects of social structure because they are here strained to the breaking point is not in doubt. Moreover, certain problems cannot be studied at all except in and through such moments of eruption, which do not merely bring into the open so much that is normally latent, but also concentrate and magnify phenomena for the benefit of the student, while — not the

least of their advantages — normally multiplying our documentation about them.[2]

Although this study does not claim to have demonstrated these dicta fully in the South African context, it is an underlying assumption in this work that wars and certain aspects of military affairs are useful for refracting pertinent socio-political issues and for assessing a wide range of important historical experiences.

Fighting Their Own War does not purport to be a 'history from below', but to some extent my understanding of aspects of the subject has been enhanced by recent analyzes in South African historiography of the way in which 'ordinary' individuals and groups experience social reality.[3] Those familiar with the advances in the writing of social history in South Africa will recognize my indebtedness to some of the ideas emanating from scholars engaged in reconstructing the lives and experiences of 'ordinary' people.

I have also benefited from the growing Anglo-American and European literature in what is generally termed 'war and society' studies. This development is largely a reaction against the 'drum and trumpet' school of military history, a field of enquiry that may be valid in its own right, but one that often degenerates into a discussion of uniforms and badges and seldom rises above campaigns and battles — the major weakness being an inclination to divorce the fighting side of war from its socio-economic and political context. Practitioners in the field of 'war and society' therefore seek to place warfare in its total historical milieu and they share a common interest in war as an agent of social change and in the socio-political repercussions of military service.[4]

In comparison with the position in Britain, America and Europe, the historiography of 'war and society' in Africa is relatively underdeveloped. Although the subject has not necessarily been neglected in African historiography, certain deficiencies remain. The full complexities of specifically war-related change as opposed to mere change over time have only been partially unravelled, and the uneven regional impact of two World Wars still awaits detailed comparative treatment. More specifically, the quality of analyzes regarding the nature, degree and implications of wartime political and socio-economic change has yet to reach the standard attained by the best works in the European and Anglo-American field. However, the outlook is not completely bleak and there are firm indications that the 'ideas about war and society that are familiar to European history are now being moved south into Africa'.[5]

Turning to South Africa, it is not too great an exaggeration to say that until fairly recently much of the historical work on wars has been done by scholars so enveloped in the smoke of the battlefield that they could hardly see beyond battle tactics, weaponry and the number of dead and wounded. But lately, in for example certain studies on the Anglo-Boer War of 1899-1902 — the largest conflict on South African soil and one that has consistently attracted scholarly attention — there has been an encouraging shift. In the important publications of S.B. Spies and Peter Warwick as well as in the innovative interpretations of W.R. Nasson, some of the wider effects of the war on various social groups involved have been systematically analyzed.[6] While certain advances have been registered in the studies of the Anglo-Boer War, the same cannot be said of South Africa's involvement in the First World War. In fact, scholars have served the topic rather poorly. For necessary background to the war period one is dependent on general, though stimulating, overviews by S.E. Katzenellenbogen and N.G. Garson.[7] Given the lack of interest in South Africa and the First World War, it is not surprising to find that black participation on various fronts has passed almost unnoticed. Except for a pioneering and suggestive article by Brian Willan on the South African Native Labour Contingent which served in France,[8] little is known about the involvement of the black South African majority in World War I, and even less about their responses to that cataclysmic global conflict.

Broadly speaking, the object of this book is to provide some insights into the African experience of the war, and to evaluate the general consequences of the war as they impinged on the lives of blacks. More specifically, the focus is on the following aspects: the wider ramifications of the war as they affected the political perceptions and expectations of different African groupings; the issues surrounding the possibility of black participation in the war; various dimensions of the recruitment campaign to draw blacks into the war effort; the nature of military service; the effect of wartime service on the socio-political consciousness of the participants as well as the related questions of whether veterans acted as catalysts for resistance on their return to the Union; and finally the broad implications of war-related socio-economic change for certain sections of the African population. Apart from its possible intrinsic interest, this study hopes to be more than a mere 'discovery' of black men in a 'white man's war'. During the period of the First World War Africans continued their struggle against domination and oppression on several levels — in essence they fought a war within a war. Within the framework outlined above, I attempt to provide perspectives on some of the hitherto neglected areas in which they exerted themselves, the tactics they employed, the impact they had and the different ways in which the struggle was sometimes perceived by the leaders and rank-and-file. In short, I hope that aspects of this analysis have been informed by an awareness of the manner in which Africans have actively tried to shape the social and political reality in and outside the military environment.

The participation of groups other than whites in colonial warfare is a recurring theme in South African history. Since the early days of white settlement at the Cape, burgher commandos regularly employed Khoikhoi against the San and in 1795 Khoikhoi (and 'coloureds') were also active in the fruitless attempts to defend the Cape against the British. This trend continued and a marked feature of the numerous 19th century frontier wars (or wars of dispossession) was the military assistance rendered by 'coloureds' and also, in certain instances, by Africans drawn into alliances with Boer or British forces.[9] Despite the widespread use of Africans in combatant and non-combatant capacities, there was a constant undercurrent of uneasiness amongst the colonists that such a policy might perhaps boomerang and in various ways jeopardize their position. During the late nineteenth century arguments against the use of blacks in warfare (particularly against whites) became more pervasive. In part this can be attributed to more pronounced racial stereotyping under the influence of contemporary Social Darwinist notions in terms of which blacks were perceived as being by nature excessively brutal, especially in battle, and partly also to the changing nature of social relations in the wake of the mining revolution. Peter Warwick argued in this respect that

> unless blacks were excluded from military operations, it was feared that peasants and workers would rise against their landlords and employers on the pretext of supporting a rival white group. In a region ever more dominated by the demands of mining capital, the patterns of social relations in late-nineteenth century South Africa determined that participation of black people in wars was something to be avoided at all costs if the process of social change and evolving structures of social control were not to be threatened.[10]

During the Anglo-Boer War blacks were extensively employed in non-combatant capacities by British and Boer alike, but there was a tacit understanding that it would be preferable not to arm blacks. However, military exigencies dictated otherwise. At various stages of the campaign the British had at least 10 000 and perhaps as many as 30 000 armed Africans in their service, while there are indications that the Boers also armed Africans, though in far smaller numbers.[11] Although both camps drew armed blacks into the conflict, the wisdom of such a policy again came under question in the post Anglo-Boer War period, and during World War I white reservations on the issue were to exercise a powerful influence on the nature of black participation.[12]

There were also a number of other considerations between 1902 and 1914 that had a distinct bearing on the black experience during the First World War. The outcome of the Anglo-Boer War had paved the way for the formation of a modern capitalist South African state and had set in motion a train of events that led to the political unification of the four colonies in 1910. The establishment of a unified parliamentary democracy for whites meshed smoothly with the interests of evolving capitalism, inasmuch as it provided 'the locus of resolution for the competing and disunited ruling classes in capitalism' and ultimately promoted ruling class hegemony.[13] Though few participants, black or white, perceived the drift of events between 1902 and 1910 in structural terms,[14] some blacks were fully aware that the tide was running against them. Members of the educated elite — teachers, ministers of religion, lawyers, journalists, clerks and small-time businessmen — had sought inclusion in the new state, and were sadly disillusioned by the post Anglo-Boer War settlement. While they had hoped to benefit from a British victory, the terms of the Peace of Vereeniging and the calculated indifference of the subsequent British administration, not to mention the intensification of certain aspects of legal discrimination, dispelled any such optimism. This in turn led to an upsurge in formal political activity and various African organizations mushroomed during the reconstruction period in the often vain hope that they would be able to influence official decision-making.

A major blow was the constitution of the Union of South Africa. While certain Africans in the Cape continued to enjoy the qualified franchise, they were denied the right to sit in parliament. Their counterparts in the other ex-colonies fared even worse, remaining voteless and, in terms of formal political process, powerless. This development proved to be a further potent stimulus in promoting not only African political organization but also unity, for the myriad of fledgling associations scattered across the country now started to cooperate formally at an inter-colonial level. A manifestation of this new political activity was the deputation sent to Britain in 1909 to protest, albeit in vain, against the colour bar in the draft Union constitution. But of far greater and more enduring significance were the moves which led to the formation of a national body, the South African Native National Congress (SANNC), in 1912 to protect African interests.[15] The founding of the SANNC two years before the advent of the First World War meant that, at a formal level at least, African political opinion was consolidated. There was now one national body which could, within limits, exert itself on behalf of Africans in the subsequent tumultuous years. As will be shown, however, Congress represented only one strand of African opinion; outside the organized body of black politics there existed a whole gamut of often divergent viewpoints.

Immediately prior to the war, African political consciousness was also shaped by the momentous implications of the 1913 Natives Land Act. The act, which prompted a Congress deputation to Britain, restricted black ownership of land to a woefully inadequate 7.3 per cent of the total area of the Union, while the anti-squatting measures contained in the legislation caused, particularly in the Free State, great hardships amid the eviction of black sharecroppers and other tenants from white farms. This act can be seen as a full-scale attack on the peasantry, designed to turn independent and semi-independent producers into wage labourers.[16] During the war years the ramifications of this legislation were very much in evidence: on account of the Land Act blacks were dissuaded from supporting the Union government's war effort and, at a different level, the act continued to form the legal basis of the uneven struggle between landlord and tenant in the 'white' countryside during increased wartime agricultural capitalization.[17] But legal restrictions on access to land were not the only source of African unrest. Indeed, in the immediate pre-war years there was a considerable ferment of protest activity. In the years 1912-1914, the black women of Winburg and Bloemfontein launched their celebrated anti-pass campaign, a large-scale African strike occurred on the Jagersfontein diamond mines, and the well-known Indian passive resistance movement was successfully launched.[18] The Union government also feared possible industrial action by blacks on the Witwatersrand gold mines. It appointed a commission during this period to investigate 'native grievances' and, of greater importance, 'to inquire into the control capable of being exercised over natives housed in compounds' and to suggest effective ways of coping with industrial 'disturbances'.[19] However, there was neither African unrest nor strike action in progress when European hostilities broke out in August 1914. Had it been otherwise, it would almost certainly have complicated South Africa's entry into the war.

While South Africa as a British dominion technically could not remain neutral and was therefore automatically at war with Germany once the British ultimatum had expired on 4 August, the Union had the right to decide on the extent to which it was prepared to render active support to the Imperial war effort. The government was faced with this decision three days after the declaration of war. On 7 August Britain approached South Africa to invade German South-West Africa, to occupy Swakopmund and Luderitzbucht and to take over the German radio stations in the interior. The South African parliament was not in session at the time, but after initial differences of opinion in the cabinet, the Union government informed Britain on 10 August of its willingness to accede to the request. A month later at a special session of both houses of parliament the decision was confirmed by 92 votes to 12 in the Assembly and by 24 votes in the Senate. Various factors informed Botha's decision to invade German South-West Africa, perhaps the most important of which was the prospect of including the territory in the Union, though this was never openly acknowledged.[20]

Blacks, of course, had no say in the decision to enter the war, but this did not in any way imply that they failed to react to the world crisis. Indeed, the outbreak of the war was the occasion for a variety of responses to emerge, and blacks also featured prominently in the consciousness of many whites.

Notes

 1. Two recent publications have dealt with current developments in the South African armed forces: P.H. Frankel *Pretoria's Praetorians: Civil-military Relations in South Africa* (1983) and K.W. Grundy *Soldiers Without Politics: Blacks in the South African Armed Forces* (1982). It should be noted though, that the title of Grundy's publication is a misnomer. It is difficult to see how blacks currently in the South African

armed forces can be described as 'soldiers without politics'; all but the most conservative black organizations in present-day South Africa would without hesitation describe their involvement as the 'politics of collaboration'. Grundy also concentrates mainly on official policies towards blacks in the military and the police, and provides only occasional insights into the motives and experiences of the men themselves.

2. E.J. Hobsbawm, 'From social history to the history of society' in F. Gilbert and S.R. Graubard (eds.), *Historical Studies Today*, p.20.

3. For a discussion of some of the literature and the problems involved in writing the history of 'ordinary people' see B. Bozzoli, 'Class, community and ideology in the evolution of South African society' in B. Bozzoli (ed.), *Class, Community and Conflict* (1987), pp.1-43.

4. See for instance, M.R.D. Foot (ed.), *War and Society* (1973); A. Marwick, *War and Social Change in the Twentieth Century: A Comparative Study of Britain, France, Germany, Russia and the United States* (1974); A. Marwick, *Women at War, 1914-1918* (1977); M.A. Nettleship, R.D. Givens and A. Nettleship (eds.), *War, Its Causes and Correlates* (1975); R.F. Weigley (ed.), *New Dimensions in Military History* (1975); B. Bond and I. Roy (eds.), *War and Society*, I and II (1975 and 1977); M. Howard, *War in European History* (1976); C.H. Enloe, *Ethnic Soldiers: State Security in Divided Societies* (1980); V.G. Kiernan, *European Empires from Conquest to Collapse, 1815-1960* (1982).

5. D. Killingray, 'War and society in British colonial Africa: themes and prospects' in D.I. Ray, P. Shinnie and D. Williams (eds.), *Into the 80s: The Proceedings of the Eleventh Annual Conference of the Canadian Association of African Studies*, I, p.251. B.A. Ogot tentatively raised some of the issues in 1974 (B.A. Ogot (ed.), *War and Society in Africa*), while two conferences held at London University (one in 1977 on Africa and the First World War and one in 1984 on Africa and the Second World War) have done much to stimulate scholarly interest. Some of the papers delivered at the 1977 conference were published in the *Journal of African History*, XIX, 1, 1978, and the topic has also filtered through to 'popular' and more general historical journals as is evident from M. Crowder's recent article, 'The impact of two World Wars on Africa' in *History Today*, 34, January 1984.

6. S.B. Spies, *Methods of Barbarism? Roberts and Kitchener and Civilians in the Boer Republics, January 1900 to May 1902* (1977); P. Warwick and S.B. Spies (eds.), *The South African War, 1899-1902* (1980); P. Warwick, *Black People and the South African War, 1899-1902* (1983); W.R. Nasson, 'Doing down their masters: Africans, Boers and treason in the Cape Colony, 1899-1902' in *Journal of Imperial and Commonwealth History*, 12, 1, 1983; W.R. Nasson, 'Moving Lord Kitchener:

black military transport and supply work in the South African War, 1899-1902, with particular reference to the Cape Colony' in *Journal of Southern African Studies*, 11, 1, October 1984.

7. S.E. Katzenellenbogen, 'Southern Africa and the war of 1914-1918' in Foot (ed.), *War and Society* (1973), pp.107-121; N.G. Garson, 'South Africa and World War I' in *Journal of Imperial and Commonwealth History*, VIII, 1, 1979, pp.68-85.

8. B.P. Willan, 'The South African Native Labour Contingent, 1916-1918' in *Journal of African History*, XIX, 1, 1978, pp.61-86. In publications which appeared soon after the war the topic was dealt with dismissively. See for example, A.B. Keith, *War Government of the British Dominions* (1921); C. Lucas (ed.), *The Empire at War*, IV, *Africa* (1924); *Official History: Union of South Africa and the Great War* (1924). It does, however, merit more attention in S.C. Buxton, *General Louis Botha* (1924) while S.T. Plaatje's *Native Life in South Africa* (1916) contains some useful insights into the early war period as such. In a different category and of particular value were the recollections of an African who had served in France, published in 1975: J. and C. Perry (eds.), *A Chief Is a Chief by the People: The Autobiography of Stimela Jason Jingoes*.

9. Warwick, *Black People and the South African War*, pp.10-14.

10. *Ibid.*, pp.14-15.

11. *Ibid.*, pp.4-5, 25-26.

12. See Chapter 2.

13. D.E. Kaplan, 'The South African state: the origins of a racially exclusive democracy' in *The Insurgent Sociologist*, X, 2, Fall 1980.

14. See, however, A.K. Soga's interpretation in A. Odendaal, *Vukani Bantu! The Beginnings of Black Protest Politics in South Africa to 1912*, pp.68-69.

15. Odendaal, *Beginnings of Black Protest Politics*, pp.288-289.

16. C. Bundy, *The Rise and Fall of the South African Peasantry*, p.242.

17. See Chapters 3 and 6.

18. J. Simons and R. Simons, *Class and Colour in South Africa, 1850-1950*, pp.136, 168.

19. U.G. 37-14, *Report of the Native Grievances Inquiry, 1913-1914*, p.1.

20. S.B. Spies, 'The outbreak of the First World War and the Botha government' in *South African Historical Journal*, 1, 1969, pp.47-57.

CHAPTER 1

Assessing New Possibilities:
Black Responses to the Outbreak of
War and Afrikaner Discord

This chapter deals briefly with the alarmist way in which blacks were perceived by many whites in August and September 1914, before considering actual African responses to the outbreak of war and to the unrest which arose amongst a section of the Afrikaners following the government's decision to invade South-West Africa.

In parliament National Party members were virtually unanimous that participation in the war would weaken the dominant position of whites and present blacks with an ideal opportunity of forcefully challenging the *status quo*. Amongst others, P.G.W. Grobler, member for Rustenburg, voiced this concern when he asked: 'What would be the position if the able-bodied men went to war and a native rising took place?'[1] The National Party, of course, also had other reasons for opposing South Africa's entry into the war and it may be argued that they only adopted this line to strengthen their case. However, it is significant that even within Botha's cabinet similar fears were expressed. F.S. Malan, Minister of Mining, Industry and Education, initially maintained that besides other considerations, the Union would require the full extent of its military power to defend the whites against possible black insurrections.[2]

Outside of parliament a persistent and pervasive atmosphere of apprehension and insecurity amongst both Afrikaans and English speakers is even more starkly recognizable. As far as Afrikaans speakers were concerned, these fears are best reflected in the misgivings of a Boer woman from the Marico district in the Transvaal. 'Our defence force is being sent to GSWA', she wrote, 'and here we sit amongst all the black people . . . . Already the servant girls are talking amongst themselves, saying that the kaffirs are only waiting till the majority of menfolk are away from the farms and then they would use the opportunity'.[3] Such views were echoed by Afrikaans speakers throughout large parts of South Africa; from Senekal, Ficksburg and Ladybrand in the Free State to Barkly East, Klipplaat and Postmastburg in the Cape Province. Some English speakers in Johannesburg and Port Elizabeth were similarly concerned, whilst in Natal, where the white population was outnumbered ten to one, fears that 'the natives will use the opportunity to rise and murder the whites in their houses' were particularly pronounced.[4] White perceptions in this respect were based on what they considered to be historical precedents: thus Afrikaans speakers referred to attacks by blacks on Boer commandos during the Anglo-Boer War of 1899 to 1902, and English speakers turned to the Bambatha rebellion of 1906 in Natal to justify their apprehensions.[5]

Although blacks, as will be indicated later in this chapter, were not completely quiescent at the outbreak of war, fears of black conspiracies 'to drive the whites into the sea'[6] were grossly exaggerated and gained greater currency through persistent rumour. 'Of course', J.C. Smuts as Minister of Defence remarked, 'one hears a good many rumours but in times like the present one was always bound to hear rumours [to] which one could not attach too much attention.'[7] Rumours are common in times of war and stress when, as one sociologist has noted, they can serve the social function 'of maintaining patterns that are important to the stability and cohesion of society'.[8] For whites, despite the differences between Afrikaans and English speakers on South Africa's participation in the war, it was perhaps a socio-psychological way of emphasizing those patterns and mentally preserving the established order as far as blacks were concerned. Indeed, some blacks realized that the rumours about their alleged conduct were directly related to white antagonisms and prejudices. 'The white men often say there will be native risings. It is because of their consciences and the sin in the hearts of whites', S.M. Makgatho of the Transvaal Native Congress observed.[9] Certain blacks also resented being made the focal point of white insecurity and publicly protested against the 'unfair and unjustifiable action on the part of the Europeans always to invoke "native unrest" whenever there are disturbances amongst themselves'.[10]

Although the Union government was not unduly concerned about the possibility of an African uprising at the outbreak of war, it nevertheless sought to monitor and influence African reactions where possible. In a confidential circular to all the officials of the Native Affairs Department, magistrates and district commandants of the South African Police, Botha emphasized the importance of keeping blacks 'peaceful'. These officials were instructed to move about 'among the people' and to notify the government immediately of 'any untoward occurrences'.

A perfunctory attempt was also made to soften the blow of the 1913 Land Act by a belated directive that, where legally possible, farmers should refrain from evicting Africans from their farms. Furthermore, numerous posters and handbills were printed for distribution amongst the African population, informing them that any movement of South African soldiers which they might witness was only to protect the interests of blacks and whites alike. This was obviously intended to counteract possible African expectations that white influence in the country was being diminished by the withdrawal of troops. In addition, Africans were urged to believe only in 'true government messages' and to discount any 'untruthful reports' which might cause 'unrest in their minds'.[11]

It is difficult to assess the overall effect of these measures on African perceptions at the outbreak of war, but at least some prominent members of the educated black elite welcomed these initiatives. J.L. Dube, president of the SANNC, interpreted it as a hopeful sign that the government was concerned about the welfare of the African population and that Africans were regarded as sufficiently important to be taken into its confidence. He commented:

> The native mind has been composed at a juncture when it might be particularly susceptible to vague alarms, but the black population has received the assurance of the Government's readiness to afford every information as to events, and to take natives into their confidence regarding any measures affecting them . . . . Perhaps a good deal of trouble might have been averted in the past if such measures had been more systematically adopted, since it has always been the complaint of the intelligent natives that they have been kept in the dark on subjects of national concern: but the Government are now carrying out a less reticent policy . . . .[12]

However, other educated Africans had their reservations. With a vague sense of uneasiness an anonymous African newspaper correspondent from Natal questioned the government's motives. 'It is not often that the Government takes the trouble to give the Natives general news about what is taking place,' he wrote. 'The natives naturally ask, why this . . . time?'[13]

As an indication of the more general response of the educated black elite at the outbreak of war, the position adopted by the SANNC is of particular interest. The SANNC was in session in Bloemfontein when the news was conveyed that hostilities had broken out in Europe.

Congress immediately affirmed its loyalty to King and Empire, pledging to suspend all public criticism of the Union government and to desist from agitation in connection with the 1913 Land Act. A delegation further assured the authorities of African support for the duration of the conflict.[14] This policy, as well as the outbreak of war itself, meant of course that the work of the deputation in Britain protesting against the 1913 Land Act was terminated. Although it was abundantly clear even before August 1914 that the British government was not prepared to pressurize the Union cabinet, the belief nevertheless persisted amongst certain SANNC members that the deputation 'might have had a real effect had not the First World War been declared in the midst of that agitation'.[15] Besides the obviously wishful element in this claim, it can also be viewed as an indication that at that particular time members of the SANNC were in their own minds still hopeful that Britain would not completely abandon African interests in South Africa. This in turn contributed to their loyalist stance at the outbreak of the war.

However, there was some dissension on this important issue. J.T. Gumede, a more militant member of Congress, considered it essential to keep up criticism of the South African government despite the war. He argued in March 1915 that such a policy would be more beneficial to African interests 'than the present attitude of folding their hands in idle talk of the war, which they have no right to claim as theirs . . . .'[16] Later, Congress's policy was subjected to even more scathing comment. For Albert Nzula, writing in 1933 as a member of the South African Communist Party, the decision of Congress to remain loyal during the war was the 'first act of betrayal' by the 'chiefs and petit bourgeois native good boys' which weakened the 'liberationist struggles of the native people'.[17]

The argument advanced by Gumede and, particularly, Nzula illustrates the precarious position of a middle-class constitutionalist body like the SANNC. Since it operated through constitutional channels, it was ultimately dependent on official goodwill and could hardly have afforded to alienate the authorities on such a major issue as the war. It would be wrong, however, to construe this loyalist response and cooperative stance simply as an indication of passive acceptance of a subservient position. Given their limited range of options to bring about constitutional change, the SANNC leaders regarded loyalty during the war as an additional method to be utilized in the unequal struggle. In identifying themselves with the white ruling class in a common cause and openly proclaiming a common allegiance to the

British crown, they expected in due course to be rewarded for their loyalty. They also hoped that such an attitude might enable them to pressurize the authorities into granting meaningful recognition. In this respect they were given a degree of assurance by the government. F.S. Malan, acting as Minister of Native Affairs at the time, approvingly told a delegation from Congress in October 1914 that they had taken a 'very wise step' at the outbreak of war 'which would be likely to impress Parliament to consider their cause sympathetically'.[18] Moreover, they had implicit trust in the ability of the British government to effect favourable change. This clearly influenced their view that an event as catclysmic as the First World War would change the nature of the Empire with corresponding benefits accruing to the African population.[19] The African elite, as Dube explained later, 'were not loyal because their treatment was good in South Africa, but because they wanted to show that they were loyal and that they were deserving of fair and just treatment'.[20]

While the position adopted by the black elite was undoubtedly valid in their own terms, the efficacy of their strategy remains a debatable point. It is clear that other alternatives were given no or little consideration and it can be argued that their stance was based on hope rather than realities. Throughout the war years they did not really try to broaden their constituency to include the growing numbers of urban workers, or through more decisive action attempt to challenge the state in sensitive areas at a time when the government was perhaps more vulnerable than otherwise. They did, it is true, give half-hearted support to strike action on the Rand in late 1918 and the immediate post-war period,[21] but other than that they did not try to secure substantial gains during the crucial war years. According to Dube the African elite was 'far too loyal to England to entertain for one moment the idea of active resistance to the laws of this country'.[22]

The African elite also came under the spell of British war propaganda which claimed that Britain was fighting on behalf of the oppressed and weak (Belgium) as well as for the protection of democratic ideals like personal freedom and equality. Members of the SANNC were quick to equate this with their own position in South Africa and to express the hope that once the freedom of Europe had been guaranteed, Britain would also demand an alleviation of the plight of Africans in the Union.[23] War propaganda, however, is seldom translated into reality and moreover the propaganda during the war was intended for a European and not an African audience.

In another respect, though, the black elite drew some more meaningful conclusions from the European conflagration. In considering the devastation wrought by the war, they became more critical of the assumed cultural and moral superiority of the whites, often invoked by the rulers in South Africa to justify white dominance. The outbreak of the war brought into sharp relief the weaknesses of the much vaunted white civilization and culture, and its credibility as a model to which every educated African should aspire became somewhat tarnished. D.D.T. Jabavu, son of the well known newspaper editor, Tengo Jabavu, later pointed out that 'the Bantu were taken by surprise that the European nations who led in education and Christianity should find no other means than the sword and accumulated destructive weapons to settle their diplomatic differences'.[24] While it would be wrong to regard educated blacks as being in awe of white civilization, the outbreak of the war did emphasize the white man's fallibility and the hope was expressed amongst the elite that 'perhaps, when the war is over there will be less boasting of the supposed civilization that lays so great a burden on the people'.[25]

Black reactions to the outbreak of war must not only be guaged in terms of the overwhelming loyalist rhetoric from the educated elite. They were a small fraction of black society and their views did not necessarily reflect opinions and perceptions of the majority of illiterate and semi-literate blacks. In addition, as has been demonstrated for the rest of Africa during the First World War, the relative passivity of the educated black elite during the war often concealed the 'ferment in the rest of society'.[26] It is therefore essential to explore the way in which other African social groupings in South Africa responded to the outbreak of war.

In contrast with the loyal response of the educated elite, dissenting views were expressed by the African working class on the Witwatersrand gold mines. They were quick to draw their own conclusions from the European struggle and relate them to their experiences as an exploited labour force on the mines. Britain was associated with the oppressive system in which they found themselves and therefore Germany was seen as worthy of their sympathies. On the Nourse mines L. Ralitane informed his fellow labourers that 'the Germans are beating the English, and you boys are foolish to work for the English when the Germans are giving them a hiding'. Ralitane's 'inflammatory' views earned him the option of a £25 fine or six months' imprisonment.[27]

Another labourer expressed his animosity even more trenchantly. 'God be with Germany and clear out all Englishmen on earth,' was his fervent wish. 'Indeed', he continued, 'if the German came out in South A.[frica] we shall be glad if we can help them too.'[28] Moreover, some mineworkers also perceived that the war held out opportunities for resistance against the repressive system in which they found themselves. The chief compound manager at the Crown mines reported in September 1914:

> I notice a great change the last weeks in the attitude of the natives towards Europeans, the natives being very cheeky and insubordinate. They appear . . . to have the idea that the Government are in difficulties owing to the war and are in consequence weak and frightened of the natives . . . .[29]

Occasionally such perceptions also contributed to explicit acts of resistance on the mines. On the Geduld mine, for example, black mineworkers withdrew their labour, or deserted as the management viewed it, at a rate of 60 men per week during October 1914. A subsequent investigation revealed that these actions were inspired by rumours that South Africa's war involvement had weakened the white man's hold over Africans and thus presented mineworkers with a chance of escaping from a hostile environment.[30]

Outside the Witwatersrand, in gold-mining areas like Pilgrim's Rest, the attitudes of black mineworkers towards the war were likewise being shaped by the harshness of their daily experiences. From Pilgrim's Rest 'extreme dissatisfaction amongst the natives' was reported, 'due to the treatment meted out to them over a period of many years by the Transvaal Gold Mining Estates Ltd.' As a result, the report continued, 'the sympathies did not seem very much against the idea of the British regime being deposed (a feeling which is shared by many natives who have suffered at the hands of the Transvaal Gold Mining Estates Ltd.).'[31] Clearly, the attitude of these mineworkers was a far cry from the stereotype that Africans generally favoured and supported Britain at the outbreak of the war.

Amongst other categories of workers, too, the outbreak of war was perceived as an appropriate occasion to voice anti-white sentiments and to demonstrate the lack of black support for the war effort. In response to the government's circular that Africans should be loyal during the war, an anonymous manual labourer from Johannesburg wrote: 'We are no friends of the whites. When you the whites are in a fix you begin to recognise us as your friends . . . . The war is not ours but yours.' He regarded it as preposterous that the whites, who always treated the

Africans 'more or less like dogs' should suddenly in a time of crisis be concerned about black friendship.[32] Some black male domestics, the so-called 'houseboys' in colonial parlance, harboured similar feelings. They pinned their hopes on British defeats 'all along the line', which they argued would mean an increasing number of white men leaving Johannesburg for the front and a corresponding weakening of white control over African lives.[33] At a later stage, Ben Machumela, a waiter in Rosebank, interpreted the war in even more drastic terms. In April 1917 he declared unequivocally: 'If we rise against the white people now we shall triumph over them, because the Germans too are drowning them in the water.'[34] The fact that such an interpretation of war-time occurrences was obviously mistaken is of little importance; of greater significance is the way in which these black workers perceived and experienced such events.

To some of them, the outbreak of war raised hopes of imminent social change and a better dispensation. This expectation they shared with the black elite, but their reasons and premises for doing so differed fundamentally from those of the elite. Whereas the strategy of the elite was based on a demonstration of loyalty and an alignment with the ruling classes in the hope that such an approach would yield beneficial results, the response of some workers revolved to a far greater extent around the way in which they perceived the outbreak of war to have altered the balance of power between black and white and the possibilities this offered for greater resistance. At the outbreak of war at least some workers were infused with a sense of urgency and opportunity, whilst the elite were complacently sure that through patience and cooperation events would ultimately turn in their favour.

A more militant pattern of response was not confined to the largely urban proletariat. In rural Natal, for example, there were peasants who viewed the war as a source of new opportunities to be exploited. The war-time predicament of Britain and South Africa meant little to them: they were more concerned about ways in which the war could possibly alleviate their own plight. Decidely pro-German sympathies surfaced rapidly. Some peasants associated the British with the white colonization of Natal; if Britain could be defeated, it was argued, their position might also change. From their perspective any change in the *status quo* was regarded as preferable to the existing dispensation. In the Harding district, for instance, it was a 'current topic of conversation . . . that a German force is coming here and the consensus of opinion is that the natives should assist them to fight the English . . . .

It is said that if the natives help the Germans to kill the English, they will give natives back the land.'[35] Likewise, in the Umzinto district 'it was common talk at beer drinking parties that the Germans were to land and that they would restore to them the Natives the lands the English had taken from them, and for this reason the natives . . . should assist the Germans . . . .'[36] Furthermore, an elderly Zulu in Durban was quite explicit that the Germans were 'fighting for the right, because the Germans say that the English are taking all the native places away. It is true what the Germans say . . . because our place has been robbed by the English people.'[37] Clearly, there was a groundswell of opinion that dispels any notion of absolute docility amongst African peasants during the war, or complete acceptance of their subservient position within the white order.

African responses at the outbreak of the war also found expression in millenarian fantasies. These combined religious and political strands in African life and were manifested in prophesies about the second coming and the commencement of a golden era in which Africans would be delivered from white domination. In the Pietermaritzburg district S. Nkabindi gained a considerable following as a prophet, predicting that the whites in South Africa would be annihilated by the Germans who would then restore the land to its rightful African owners.[38] Somewhat different in content though not in spirit was the prediction of an anonymous prophet in the Dundee district who claimed that Dinuzulu (former head of the Zulu royal house who had died in 1913 after being deposed in 1909 and sentenced to four years imprisonment for his part in the Zulu rebellion of 1906) was still alive and that the Germans would bring him to South Africa and reinstate him as the supreme African ruler.[39] Millenarianism also surfaced on the Witwatersrand where prophets interpreted the outbreak of the war as an omen that Africans should rid themselves of acquired western customs in preparation for the dawn of a new era in which they would once again rule in their own land.[40] These manifestations of millenarianism are of considerable interest since 'such movements usually reflect a pessimism about the efficacy of human agencies and a belief that social transformations can only come about by cataclysmic means.'[41] Those Africans who sought solace in millenarian fantasies must have been in desperate straits if for them an event such as the war heralded the start of black liberation.

Others had less faith in outside intervention or salvation, and perceived the war as an opportunity to deliver themselves from bondage. The magistrate of the Greytown district in Natal declared explicitly:

> Certain natives are going amongst the tribes . . . saying that now the English are at war with another nation, you have a good chance to fight them, as England cannot send men to assist. Why should you forever be under a contract to a white man . . . ? What are you to do? Your chance to ease your burdens is to fight the white man and get your country back.[42]

From the same district the police reported towards the end of August 1914 that 'there have been several remarks passed by the Natives . . . here to the effect that "Now is the time . . . ."'[43] It must, of course, be kept in mind that at the outbreak of the war whites were prone to exaggerate the possibility of African uprisings — a psychological over-reaction which had more to do with white stereotyping and fears than the actual African response — but in these particular cases there is no reason to doubt the veracity of the reports. Certainly there were peasants who considered turning the white man's predicament into their opportunity. However, to have implemented these ideas would have required a sustained level of organization and mobilization, as well as a focussing of discontent on some central issue. In the absence of such prerequisites no widespread concerted mass action occurred in 1914, but this does not detract from the logic of African perceptions that the outbreak of war weakened the white dominated state and thus offered an opportunity to strike at the system.

On one particular occasion, African peasants did in fact attempt forcibly to exploit the situation brought about by the war. Between 12 and 19 November an uprising occurred in the Matatiele, Mount Fletcher and Mount Frere districts of East Griqualand (the northernmost part of the then Transkeian territories) when two to three thousand peasants destroyed cattle-dipping tanks and burnt and looted a number of trading stores. The situation seemed critical at the time and the whites in the countryside hastily fled into the town for protection. The Chief Magistrate, W.T. Brownlee, immediately acted to reassert white dominance in the district; every available member of the Citizen Force was called out, armed, and rushed by motor car to the scene of disaffection. Confronted by the armed might of their white overlords, open resistance on the part of the peasants petered out. A subsequent report revealed that they were seriously aggrieved at the way in which the authorities applied compulsory cattle-dipping regulations against East Coast Fever. Although the area was not declared fever-stricken, African peasants were nevertheless forced to comply with the dipping regulations. In addition, they had to make weekly payments for such dippings, whilst white farmers of greater financial means managed to evade these regulations with impunity. Moreover, opposition to cattle dipping also had a political dimension in that peasants experienced compulsory dipping as a drastic intervention in traditional rural life which emphasized their inability to exercise control over the way in which they were governed. Dipping regulations were admittedly the focal point of the revolt, but the timing of peasant resistance to these measures is of considerable significance in assessing the African response to the outbreak of the Great War. The revolt took place at a time when white authority in the Transkei was particularly vulnerable since many policemen had been drafted into the South African Defence Force. It is clear from a series of meetings held prior to the revolt that the withdrawal of a substantial section of the police had not gone unnoticed amongst the peasants. With the white man's attention diverted by hostilities elsewhere, the opportunity for meaningful resistance had presented itself. Though more armed men turned out to quell the revolt than they had anticipated, it is nevertheless significant that they considered the outbreak of war as an opportune time to attempt to rid themselves of the obligations imposed by white rulers.[44]

Responses by Africans to the outbreak of the war ranged, then, from declarations of loyalty through to expressions of anti-white sentiment, millenarianism, and contemplated or actual revolt. Reflecting the complex diversity of African society, these responses all began in a general awareness of a possible shift in power relationships due to the war. However, not all African groups demonstrated this awareness of the changing situation. For some the war was merely a white man's quarrel. 'The feeling came to be pretty common amongst them', it was reported, 'that this was only one more of those wars to which the Europeans, who ought to know better, were accustomed, and that it was not in any vital sense a Bantu concern.'[45] In as far as these Africans were informed about the war, they were unconcerned about its possible implications. They had, outwardly at least, come to terms with white dominance and the forms of government under which they had to live. Whatever happened in the war, it would not really affect them. In a resigned way a Transkeian chief explained: 'The Umlungu [white man] has come here to stay, and we know well enough by this time that nothing will move him.'[46]

Perhaps one of the most dramatic events to occur on South African soil during the First World War was the Boer rebellion which flared up in the last quarter of 1914. Approximately 12 000 rebels tried in vain to overthrow the Botha government and the affair ended with 190 rebels and 132 members of the government forces killed. Since Botha used mainly Afrikaner troops, the revolt can be likened to a civil war in which Afrikaner fought Afrikaner.

Dissident elements in Afrikaner ranks, like those blacks who considered Britain's adversity their opportunity, responded with alacrity after it became known that the Union government had decided to support Britain actively during the war and to invade South-West Africa. To varying degrees the rebel leaders were prompted by a general feeling of dissatisfaction with the Botha government (especially after the exclusion of General J.B.M. Hertzog from the Botha cabinet in 1912), a desire to reestablish republican independence after the defeat of the Anglo-Boer War and, of perhaps overriding importance, strong opposition to the projected South-West African campaign. Amongst the rank-and-file rebels there was also a fair sprinkling of impoverished *bywoners*, lured by the promises of the leaders that a successful rebellion would herald a new and prosperous era for poor Afrikaners.[47]

Although a considerable amount has been written on the resistance of some Afrikaners to the Botha government, no attention has been paid to the way in which blacks viewed and were affected by the fraternal strife amongst Afrikaners during the war.[48] It is interesting to reflect that at this time there were both black and Afrikaner groups who saw the war as an opportunity to satisfy their respective aspirations. This does not imply, however, that blacks, and in particular the educated elite, had any sympathy for the Afrikaner rebels. Some of them roundly condemned the rebels for resorting to violence. Afrikaners, unlike blacks, they argued, had constitutional means at their disposal to effect change and it was therefore ironic that 'thousands of Dutch South Africans living under the constitution of their own making were prepared to take up arms against a Government composed almost exclusively of men of their own blood, leaders of their own party, placed in power by their own people'.[49] Congress also expressed its dismay: 'We have a spectacle today', Dube remarked, 'of a practically uncivilized people . . . remaining loyal and true even under many unjust and oppressive laws such as Pass Laws, Native Land Acts, and what not, to the everlasting shame of the white South African rebel!'[50] It furthermore appeared to Dube that the rebels had insufficient reason to take up arms. 'They are denied no political rights or privileges, no freedom of movement or of action, enjoyed by their English and Dutch fellow-countrymen', he commented. 'To all intents and purposes they are quite as free and unfettered as they were before the Boer war'. The elite's assessment of rebel grievances and conduct might have been somewhat narrow and unbalanced, yet their arguments were in line with their general strategy of supporting the Botha government's war effort. They also had an additional reason for damning the rebellion. Some argued with considerable force that a successful rebellion would have left them under Afrikaner nationalist dominance and in 'what state would we poor wretches be in then!'[52]

The white rebellion further provided the black elite with an excellent opportunity of contrasting their loyalty to the British crown with that of white disloyalty. With thinly disguised delight H.M. Tyali, a member of the Transkeian Bunga, pointed out that 'it is the white race who rebelled during the war, but all eyes were looking on the Natives to rebel against the Government.' This, Tyali hoped, should prove to the government that blacks were worthy of being trusted.[53] Others were even more optimistic that their loyalty 'during these strenuous times' might actually lead to a change in alliances. 'We do not expect payment for our loyalty', it was argued, 'but . . . when this war is over, Britishers in South Africa will have to cease to pat brother Boer on the back, because the Boers hate the British too much. The British should therefore rather look after the natives'.[54] The government was not oblivious to the possible effect of the rebellion on African perceptions. Immediately after violence flared up, Botha issued a general appeal to the black population, urging them to ignore the strife in the white community since it did not concern them.[55]

Although the official view was that blacks should be passive, unthinking witnesses to the drama in white society, in practice this did not happen. Not only was the black elite quick to draw pointed conclusions from the conflict, but others actually became intimately involved in hostilities.

In parliament Botha denied, somewhat vaguely, that the government had used Africans in military operations against the rebels,[56] but there is convincing evidence to prove the contrary. Prominent rebel leaders as well as National Party members claimed that blacks had actively assisted the government forces during the rebellion.[57] These assertions are substantiated by circulars sent to senior officials in the Native Affairs Department shortly after the outbreak of the rebellion, informing them that a special 'Native Intelligence Branch', which would cooperate with the Defence Force, had been formed. This intelligence service was controlled by A. King (Assistant Native Commissioner at Hammanskral who was later killed in a clash with rebel commandos). It operated informally in the Pretoria, Rustenburg and Waterberg districts to gain information on rebel movements, and Native Commissioners in these districts received instructions that they 'should quietly advise Chiefs, Headmen and leading Natives of the arrangement made by the Government and should impress upon them that in their own interest they should find means of sending word of any rebel band or commando that is seen'. This information would then be conveyed to the Defence Force.[58] The Defence Force found this network particularly useful: African headmen in these areas provided them almost daily with often detailed information on the activities and strength of rebel commandos.[59] On a somewhat smaller scale, blacks were also employed as informers and scouts by government forces in the Free State at a rate of 3s.6d. per day.[60]

There is no clear-cut evidence on whether these blacks were armed or not. Government spokesmen denied that the Defence Force had armed any blacks during the insurrection, but rebel supporters insisted that the government had committed the cardinal sin of arming black men to fight against whites.[61] In practice it seems unlikely that the Defence Force would have deployed blacks without arming at least some of them; confronted by armed rebels an unarmed scout would have had no chance of returning with useful information. It therefore appears logical to assume that some black scouts must have been armed, though the Government refused to admit this. Besides actively assisting the government forces, blacks were further employed in a non-combatant capacity in the field of operations and did all the menial work in the camps.[62] As had happened during the Anglo-Boer War twelve years earlier, the pattern of the master-servant relationship was rapidly transferred from civilian to army life.

Participation on the side of the government forces had its advantages — especially in terms of the higher than average wage to be earned as a scout — but it was also a decidedly risky business. If they were captured by the rebels, particularly harsh treatment awaited them. The usual punishment was 25 lashes with a *sjambok*, but reports also filtered through that rebel forces had castrated black spies and in certain cases shot them out of hand.[63] Although these reports, emanating as they did from rebel sources, might have been exaggerated and designed to deter other blacks from actively assisting the government, it does not detract from the general impression that the rebels showed little mercy to those blacks unfortunate enough to be captured.

As far as black involvement on the side of the rebels is concerned, there is some scanty but tantalizing evidence suggesting that the rebels might have considered courting black support for their cause. The Free State rebel leader Wessel Wessels wrote to the Sotho chiefs Mopedi, Griffith and Joel, urging them to 'remain quiet' in the 'war of white against white', but also hinting at the possibility that the Sotho might consider helping them in the event of the government arming Indians to fight the rebels.[64] This initiative on the part of the rebels was, however, not pursued, nor did the Sotho display any interest in getting involved in the conflict. Although cooperation between some blacks and the dissident elements in Afrikaner ranks is not completely far-fetched as will be demonstrated later in this chapter, during the rebellion blacks generally showed little inclination to side with the rebels. In some isolated instances, however, rebel leaders in the western Free State claimed that black labour tenants understood and sympathized with the rebel cause. Apparently the rebels' antipathy towards 'the English' was shared by those blacks.[65] Whether such sympathy for the rebels was genuine or merely a reflection of enforced deference to white landlords, remains, however, a moot point.

Some blacks nevertheless served on the side of the rebels as noncombatant *agterryers*; like the *agterryers* during the Anglo-Boer War they performed such tasks as carrying provisions for the Boer 'masters', attending to the horses and herding cattle when necessary. To the Boer rebel this service was merely an extension of the contractual obligations between employer and employee; instead of working on the farm, the labourer now rendered his services as an *agterryer* on commando. Moreover, the rebels had no compunction in forcefully pressing blacks into service. In the Kakamas district the prominent rebel leader, S.G. Maritz, a lieutenant-colonel in the Defence Force before coming out in rebellion, threatened to shoot certain blacks if they refused to join the rebel forces as auxiliaries to attend to the horses.[66] The rebels apparently often used such intimidating tactics to acquire the services of blacks. In 'different centres of South Africa', Sol Plaatje pointed out, 'native peasants were horsewhipped into the enemy's service as soon as the standard of rebellion was unfurled'.[67]

It is impossible to determine the number of blacks who served with either the rebels or the government forces. Such involvement as there was had its precedents in South African warfare, immediately and notably in the Anglo-Boer War. Compared to that all-embracing conflict the rebellion was of course a minor affair, but in certain respects a similar pattern repeated itself: whites fought whites on South African soil; blacks were probably armed despite official denials; blacks were employed to perform non-combatant behind-the-lines services; and blacks were often drawn into hostilities against their will.[68]

Furthermore, as in the Anglo-Boer War, African peasants who cultivated land in the vicinity of military operations were often adversely affected. During the rebellion many peasants suffered material losses as both rebel forces and government troops summarily commandeered sheep, cattle, horses and foodstuffs. At times government forces issued receipts for what they had taken — an arrangement which was invariably to the disadvantage of often illiterate peasants — whilst rebels did not even bother with such legal niceties and seized whatever they required without further ado. Although peasants voiced their objections, they often had no option but to submit to white demands. Thus S. Kalomane of the Kuruman district testified that he had tried in vain in November 1914 to prevent a rebel commando from appropriating his wheat crop.[69] The conduct of rebels in the western Transvaal was recalled vividly by Kas Maine, a sharecropper in the area:

> If they came to the village, they chose the best horses and drove them away. They didn't ask the owner's permission to drive them away . . . .
> When I asked them why they drove the flocks away, I was told to shut up . . . (*Kaffer hou jou bek*).'[70]

Likewise D. Aphane objected when the rebels in the Pretoria district wanted to take his horse. They simply ignored him, and 'there and then . . . surrounded my horse and caught it', he declared.[71] Numerous similar complaints by African peasants were registered.[72]

In addition, unscrupulous white stock speculators exploited the unsettled state of the country. They informed peasants in the western Transvaal that the rebellion would be a repetition of the Anglo-Boer War during which blacks lost much of their stock, and that it would be better for them to get rid of their cattle as soon as possible rather than lose all at a later stage. In this way speculators paid well below the normal market price for animals which they resold later at a considerable profit.[73]

However, Africans were not always the victims of white greed; some of them had their own ways of reversing the situation. In contrast to those Africans who suffered losses during the uprising, there were others who actually used the opportunity to their own benefit. They were mostly farm labourers who took advantage of the absence of their white landlords on commando to abscond with some of their stock — an easy and effective way of supplementing their own resources while simultaneously striking an unsympathetic employer a parting blow.[74]

Nevertheless, the general state of affairs in the rural districts during the rebellion disturbed African political leaders and in October 1914 the SANNC requested an interview with the acting Minister of Native Affairs, F.S. Malan, to discuss African losses. On meeting Malan, R.W. Msimang pointed out that 'they . . . were very serious on the protection of life and property of the people in the country districts against violence, commandeering of property and other provocative acts by the rebels'. Africans were unprotected in the rural areas, Msimang explained, and they had no assurance that they would be compensated for any losses they might suffer. Their stock was often their only livelihood and consequently losses fell heavily on them. Malan replied that during armed insurrection both blacks and whites were exposed to certain risks for which the Government could not be blamed. Nonetheless, the government was prepared to go into the matter and compensate deserving cases.[75]

When calm had returned to the country, the Rebellion Losses Commission was instructed to investigate the claims of whites and blacks. Although the commission did attempt to meet the demands of African claimants, compensation did not always proceed smoothly. Some Africans did not know that they could claim compensation, while others did not have the necessary proof to substantiate their claims. Despite such problems, the commissioners were satisfied with the way they had completed their task.[76] It is highly doubtful, however, whether this view was shared by the numerous peasants who had suffered heavy losses during the rebellion.

The existing literature on the Boer rebellion has not only failed to look at black involvement, but has also created the impression that once the Union government had quelled the revolt, Afrikaners were content to follow constitutional methods in opposing the Botha government. It is true that an increasing number of Afrikaners supported the National Party under General J.B.M. Hertzog after the rebellion, but this does not imply that it was the only avenue open to dissident Afrikaners and that no other more drastic extra-parliamentary measures were contemplated.

Towards the end of 1916 and again during the last months of 1917 and the first half of 1918, there were constant allegations that dissatisfied Afrikaners were plotting another revolt. The government took a serious view of the matter and in December 1916 two men who were regarded as leaders of the so-called 'second rebellion', G. van N. Schonken, a teacher in Johannesburg, and C.P. van der Merwe, an insurance agent in Reitz, had to appear in the Bloemfontein High Court, charged with treason. It was alleged that they had planned a strike of all white municipal employees and railwaymen in Johannesburg to coincide with an armed rising in the country districts which would put the government under pressure to declare a republic in South Africa. According to Judge J.H. Lange who tried the case, the state had prepared its brief very badly and on technical grounds he was forced to acquit the accused. However, a third man who was tried separately, J.J. Rabie, a police constable from Harrismith, was found guilty and sentenced to eighteen months imprisonment.[77] Towards the end of 1917 there were once again rumours of revolt — the so-called 'third rebellion' — when a number of dissident Afrikaners threatened to capture Botha, stir up the countryside and simultaneously organize a large-scale strike on the Rand. This ambitious plan, however, had no further repercussions.[78]

Although the exact nature of and support for these projected risings remain vague and sketchy, they nevertheless demonstrated that below the surface there was still considerable ferment in Afrikaner society. Besides the ill-conceived 'second' and 'third' rebellions there was, as will be shown, a sustained element of militancy in grassroots Afrikaner politics in the rural areas. Of particular interest in the context of this study are the persistent claims that dissident Afrikaners in the countryside attempted to involve blacks in their plans.

In August 1917 it was confidentially reported that 'Dutchmen from the Free State' tried to persuade blacks on the western border of the province to side with the 'rebels' in the event of a revolt. A black man who remained anonymous in the documents, gave evidence that they were offered arms and ammunition and that in return for their help 'the Dutchmen promised absolute freedom and that they would divide the country, giving us half and keeping the other half for themselves'.[79] Major K.M. Fisher of the South African Police who investigated these allegations declared that 'undoubtedly political emissaries' were active in the area and that with the cooperation of a 'certain class of nationalist farmer' were making 'mischief' among the Africans 'with a view to arms and ammunition being supplied to persons who at present are not able to obtain the same.'[80] Another, somewhat similar case in the Free State involved J.J. Rabie who, it will be remembered, was convicted in the Bloemfontein High Court for his part in the so-called 'second rebellion'. Rabie was found guilty of attempting to secure the support of the Sotho chief, Griffith. He was apprehended before he could contact Griffith, but his intentions were clear. Rabie had in mind that in the event of a general Afrikaner revolt, Griffith should instruct Sotho mineworkers on the Rand to strike, and then sabotage railway lines and cut telephone wires. In exchange for their help, Rabie promised the Sotho the districts of Harrismith, Witzieshoek, Thaba Nchu, Aliwal North and an unspecified part of the Transvaal. It also transpired that Rabie had based his hopes for Sotho support on the interesting assumption that both groups, the Afrikaners as well as the Sotho, were oppressed by 'the English' and therefore had a common interest in opposing the *status quo*.[81]

Attempts to draw blacks into militant rural Afrikaner politics were not restricted to the Free State. In the Transvaal, police in the Rustenburg district were convinced that N.J.R. Roets, a fieldcornet during the 1914 rebellion, had conspired with African headmen in the area who were given the assurance that the 'white men will join them in a rising'. According to the police report it was 'general talk' in the district during September 1917 that 'the rebels are working with the natives, promising them every assistance and telling them they are brothers and that the natives can marry their daughters'.[82] From the same district J.S. Malan, a supporter of General Botha, wrote to the prime minister informing him that he had heard that some Africans 'wanted to fight and that certain whites who were in league with them had promised them rifles'.[83] Similar reports also emanated from the northern areas of the Transvaal. A black man, identified only as Klaas in the reports, categorically declared in December 1917: 'The Dutchmen in the Northern Transvaal are going amongst the Sesuto inciting them to rebel . . . .'[84]

News of these political undercurrents also appeared in the English language press and was presented as proof of how 'degraded' some Afrikaners had become in order to achieve their aims. The *Rand Daily Mail* reported:

> We do not believe that the mass of Nationalists would descend to the stirring up of native unrest for the purpose of damaging the Ministry, but some of them are so bitter and so blinded by political hatred that they are quite capable of even so wicked a policy.[85]

The Imperialist, a Natal newspaper, was even more outspoken:

> There is no use mincing matters in times such as these and we would therefore point out that we have it on unimpeachable authority, that the Nationalist leaders are informing their followers that in the event of trouble, they can look for support from the Basuto . . . .[86]

The report from *The Imperialist* was undoubtedly an overstatement. National Party spokesmen denied any involvement whatsoever,[87] and there is no evidence linking the Party as such to grassroots Afrikaner militancy.

However exaggerated some reports were, it is clear that there was considerable and widespread activity amongst certain rural Afrikaners. However, what is the significance of these overtures to blacks? In a general statement on the effect of the First World War on South Africa, the historian S.E. Katzenellenbogen has made the following relevant comparison:

> Afrikaners would be most unwilling to accept that they had anything in common with African nationalists, but in addition to the desire to be free to develop their own culture . . . and to eliminate foreign political dominance and economic exploitation, black nationalists . . . shared with Afrikaners the experience of the war of 1914-1918 as a significant turning-point in their development.[88]

Whether the war was indeed such a watershed remains to be examined, but Katzenellenbogen's comparative focus is undoubtedly justified. Furthermore, during the war years there was a certain convergence of interest between Afrikaner militants and a number of blacks since they both opposed, though for different reasons, the Botha government. The fact that dissident Afrikaners explored the possibility of involving blacks in their schemes suggests a hidden dimension in the pattern of interaction between black and white in the rural areas during this time. As yet we have a very imperfect knowledge of the implications of socio-economic developments in the countryside and the forms of consciousness they spawned, but it seems that at least some Afrikaners were alive to the possibilities of ignoring racial distinctions and forging links based on mutual interest. However, the tentative and opportunistic nature of their attempts precludes a firm interpretation of the issue. Moreover, the main concern of Afrikaner militants in the rural areas was not actually to side with the blacks in an alliance against the authorities, but to exploit their grievances and, as a government memorandum on the unrest concluded, to work 'towards having a little native trouble as a means to an end'.[89] Similarly, from Rustenburg district the police reported that those who approached the blacks in the area aimed at a 'native scare to obtain the sympathy of the Government for arms'.[90] John X. Merriman also informed Botha that he had a 'shrewd suspicion' that certain Afrikaners 'would not be sorry to see you entangled in some native disturbance'.[91] Even if racial prejudice did become somewhat blurred around the edges, its central core remained intact. The importance of these efforts must therefore not be exaggerated, but it nevertheless appears that relations between black and white in the rural areas were more nuanced than has often been assumed.

Black responses to these attempts were calculated and revolved around the options and benefits which an arrangement with dissident Afrikaners could offer. Those who were approached by Afrikaners from the Free State were fully aware of the potential advantages. 'We could beat the English and would then be free men as we were before the English came and then we would not have to pay hut tax', was their opinion.[92] In the Rustenburg district an even more ambitious possibility occurred to those who considered Afrikaner overtures. 'The natives amongst themselves say', it was reported, 'that we will accept all your [Dutch] support and when we rise we will cut your throats as well, we will beat the English and Boers as well . . . .'[93] Those in the northern Transvaal, however, stated that they did not wish 'to side with either party but wish to become strong and independent as they were long ago'.[94] To a greater or lesser extent Africans were thus prepared to consider the schemes which emanated from certain Afrikaner circles, but it is clear that such consideration was shaped by their intense resentment of any form of white supremacy.

These Africans were not the only ones to ponder the potential of cooperating with Afrikaners opposed to Botha. The possibility of exploring new tactical alliances was also mooted at a meeting of the Transvaal Native Congress in October 1916. During the discussion of black grievances about the 1913 Land Act, a proposal was made from the floor that if Botha were not prepared to consider black demands, then 'General Hertzog should be approached . . . to see if it would not be wise to follow him . . . . General Hertzog was against Botha and no good but he might be of use to the Natives in assisting to have their wrongs righted.'[95] Although the idea was not pursued, it is apparent that certain blacks saw in the political divisions amongst whites, accentuated by the war issue, an opportunity to further their own cause.

Notes

1. *Debates of the House of Assembly*, 10 September 1914, col. 82.
2. F.S. Malan Collection, 65, Notes on 'De Brits-Duitse Oorlog', 7 August 1914.
3. *De Volkstem*, 25 September 1914 ('Vrees voor de Kaffers'). Translation.
4. P.M. 1/1/145, C.J. Lotter to Botha, 6 August 1914 and A.J.H. Vorster to Botha, 25 August 1914; P.M. 1/1/148, A.H. Lamprecht to Botha, 25 September 1914; SAP File 6/245/14/16, Assistant Commissioner of Police Bloemfontein to Secretary South African Police Pretoria, 10 August 1914; D.C. 623/194/9199, Secretary of the Divisional Council Barkly East to Provincial Secretary Cape Town, 12 September 1914 (copy); J.X. Merriman Collection, 560, E. Sheppard to Merriman, 30 December 1914; *Church Times*, 11 September 1914 ('South Africa and the Empire'); S.N.A. 1/4/25/c/13/1914, Magistrate Estcourt to Chief Native Commissioner, 12 September 1914. (The quotation is from the last document).
5. *Debates of the House of Assembly*, 10 September 1914, col. 82; S.N.A. 1/4/25/c/13/1914, Magistrate Estcourt to Chief Native Commissioner, 12 September 1914.
6. J.X. Merriman Collection, 560, E. Sheppard to Merriman, 30 December 1914.
7. *Debates of the House of Assembly*, 10 September 1914, col. 88.
8. I.C. Brown, *Understanding Race Relations*, p.58.
9. N.A. 108/521, Report on a meeting of the Transvaal Native Congress, 19 June 1921.
10. *Tsala ea Batho*, 6 June 1915 ('A native protest').

11. S.A.P. file 6/245/14/17, Confidential and urgent circular, 12 August 1914; J.205/474/14, Confidential and urgent circular, 15 August 1914; G.N.L.B. 192/1329/14/48, Message to the Native population, 21 August 1914; *Imvo Zabantsundu*, 25 August 1914 ('Natives and the War').

12. *Ilanga Lase Natal*, 28 August 1914 ('Native tranquillity').

13. *Ilanga Lase Natal*, 25 September 1914 ('Unsettled Native minds').

14. G.N.L.B. 187/1217/14/Dll0, SANNC to Minister of Native Affairs, 6 August 1914; *Tsala ea Batho*, 22 August 1914 ('SANNC resolutions'); Plaatje, *Native Life*, pp.260-61; Walshe, *African Nationalism*, pp.51-52.

15. *Contact*, 3, 7, 2 April 1960, Interview with Selby Msimang.

16. *Izwe La Kiti*, 17 March 1915 ('The Native question').

17. A.T. Nzula and others, *Forced Labour in Colonial Africa*, p.205.

18. G.N.L.B. 187/1217/14/D110, Report of a meeting with the acting Minister of Native Affairs, 31 October 1914.

19. Compare *Ilanga Lase Natal*, 5 March 1915 ('The native disposition'); *Ilanga Lase Natal*, 9 October 1914 ('Native loyalty'); *Tsala ea Batho*, 12 December 1914 ('Native loyalty').

20. *Cape Times*, 17 March 1917 ('Mr. Dube's speech').

21. See Chapter 6.

22. *Ilanga Lase Natal*, 4 October 1918 ('The Imperialist').

23. T.H. Qualter, *Propaganda and Psychological Warfare*, pp.55-58; *Ilanga Lase Natal*, 6 April 1917 ('A worthy defence').

24. D.D.T. Jabavu, 'Native unrest in South Africa' in *International Review of Missions*, 1922, p.254.

25. *Ilanga Lase Natal*, 27 November 1914 ('Civilization demands').

26. R. Rathbone, 'World War I and Africa: introduction' in *Journal of African History*, XIX, 1, 1978, p.5.

27. G.N.L.B. 192/1329/14/D48, Copy of a report by the compound manager, 18 November 1914; *Tsala ea Batho*, 21 November 1914 ('Seditious language').

28. G.N.L.B. 192/1329/14/D48, Anonymous letter intercepted by Native Affairs Department, 6 September 1914.

29. S.A.P. file 6/245/14/37, Copy of a report by the compound manager, 4 September 1914.

30. G.N.L.B. 192/1329/14/D48, Rex versus T.M. Paulsen, 10 November 1914; *Transvaal Leader*, 13 November 1914 ('Fruits of sedition').

31. J. 196/3/317/14, J. Cullen and others to Assistant Magistrate Pilgrim's Rest, 22 May 1915.

32. G.N.L.B. 192/1329/14/D48, Anonymous intercepted letter, date stamped 3 September 1914.

33. G.N.L.B. 192/1329/14/D72, H.E. Mathie to J.C. Smuts, 27 October 1914.

34. S.A.P. file 6/499/17/2, letter from Ben Machumela intercepted and translated by the Native Affairs Department, 9 April 1917.
35. J. 205/14/467/14, Sworn declaration by S. Sincuba, 26 September 1914.
36. S.N.A. 1/4/25/c/2/1915, Magistrate Umzinto to Chief Native Commissioner Natal, 26 January 1915.
37. *Rand Daily Mail*, 10 August 1914 ('Zulu gives his version of how the war started').
38. C.N.C. 247/1196, Chief Native Commissioner Natal to Attorney General Natal, 10 August 1914.
39. S.A.P. file 6/245/14/37, District Commandant Dundee to Commissioner of Police, Pietermaritzburg, 6 September 1914 (copy).
40. *Transvaal Leader*, 8 April 1915 ('Native prophets').
41. G. Shepperson, 'The comparative study of millenarian movements' in S. Thrupp (ed.), *Millennial Dreams*, p.44.
42. J. 205/4/467/14, Report of the magistrate of Greytown, 18 August 1914.
43. S.A.P. file 6/245/14/37, District Commandant Greytown to Commissioner of Police Pretoria, 31 August 1914.
44. This account is based on C.M.T. 3/926/778/2, Official government report, 8 December 1914 (published as S. 3-15, *Union of South Africa, Senate, Report of the Government's Special Commissioner*, April 1915); S.A.P. file 6/245/14/209, Police and magistrate's reports, 31 October, 10 to 21 November, 1914; C.O. 551/62/45389, Buxton to Harcourt, 17 November 1914; S.N.A. 1/4/25/c/16/1914, Chief Native Commissioner Natal to Native Affairs Department Pretoria, 19 November 1914; *Imvo Zabantsundu*, 15 November 1914 ('Matatiele troubles'); *Territorial News*, 28 November 1914 ('Matatiele matters'); *Cape Times*, 25 November 1914 ('Unrest among the natives'); *Cape Times*, 26 November 1914 ('The native unrest'); W.T. Brownlee, *Reminiscences of a Transkeian*, introduction; C. Bundy, 'Dissidents, detectives and the dipping revolt: social control and collaboration in East Griqualand in 1914', Centre for Southern African Studies, University of York, Seminar paper, 1982.
45. R.H.W. Shepherd, *Lovedale, South Africa: The Story of a Century*, p.323.
46. Quoted in G. Callaway, 'Umlungu: or the European in South Africa' in *East and West*, February 1917, p.196.
47. On the rebellion see G.D. Scholtz, *Die rebellie van 1914*, pp.134-192; T.R.H. Davenport, 'The South African Rebellion of 1914' in *English Historical Review*, 78, 1963, pp.73-94; S.B. Spies, 'The outbreak of the First World War and the Botha government', p.52; J. Bottomley, 'The South African rebellion of 1914: the influence of industrialization, poverty and poor whiteism', African Studies Institute, University of the

Witwatersrand, Seminar Paper, June 1982.

48. The literature is reviewed in A.M. Grundlingh, 'Die rebellie van 1914: 'n historiografiese verkenning' in *Kleio*, XI, 1 and 2, 1979, pp.18-30.
49. *Izwe La Kiti*, 10 March 1915 (Letter from 'Anti-Rebellion').
50. *Ilanga Lase Natal*, 30 June 1916 ('When is rebellion justifiable?').
51. *Ilanga Lase Natal*, 11 October 1918 ('Republican propaganda').
52. *Izwe La Kiti*, 24 March 1915 ('Letter from Nonkonwa').
53. 1/T.B.U. 25/66/1, H.M. Tyali to Chairman of the Bunga, 2 December 1916.
54. *Ilanga Lase Natal*, 27 November 1914 (Letter from 'Loyalty').
55. G.N.L.B. 192/1329/14/D48, Circular from Botha, 24 October 1914.
56. *Cape Times*, 7 June 1916 ('Parliamentary debates'). When questioned on this point Botha's response was that 'the rebellion now belongs to the past, and he hoped members would not continually bring up matters connected therewith.'
57. A. 787, Preller Collection, 190, p.126, Manifesto to the People of South Africa, undated, signed by C.F. Beyers, C.R. de Wet, M. Maritz, J. Kemp, Wessel Wessels, J. Fourie and J.J. Pienaar.
58. S.A.P. file 6/240/14/23A, Circular to Native Commissioners, 6 November 1914.
59. A. 787, Preller Collection 264, p.127, 'Aantekeninge oor rebellie', 12 November 1914.
60. J. 248/5/194/16, Magistrate Bethlehem to Minister of Justice, 25 February 1916; S.A.P. file 6/245/14/214, R. Gaboo (from Frankfurt) to A. King, 28 November 1914.
61. *Cape Times*, 17 March 1915 ('Parliamentary debates'); *Cape Times*, 7 June 1916 ('Parliamentary debates'); J.M. de Wet, *'n Lewensskets van Jopie Fourie*, p.91.
62. *Cape Times Annual*, 1919 (article by Lt. F.C. Cornell).
63. A. 787, Preller Collection, 264, p.128, 'Aantekeninge oor Rebellie', 12 November 1914.
64. Copies of the letter, dated 15 November 1914, are in G.G. 486/9/59/49 and in the Merriman Collection, 438. On this issue see also Merriman Collection, 49, Merriman to F. Dormer, 2 February 1915; *Cape Times*, 2 and 4 December 1915 (Parliamentary debates); U.G. 46-16, *Report of the judicial commission of inquiry into the causes and circumstances relating to the recent rebellion in South Africa*, p.54; Plaatje, *Native Life*, p.322.
65. H. Oost, *Wie is die Skuldiges?*, p.373.
66. P.V.L. 127/2797/K-series, Sworn declarations by M. Esau, T. Myburg, I. Mohlabane, G. Joseph, H. Cloete, J. Farmer and G. Booysen, 16 January 1915.
67. Plaatje, *Native Life*, p.342.
68. For the Anglo-Boer War see Warwick, *Black People and the South*

African War, pp.19-27 in particular.

69. K. 1/28/61/30, Sworn declaration by S. Kalomane of Kuruman, 23 November 1914.

70. Transcript of an interview with K. Maine, p. 11, 17 September 1980, Oral History Project, African Studies Institute, University of the Witwatersrand.

71. K. 1/36/973/23, Sworn declaration by D. Aphane of Hammanskraal, 13 March 1915.

72. See for instance K. 1/36/393/29, Sworn declaration by H. Mganebi of Potchefstroom, 10 May 1916; K. 1/36/975/84, Sworn declaration by A. Lepaku of Hammanskraal, 12 March 1915; K. 1/28/568/3, Sworn declaration by E. Esail of Krugersdorp, 2 July 1915; K. 1/26/1222/56, Sworn declaration by J. Mosheni of Kroonstad, 26 July 1915; K. 1/59/unsorted, Sworn declaration by F. Tlharipe of Bothaville, 8 June 1916.

73. J. 199/3/919/14, Secretary of Justice to Secretary of Native Affairs, 27 November 1914 (copy).

74. U.G. 40-16, *Report of the Rebellion Losses Commission*, 1916, p.7.

75. G.N.L.B. 187/1217/4/D110, Report of an interview with the acting Minister of Native Affairs, 31 October 1914.

76. K. 1/60/7/11, Secretary of Native Affairs to Rebellion Losses Commission, 3 February 1915; U.G. 40-16, *Report of Rebellion Losses Commission*, p.7.

77. P.F. van der Schyff, 'Die rebellie wat nooit plaasgevind het nie' in *Die Huisgenoot*, 21 June 1968, pp.14-16; *De Burger*, 6 December 1916 ('De tweede rebellie valt in het water'); *Rand Daily Mail*, 6 December 1916 ('That second rebellion').

78. A.H. Marais, 'Die "derde rebellie"' in *Acta Diurna Historica*, 1, 4, December 1972, pp.3-6.

79. S.A.P. file 6/499/17/1, Sworn declaration by an anonymous African, 15 August 1917.

80. S.A.P. file 6/499/17/1, Maj. K.M. Fisher to Staff Officer Pretoria, 14 August 1917.

81. *De Burger*, 7 December 1916 ('Rabie veroordeeld'); *De Burger*, 11 December 1916 ('Rabie ontvangt tronkstraf'); *Rand Daily Mail*, 6 December 1916 ('That second rebellion'); G.G. 1271/51/4330, Report on petition for remission of sentence, J.J. Rabie, 3 September 1917.

82. J. 255/3/527/17/64, Report by Constable F. Hicks, 13 September 1917.

83. J. 255/3/527/17/56, J.S. Malan to Botha, 27 October 1917 (copy).

84. D.C. 321/41/34285, Sworn declaration by Klaas, 6 September 1918.

85. *Rand Daily Mail*, 22 October 1917 ('German agents in the Transvaal').

86. *The Imperialist*, 19 April 1918 ('Rumours of native participation').

87. S.A.P. file 6/499/17/3, Tielman Roos to Minister of Defence, 5 November 1917.
88. Katzenellenbogen, 'Southern Africa and the War of 1914-18', p.117.
89. D.C. 320/27/34285, Memorandum by Major J. Leipoldt on the unrest in South Africa, 19 December 1917.
90. D.C. 320/28/35017, Corporal A. Cockrell to District Commandant Rustenburg, 6 December 1917 (copy).
91. Merriman Collection, 227, Merriman to Botha, 18 August 1916.
92. S.A.P. file 6/499/17/1, Sworn declaration by an anonymous African, 15 August 1917.
93. J. 255/3/527/17/64, Report by Constable F. Hicks, 13 September 1917.
94. D.C. 321/41/34285, Sworn declaration by Klaas, 6 September 1918.
95. G.N.L.B. 192/1329/14/48, Report on a meeting of the Transvaal Native Congress, 17 October 1916.

CHAPTER 2

Official and Public Discourse on the Issue of Black Participation in the War

In the past, as indeed in the present, military establishments have assiduously cultivated the image of non-partisan concern with the protection and defence of all layers of society. In reality, however, they reflect and often reinforce divisions in society. Although the organization and composition of the armed forces may stem in part from specific military requirements, ultimately their nature is determined by the power structures and prejudices prevalent in the society from which they emerge. Particularly in critical times of war, when the armed forces assume a central role and there is a greater fusion between military and civilian affairs, military establishments become even less immune from wider social tensions. This chapter explores the interactive process between the military and society by focussing on the issues surrounding the involvement of blacks in the First World War and by analyzing the nature of the responses it gave rise to.

Article 7 of the South African Defence Force Act of 1912 (Act No. 13 of 1912) specified that Africans could be called upon to enrol as non-combatants, but the obligation to do armed service was restricted to persons of European descent. The relevant article could of course be changed by a majority vote in parliament, but to cope with unforeseen circumstances a qualifying clause was added stipulating that the article might be repealed summarily in times of war.[1]

The decision that whites alone should carry the burden of defence was not, as implied by certain parliamentarians during the discussion of the bill in 1911 and 1912, inspired by magnanimity.[2] On the contrary, the exclusion of blacks was a direct result of the apprehensions and prejudices which permeated white society. It was feared that, if blacks were allowed to join the Defence Force on a basis of equality in an armed capacity, the existing nature of social relations might be threatened, and the position of the white minority jeopardized by blacks trained in the use of firearms. During the parliamentary debate on the Defence

Force Bill it emerged clearly that the training of black troops 'would only be a menace' and that it 'would be an immoral thing in South Africa to place black and white troops on the same footing'.[3] J.B. Wessels (National Party member of parliament for Bethlehem) explained the 'immorality' of the issue at a later stage in parliament when he asked: did they realize that the coloured man, when he donned uniform, said to the white man, "I am now your equal — the equal of your wives and children"?[4] And from a 'security' point of view P.A. Silburn, a contemporary military writer and Unionist Party member of parliament for Durban Point, maintained that 'to teach and encourage the use of the rifle by native races may result in trouble if not disaster'.[5]

Intimately related to these concerns were the perceived objectives and functions of the force. The military was not merely conceived in terms of a safeguard against external threats, but was also seen as a force to be deployed in the event of black insurrection. Although the Committee of Imperial Defence in a memorandum on the defence of South Africa in 1911 considered the possibility of a black uprising as remote, the 'danger of internal native disturbances' could not be lost sight of.[6] Major-General G. Aston, the British military adviser involved in formulating the Defence Bill, largely saw the role of the Defence Force in this light, whilst General J.C. Smuts as Minister of Defence declared explicitly when the bill first came up for discussion in March 1911: 'If they had a scheme of defence, by which they insured themselves against those internal native troubles which might arise in South Africa, they would have done a good day's work'.[7] Right from the outset, then, the establishment of the Union Defence Force by the ruling class was in part an effort to ensure their continued dominance and control of the subordinated majority.

The nature and implications of South Africa's first Defence Force Act did not go unnoticed amongst some blacks. Their exclusion from the Defence Force was regarded as yet another discriminatory act and was one of the grievances cited at the time of the founding of the SANNC in 1912.[8] Furthermore, according to T.L. Schreiner, Unionist member of parliament for Tembuland who often tried to act as a spokesman for blacks in parliament, unspecified black newspapers were perturbed about the projected role of the Defence Force as an additional coercive arm of the state in its relations with Africans.[9] Indeed, certain blacks showed a keen awareness of the significance of defence developments. 'The Defence Force Act . . . was originally intended to terrorise the Natives who had been all along looked upon as enemies of the peace. Of course, we have never been deceived, and we know why this Force was organised', was the pointed commentary of *Ilanga Lase Natal*.[10]

With the advent of the war the African elite hoped that the exigencies of war would create sufficient openings in the Defence Force edifice to allow the entry of blacks, but in the event the foundations and structures of the military establishment were to remain firmly intact. Thus an offer by the honourary president of Congress, W.B. Rubusana, to raise 5 000 blacks for army service, elicited the following candid reply from the Secretary of Defence:

> I am to refer you to the Provision of Section 7 of the South African Defence Act 1912, and to state that the Government does not desire to avail itself of the services in a combatant capacity, of citizens not of European descent in the present hostilities. Apart from other considerations the present war is one which has its origin among the white people of Europe, and the Government are anxious to avoid the employment of coloured citizens in a warfare against whites.[11]

The underlying meaning of the unspecified 'other considerations' is not hard to detect in the light of those preoccupations which informed the Defence Act; in all likelihood it referred to white perceptions of the possible 'harmful' repercussions of arming blacks. Such sensibilities amongst South African whites were well recognized by A. Bonar Law, the Secretary of Colonies in 1915, who stated that 'no proposal for training Natives upon a large scale is likely to be acceptable to . . . the British and Dutch inhabitants of the Union, as the return, after peace, of a large body of trained and disciplined men would create obvious difficulties and might seriously menace the supremacy of the whites'.[12]

It might be argued that had the war impinged more tangibly on white South Africans, perhaps to the extent that they had to face German domination in the country, the authorities might well, in order to bolster defence, have given greater thought to arming blacks. This, however, is speculative. In 1916 when the Colonial Office, urged by the War Office, did tentatively approach the South African government on the possibility of raising an armed black corps for service in Europe, the South African reaction was predictable: under no condition would the government allow a black combatant force to proceed to Europe as this could endanger white South Africa. The Colonial Office accepted this reply without demur and the War Office acquiesced.[13] This meek response is perhaps not surprising, for although the British government was hard pressed for manpower, there were strong reservations in relevant quarters in Britain which echoed South African concerns that

> there would be no more peace for South Africa if it were to be put in the power of the natives to say to the Whites there: 'You tried to beat your White enemies in Europe without us, but you failed and had to call us in to finish the war'. The moral effect throughout the Union of sending native contingents to fight on the battlefields of Europe would be incalculably disastrous to the prestige of the Whites there.[14]

In contrast to white objections against the arming of blacks, the use of blacks in a non-combatant capacity in South-West Africa and German East Africa did not provoke any criticism. In part this can be ascribed to the established precedent that blacks, as unarmed workers, had previously and without any qualms on the part of whites, been employed in South African wars like the Anglo-Boer War where both sides utilized non-combatant blacks. Moreover, the structure of the division of labour between black and white in the Union also offered a partial 'explanation'. 'To plough, to dig, to hoe, to fetch and carry, to cook — all laborious and menial toil is the duty of the black man. The average white man would consider it degrading to be seen doing any of these things', according to Maurice Evans, a contemporary sociologist.[15] Even if this was perhaps an oversimplification in class terms, it shaped military policy to the extent that in the German East African campaign General Smuts considered it imperative to employ blacks as labourers 'as white men cannot be asked to perform work associated with Natives'.[16] Furthermore, the use of blacks in an inferior role as non-combatant labourers, as opposed to armed soldiers, in colonial territories was also ideologically acceptable. Not only did the orthodox black-white relationship remain undisturbed with the black man in a familiar subservient position, but there was also less chance that blacks might lay claim to political and social equality on account of having served in the same armed capacity as whites. Sol Plaatje recognized this when he stated that 'it seems to have occurred to the authorities that the best course is to engage the Natives in a capacity in which their participation will demand no recognition'.[17] Of course, service in the colonial territories also meant that there was little chance of South African blacks being exposed to significantly different ideological influences so that the risk of these Africans posing a threat to white supremacy was considerably reduced.

However, a particularly noteworthy feature of black South African involvement in the war was the employment of Africans as labourers outside colonial territories in the main theatre abroad. The initiative for this development came from the imperial government and at first consideration was given to the use of South African blacks in Britain, but eventually France was decided upon.

On account of the enormous loss of life on the Western Front more and more voices were raised in Britain in 1916, advocating that Africans be enrolled to alleviate the threatening manpower shortage. The intention was that blacks should replace labourers in Britain and France so as to release more whites for active service. In some quarters the raising of an auxiliary arm of a million black troops from Africa was mooted and the idea was widely discussed in influential British newspapers.[18] And in the House of Commons, Winston Churchill, then a Liberal member of parliament, argued: 'Consider all the services in the Army which might be rendered by natives, thereby releasing white men in full efficiency for the fighting line. Their interests are identified with ours. The result of this War will settle the fate of the African population as much as it will our own'.[19] Another Liberal member of parliament, Josiah Wedgwood (who had been a magistrate in the Eastern Transvaal after the Anglo-Boer War) strongly supported Churchill on this issue and his views were also publicized in the South African press.[20] However, in the Colonial Office these suggestions met with little enthusiasm and the idea of employing black South African labourers in Britain was given short shrift; objections were raised on the grounds of race, discipline, efficiency, and housing. In addition, British trade unions were implacably opposed to the possible displacement of their members by foreign workers.[21]

Although South African blacks were not to be used in Britain, large-scale military offensives in France during 1916 and the urgent need for manpower to maintain the infrastructure required for these operations decisively influenced the decision to use African labour in France. In March 1916 General D. Haig, commander of the British forces in France, emphasized the dire shortage of labour:

> It is not possible for us to work the quarries and forests in this country until we get more Labour Battalions for this purpose. Labour is our great difficulty, and it is an increasing one, owing to the very extended front recently taken over by me from the French.[22]

The British military authorities estimated in August 1916 that they needed an additional 60 900 labourers in France. With the War Office continuously clamouring for more manpower, the Colonial Office reluctantly agreed, after obtaining the approval of the French government, to the use of South African blacks as workers in France. H. Lambert, a senior Colonial Office official, regarded 'the whole thing as an experiment and a very doubtful and hazardous one' and considered it 'a pity that we could not have managed without employing them [black South Africans] in Europe'.[23]

If the Colonial Office was perturbed about the scheme, it is not surprising that the South African government was even more so. The government recognized the war-time need for labour, but to send blacks to a European country in the turmoil of war meant that these Africans might be exposed to less inhibited contact between black and white. From the point of view of the ruling class in South Africa it was therefore an undertaking fraught with danger for the existing ideological order. Whereas service in colonial territories presented no problem as the nature of black-white relationships was very similar to those in South Africa, white South Africans were, as H. Sloley (a former Resident Commissioner in Basutoland and at the time of the First World War a member of the Aborigines Protection Society) explained, 'particularly concerned with the question of whether the natives, by their experience in the new environment and under new political and social conditions, would not be entirely unfitted to return to their homes and resume, contentedly and usefully, their former status and position in the South African community'.[24] And in his negotiations with the British government, Prime Minister Botha emphasized that 'the employment of Natives in Foreign parts may result in social evils or difficulties on their return by reason of the freedom of social intercourse with other races'. The cabinet thus viewed the scheme 'with great interest and no little anxiety'.[25]

The South African government clearly had deep-seated reservations, but nevertheless informed the British that they were willing to raise a black labour contingent for service in France. Why did they agree to such a scheme, despite the fact that they were extremely uneasy about its possible ramifications? In order to explain this apparent paradox, it is necessary to look at the underlying reasons which prompted their decision.

An important factor was the acceptance of the precondition for participation insisted on by the South African government. The proposed contingent had to be housed in close compounds in France — similar to those on the diamond mines of Kimberley — otherwise the Union government would have been unable to support the plan. Botha considered such a measure as an essential 'safeguard against the possible manifestation in this country in the future of undesirable consequences calculated to flow from their too familiar social intercourse with Europeans of both sexes in a country where colour prejudice is less marked than in South Africa'.[26] The imperial authorities readily agreed and the South African government's fears about 'social contamination' were assuaged.

A further consideration was Botha's concern that the Imperial government could possibly bypass the Union authorities by enlisting blacks from the surrounding protectorates of Bechuanaland (Botswana), Basutoland (Lesotho) and Swaziland — an alternative that was actually raised by the British government.[27] Botha, however, maintained that for the benefit of the region as a whole South Africa should take the initiative, and was particularly concerned that South African, as opposed to British officers, should be in command. The Union government 'had undertaken the recruiting of the contingent, he explained, 'because they desired to keep the subject under their control and so that the officers should be South Africans who knew the country'. He was explicit that the association of blacks 'side by side with British soldiers who have not been accustomed to deal with them, is regarded as dangerous from the South African point of view'.[28]

The South African government's approval of the scheme was thus dependent on gaining full control of the contingent in order to protect what they considered South Africa's interests. Besides these considerations, it must be borne in mind that through the South-West African and German East African campaigns, as well as the presence of a white South African brigade in Europe, Botha had already committed himself firmly to the war effort. His decision to assist the British government further in their quest for manpower therefore dovetailed with his general policy.

It has also been suggested that the authorities in South Africa might have realised that 'the scheme provided an ideal opportunity for testing — in what would, it was hoped, be carefully controlled conditions — the practicability and effects of the implementation of certain segregatory devices of social control; the lessons and results of this experiment could possibly be utilized in South Africa itself'.[29] While the general climate of the time was undoubtedly segregationist, it is doubtful whether this was a primary consideration, though it may well have been perceived as a useful spin-off of a policy which was dictated by more pressing military requirements.

In the field of white party politics the government's decision to send a black labour force to France became a thorny issue. The National Party, already opposed to Botha's policy of supporting the war effort, roundly condemned the scheme as irresponsible and detrimental to white South Africa, and at congresses of the party it was even suggested that those blacks who enrolled for the contingent should not be allowed to return to South Africa.[30] In parliament National Party members castigated Botha for once again giving preference to imperial instead of South African interests and for not consulting parliament before embarking on such a 'dangerous' course. In the face of such opposition, Botha could obviously not openly admit to any reservations that would add grist to the Nationalist mill. He counter-attacked by claiming that the National Party criticism was inspired by pro-German sentiments, and that their fears were unfounded because blacks would be placed in closed compounds and under the strict control of South African officers. He also felt under no obligation to have consulted parliament since the whole undertaking would be financed by the British and not the South African government.[31]

Although the National Party was the most vociferous in its opposition to the scheme, members of other political parties had similar criticisms. While the predominantly English-speaking Unionist Party could not, in view of its fervent, almost jingoistic support of the British war effort, object in parliament to a scheme designed to promote the British cause, rank-and-file members nevertheless voiced their concern. In two staunchly Unionist cities, Durban and East London, the letter columns of the local newspapers were filled with anguished attempts to reconcile loyalty to the Empire with opposition to the contingent; a common rationalization was the claim that blacks in France would not substantially contribute to the war effort and that the perceived negative effects of the scheme outweighed its doubtful military advantages.[32] 'To sum up the effect of these expressions of opinions', the *Natal Mercury* declared, 'it has to be said that the weight of authority in this part of Union is not favourable to the sending of a large body of Natives overseas'.[33] As for the Labour Party, T. Boydell, member of parliament for Durban-Greyville, agreed with this groundswell of Unionist opinion, considering the whole venture a 'ghastly mistake'.[34]

Even some prominent members of Botha's ruling South African Party objected to the scheme. None other than John X. Merriman, the high priest of Cape liberalism, cautioned in private that 'anything that tends to lessen or break down the almost superstitious regard that the native races have . . . for the European makes for evil'. He also informed Smuts that the matter was one of concern to politicians of all persuasions: 'It is not only the professional mischief maker who views the experiment with disfavour, but some of our wisest and most solid friends who regard the introduction of our Natives to the social conditions of Europe with the *greatest* alarm'.[35] Clearly, paternalistic Cape liberalism drew the line at developments which might involve the possibility of loss of control and authority over Africans.

Although there was no formal cooperation between the various political parties on the matter, there was a considerable degree of tacit understanding that the undertaking was not in the interest of white South Africans. Despite other sharp differences of opinion on the Union's war policy, particularly between the South African Party and the Unionist Party on the one hand and the National Party on the other, the politics of involving blacks in the war was the one issue which, at grassroots level, tended to blur party lines. In the general discussion on the subject, support for the war effort abroad had to give way to the importance of maintaining the existing order at home.

To appreciate the depth of opposition to the scheme, it is necessary to move beyond the confines of party politics to the ideological constructs which helped to forge white beliefs. Central to white objections was the argument that the venture would, in general terms, be harmful to South African 'interests'. But the specific content of these 'interests' must be unravelled and defined in order to understand more precisely and comprehensively the various strands of the issue.

A core element in the ideological perceptions of whites was the firm belief that service overseas would raise black political consciousness. 'It seems well to point out', the *Natal Mercury* commented, 'that 10 000 more or less unsophisticated boys will come back to this country after contact with an altogether new environment very different individuals from what they were when they left'. Therefore the 'political change that might come over the native when he returns to this country' was a matter of grave concern.[36] The nature of the perceived political change was spelt out by J.G. Keyter, member of parliament for Ficksburg, at a party congress. He predicted that 'when the kaffir returned, he will pretend to be a major or colonel and the white man his underling, he will have ideas above his station, he will work for no white man and incite his people to agitate for equal rights.'[37] And Advocate O. Pirow of the National Party went to the heart of the matter when he declared: 'On their return from Europe, the kaffirs will demand the vote.'[38]

Such considerations held powerful sway over white minds and in a rather unexpected way nearly wrecked the undertaking. Before recruitment of the contingent commenced the government asked for medical opinion on the possible effect of the cold in France on Africans, and upon receiving a negative report from Dr. George Turner, a specialist on diseases amongst Africans, reconsidered the whole scheme. However, Dr. F. Arnold, head of the Union's health services, had no objections and commented that Dr. Turner 'allowed himself perhaps unconsciously, to be influenced by considerations other than medical when he gave his unfavourable opinion'. Arnold was too charitable and understated his case; medical evidence was indeed wilfully distorted to fit political views. 'As regards Dr. Turner's condemnatory report', E. Dower, Secretary for Native Affairs, informed Botha, 'he has frankly admitted to me that he was influenced not so much on the purely medical side as from his opposition to the venture on political and other grounds. As a South African he strongly objects to the move (because of its possible bad after effects)'.[39]

An additional strand of this question, related to the perceived political repercussions, was the fear, expressed in general terms, that blacks might be 'socially and morally contaminated' in France. Specifically this implied that, to the detriment of white South Africa, members of the contingent might associate and consort with white women abroad. In the Cape Province *De Burger* held that the 'cancer of immorality would spread over the breadth and length of South Africa and that our women and children would no longer be safe on their farms'.[40] And in Natal a newspaper correspondent declared the scheme an 'outrage against humanity', in consequence of which 'hundreds if not thousands of Natives will indulge in an intercourse which in this province is considered one of the gravest crimes against our social life'. He further predicted: 'Truly, we shall be letting loose a boomerang, the force which on its return, will strike at the root of our social life.' Another, equally distressed correspondent asked: 'Should the native have social intercourse with a white woman, what effect will it have on the native mind?' To him it was a foregone conclusion that 'our fair daughter will be degraded'.[41] Among the organizations which took the issue up were the bourgeois-feminist Women's

Enfranchisement League and the Dutch Reformed Church.[42] Since the contingent was to be housed in closed compounds in France, the authorities felt that these fears were exaggerated. 'The South African public may be quite sure', was the official response, 'that no untoward results will eventuate'.[43] White fears, however, were not allayed and it was argued that 'despite compounds and the rest, on their arrival in Europe every black man will have a woman on each arm'.[44]

Although the authorities had insisted on the closed compound system because they shared exactly the same reservations, in some quarters the intensity of public concern clearly surpassed even the government's own misgivings and assumed a near pathological nature. According to one social scientist concerned with the dynamics of 'moral panic', such responses have a sexual basis and therefore 'even the prospect of limited physical contact . . . seems to set off the kind of sexual excitement in whites that produces anger'.[45] The vague possibility that blacks in France might be involved with white women certainly produced intense 'moral' indignation, but ultimately this explanation is unsatisfactory: it is somewhat tautological and also fails to take into account the effect of inequality and conflict on such a social phenomenon. The racism of sex is not only in the mind, but stems from and is maintained by an unequal socio-economic and political system. White objections to South African blacks consorting with white females abroad thus went beyond the narrowly defined 'moral' concerns, and such contacts were in a broader ideological sense construed as a direct attack on the structural base of society.

Such a response was not uncommon in South Africa. Before the First World War, between 1890 and 1914, public outcry against the 'dangers' of affairs between black and white was a persistent feature of the collective mentality of a section of white society. This trend was very visible on the Witwatersrand and can be related to periods of marked instability in society. In particular, from 1912 to 1913 there was a widespread, almost hysterical fear amongst whites that Africans would assault and rape women at random. Incidents that did occur were grossly exaggerated, but a parliamentary commission was nevertheless appointed in 1913 to investigate what was called the 'black peril scare'.[46] On a smaller scale and with even less tangible reasons, opposition to the 'moral' effects of the contingent was a continuation of this syndrome, the concerns of the 1913 'black peril scare' being resurrected in 1916 and formulated in similar hyperbolic terms. As a result of the unsettling war circumstances white society was again passing through a period of stress, and once more the sublimated neuroses of the white psyche emerged.

White objections to the contingent were specifically expressed in political and moralistic terms and were incorporated as such in the general ideological discourse. But the pervasive nature of such fears must not be allowed to obscure other considerations which were of equal, if not greater, concern. During the thirty years preceding the First World War, the nature and structure of South African society changed dramatically as a result of the dramatic expansion of capitalist relations, and the ready availability of cheap labour was a prime requisite for this development. It is therefore not surprising that the body which represented the interests of the major capitalists and employers of labour in South Africa, the Chamber of Mines, was decidedly uneasy about the prospect of a large number of potential workers leaving the country. However, the mineowners did not experience an acute labour shortage at the time (1916) and were further relieved by government assurances that the scheme would not materially affect their labour supply.[47] In Natal, though, the 'scarcity of native labour' weighed heavily with those who were dependent on cheap black labour for their prosperity and they did not hesitate to register their protest. Sir Liege Hulett, the wealthy sugar baron, condemned the undertaking as 'absolutely unnecessary' and was convinced that Natal could not 'spare any native labour'.[48] Likewise, Sir Marshall Campbell, who had extensive interests in the sugar industry, declared that the 'requirements of our industries imperatively dictate the retention of all available native labour in Natal.'[49] There can be little doubt that the profit motive took precedence over patriotic considerations. Caustically Governor-General Buxton remarked that the capitalist class in Natal

> want the labour and they are afraid that if they allow the Zulu to go and assist the Empire, they will suffer in their pockets. The Natal Britisher is a great man to talk of Natal as British to the backbone, but when it comes to helping the Empire in the concrete he pauses if his own interests are involved or affected.[50]

Clearly the ideological facade of patriotism crumbled under the threat of reduced financial gain.

Employers were not only concerned about the possible loss of labour, but were also perturbed that those Africans who went overseas might be exposed to socialist ideas, and as a result develop an increased sense of class consciousness and a new awareness of their position as a subjected labour class. Contact with such 'undesirable elements', some employers argued, would mean that on their return the 'natives' would no longer be 'prepared to do the work which they had done in the past'.[51] The spectre of a less tractable and servile work force obviously loomed large.

In contrast to the political, moralistic and economic objections, there were those sections of the white community who approved of the government's decision to send a contingent to France. Missionary opinion in the Eastern Cape, for instance, rejected the 'political creed which would deny to the Bantu any place in the Empire's service lest they should thus secure political and social recognition', and further stressed that 'one of the lessons South Africa would do well to learn is to lay aside racial prejudice'. Similarly, this view condemned criticism of the 'purely selfish kind which grumbles because there will be so much less labour available in South Africa'. However, not surprisingly, the compound system was welcomed as a safeguard against 'the temptations to debauchery'.[52] While these contemporary liberals thus summarily dismissed two widely held objections, they were unable to shed their paternalistic and moralistic beliefs. Blacks stood in need of protection from the 'moral dangers' abroad and, according to missionary insight, were especially vulnerable to such temptations. Moreover, paternalistic assumptions also explain why they gave their blessing to the scheme. There was no consideration of the possible benefits (or disadvantages) of the undertaking as far as the Africans themselves were concerned, other than that 'the call would bind them to the Union and to the Empire in active loyalty, a result perhaps not less valuable than the actual labour they will provide'.[53] Loyalty to the Union and Empire was automatically assumed to be in the best interests of Africans, and the overriding concern was clearly to strengthen black commitment to the existing dispensation.

Others sanctioned the scheme because they saw possible advantages accruing to the white man. To certain farmers, particularly those relatively untroubled by labour shortages, it was a way of demonstrating to blacks the military power and capability of white society. In less than subtle terms they argued that service in war-torn Europe 'could give the Natives such a graphic description of what they would be up against, should they ever dream of rising, that that phase of the native question in South Africa would be finally settled.'[54]

The dividing line between those who opposed the scheme and those who supported it was thus very thin. Ideological overlays aside, the camps had one fundamental concern in common: how and to what extent did the undertaking affect the vested power structures in South Africa? Ultimately then, despite widely different views, there was considerable consensus amongst the ruling classes that the issue at stake was the maintenance and reinforcement of the *status quo*.

Whereas the concerns which determined the degree and nature of black participation are outlined above, it remains to consider the way in which Africans responded to the delineation of their role as noncombatants and the pervasive white criticism of the labour contingent.

Despite the fact that the Defence Act of 1912 precluded Africans from armed military service, at the start of the First World War there was a strong body of black elite opinion which argued that blacks should fight for the right to fight. Congress demanded active participation in the war and, according to Sol Plaatje, 'threw themselves into the vortex of the martial enthusiasm that was then sweeping the country'.[55] Black newspapers claimed that 'it was the wish voiced by a larger number of Natives in South Africa to fight in this war'.[56] And, as has been mentioned before, W.B. Rubusana made a vain offer to raise 5 000 black combatant troops.

There were a number of reasons for the enthusiasm of certain blacks to secure participation in the war. To some degree at least, they were influenced by the fact that other 'coloured races' of the British and French colonial empires were involved in hostilities; the black press in South Africa was filled with the war-time exploits of Indian troops who had enrolled in the British army and blacks from North and West Africa who fought for the French.[57] To some extent, also, they echoed the patriotic rhetoric of the day that 'it was a duty to fight out of loyalty to the British flag'.[58] Of much greater importance, though, was the realization that a wider political protest could be registered. It was recognized that since combatant service was a symbol of full citizenship, the government's refusal to allow blacks to participate in combat duty really reflected their subjected and colonized status. Insistence on armed military service was therefore a way of challenging the creed which relegated them to an inferior position, and it was hoped that entry into the armed forces would provide an opportunity of increasing their bargaining power and bolstering their claim to citizenship. Hence Congress emphasized the link between combatant service and citizenship and its possible beneficial effects:

> If at the conclusion of the war we were able to point to a record of
> military service, the Constitution would inevitably have to be altered in
> order that brave soldiers of the Empire might be put in possession of the
> fullest rights and privileges of citizenship and all that pertain to *Subjects
> and Soldiers* of the British Empire.[59]

Others made essentially the same point using more vivid imagery.
'Without the Natives' shedding of blood for the King as all his
subjects', argued A.Z. Twala, 'there is no emancipation from the
many unscrupulous laws until the millennium'.[60] While such considerations were uppermost in the minds of the educated elite who
were struggling to be accommodated in the white dispensation, the
other classes in society showed little or no concern. To the
underclasses, often living in abject poverty, there were more
immediate and pressing battles than a white man's war in foreign
countries.

Nevertheless, the possibility that armed participation in the war
might spark off renewed political demands was, of course, precisely
the reason why the government refused to arm blacks. This was a
double blow for the black elite advocating combat duty: their loyalist
sentiments were, in effect, snubbed, and their wider political expectations arising from the war were also frustrated. Congress, understandably felt aggrieved and adopted a resolution expressing its
'disappointment', and regretting that 'the natural demand of the
returning soldier to the rights of citizenship has been excluded by
anticipation'.[61]

In the light of the government's rejection of their offer of armed
service, it is not surprising that the announcement to send a labour
contingent to France was received with mixed feelings. 'Responsible
African opinion might be said to have been in a state of mingled
bewilderment and anxiety', it was recorded later.[62] Congress nevertheless accepted the contingent as the second best option to combat
service. Now that a black combatant unit was out of the question and
the political potential of such a unit had evaporated, they hoped that
the labour contingent might serve the same purpose. Although they
realized that the non-combatant status of the contingent reduced its
political potential, it was still regarded as a possible chance 'for the
natives to acquire a just and recognised status as loyal subjects of the

Crown'.[63] There were, however, less sanguine views. Reflecting an understanding of the ultimate interests involved and the hegemony of the ruling class, L. Ndondela of East London, who apparently was not a member of Congress, commented: 'Of course it won't be to the natives' good, because whatever they will do will be for the good of the Imperial Government and the Union. Whether they go or remain here, they will not get any good'.[64] Congress, as will be shown later, objected to some organizational aspects of the contingent, but never questioned the reasons for its formation or the assumption that it was necessarily in the interests of Africans.

The class position of the black elite and their accommodationist strategy underlay their support for the contingent, and this policy was perhaps paradoxically reinforced by the opposition to the scheme voiced by many whites. The argument advanced by whites that the undertaking was 'politically dangerous', was considered in the black press as 'the best proof that this contingent is a good thing for the natives'.[65]

Other objections voiced by whites were given short shrift. Fears that blacks in France would be involved with white women were dismissed as a figment of the white imagination, and the blatantly one-sided nature of the 'black peril' syndrome caused one commentator to ask: 'What do all the half-castes bear witness to — the black or white peril?'[66] In turn, the criticism that the contingent would lead to a labour shortage was regarded as opportunistic and as an example of the perception of blacks as mere units of labour. The sincerity of the 'British element', which was supposed to make willing sacrifices during the war, was therefore called into question since they were only aiming 'to use the natives as means to enrich themselves very quickly'.[67]

The issue of black participation in the war has demonstrated how the concerns, interests and prejudices in society drastically impinged on military matters. Precisely because of such wider influences, the role of blacks in hostilities was neatly circumscribed and emasculated. It remained, however, to implement this policy, and the first hurdle to be crossed was to find the necessary black manpower.

Notes

1. *Acts of the Union of South Africa*, 1912, Act No. 13 of 1912.
2. *Debates of the House of Assembly*, 23 February 1912, col. 651 (Col. C.P. Crewe).
3. *Debates of the House of Assembly*, 8 March 1911, col. 1658 (T. Smuts).
4. *Cape Times*, 21 March 1917 ('Parliamentary debates').
5. P.A. Silburn, *The Colonies and Imperial Defence*, p.193. This work appeared in 1909.
6. C.A.B. 5/2/79-C, South Africa, Memorandum by the Committee of Imperial Defence, 3 May 1911.
7. *Debates of the House of Assembly*, 1 March 1911, col. 1473.
8. Walshe, *African Nationalism*, pp.30-31.
9. *Debates of the House of Assembly*, 26 February 1912, cols. 673-674.
10. *Ilanga Lase Natal*, 8 October 1915 ('A scandal').
11. D.C. 623/190/9199, W.B. Rubusana to Minister of Native Affairs, 20 October 1914, and Secretary of Defence to W.B. Rubusana, 6 November 1914. A copy of the letter appears in Plaatje, *Native Life*, p.281.
12. C.O. 537/604/46680, Secret memorandum by A. Bonar Law for the Cabinet on the raising and training of Native troops, 18 October 1915.
13. C.O. 616/64/60190, Memorandum on steps taken to increase the supply of Coloured troops and Coloured labour, 14 December 1916.
14. *South Africa*, 18 November 1917 ('As labourers only').
15. M.S. Evans, *Black and White in South East Africa*, p.155. Evans's work first appeared in 1911.
16. W.W.I., I.S.D.6/43, Smuts to Buxton, 28 August 1916 (copy).
17. Plaatje, *Native Life*, p.268.
18. *Daily Chronicle*, 27 October 1916 ('The Empire's native races and the war'); *Daily Chronicle*, 30 October 1916 ('Manpower from Africa'); *The Times*, 29 July 1916 ('Natives and the war'); *The Times*, 4 August 1916 ('Natives as labourers'); *The Times*, 22 November 1916 ('Native labourers'); D. Stuart-Stephens, 'Our million black army!' in *The English Review*, October 1916, pp.353-360.
19. *British Parliamentary Debates (House of Commons)*, col. 2024, 23 May 1916.
20. *British Parliamentary Debates (House of Commons)*, cols. 495-96, 1530-37, 25 July and 3 August 1916; *Rand Daily Mail*, 16 August 1916 ('Use of black troops, Major Wedgewood's views').
21. C.O. 551/90/31484, Notes on proposed Native Labour for England, 4 July 1916; C.A.B. 42/46/7, Memorandum on the importation of labour from abroad, December 1916.

22. M.U.N. 4/6527, Gen. D. Haig to W. Runciman, 26 March 1916.
23. W.O. 32/11345, Notes on a conference to consider proposals that African and Chinese labour be employed in France, 12 August 1916, and War Office to Colonial Office, 14 August 1916; C.O. 616/64/57352 and 44419, Marginal notes by H. Lambert, 15 September and 2 December 1916. Emphasis in the original.
24. H. Sloley, 'The African native labour contingent and the welfare committee' in *Journal of the African Society*, XVII, 1918, p.200.
25. G.G. 549/9/93/56, Botha to Buxton, 19 August and 5 October 1916.
26. G.G. 549/9/93/56, Botha to Buxton, 19 August 1916.
27. *De Volkstem*, 8 September 1916 ('Z.Afr. naturellen dokwerkers na Frankrijk'); *De Volkstem*, 26 September 1916 ('Gen. Botha toespraak'); *Cape Times*, 21 March 1917 ('Parliamentary debates'); C.O. 616/64/54173, Colonial Office to Buxton, 29 August 1916; G.G. 549/9/93/56, Buxton to Botha, 12 September 1916.
28. *Cape Times*, 21 March 1917 ('Parliamentary debates'); G.G. 547/9/93/120, Botha to Buxton, 2 April 1917.
29. Willan, 'The South African Native Labour Contingent, 1916-1918', p.71.
30. *De Burger*, 29 September 1916 ('Nationale Partij Kongress'); *Het Volksblad*, 13 October 1917 ('Vergadering O.V.S. Nationale Partij Kongres').
31. *Cape Times*, 14 and 21 March ('Parliamentary debates').
32. *Natal Mercury*, 20 September 1916 (Letter from an 'old veteran'), *Natal Mercury*, 12 September 1916 ('Native contingent, local opinion'); *Natal Mercury*, 20 September 1916 (Letter from 'Y.O.B.'); *Natal Mercury*, 3 October 1916 (Letter from 'A colonist of 35 years standing'); *Natal Advertiser*, 13 September 1916 ('Natives for Europe'); *East London Daily Dispatch*, 11 September 1916 ('Native labourers for France'); *East London Daily Dispatch*, 25 September 1916 (Letter from Rev J.W.W. Owen).
33. *Natal Mercury*, 12 October 1916 ('The proposed native contingent').
34. *Natal Mercury*, 12 September 1916 ('Native contingent, local opinion').
35. Merriman papers, 444, Merriman to Buxton, 5 December 1916; Hancock and Van der Poel (eds.), *Selections*, III, pp.413-14; Merriman to Smuts, 20 November 1916. Emphasis in the original.
36. *Natal Mercury*, 15 September 1916 ('The native labour contingent'); *Natal Mercury*, 12 October 1916 ('The proposed native contingent').
37. *Het Volkblad*, 13 October 1916 ('Vergadering O.V.S. Nationale Partij Kongres'). Translation.
38. *Ons Vaderland*, 8 December 1916 ('Pirow over de kaffer kwestie'). Translation.
39. D.C. 768/80/1997, F. Arnold to E. Dower, 15 October 1916 and E. Dower to Botha, 15 October 1916.

40. *De Burger*, 18 September 1916 ('De Tienduizend'). Translation.
41. *Natal Mercury*, 20 September 1916 (Letter from Y.O.B.); *Natal Mercury*, 3 October 1916 (Letter from 'A colonist of 35 years standing').
42. P.M. 1/1/19, Women's Enfranchisement League to Botha, 28 October 1916; P.M. 1/1/302, Ds. I.J.A. de Villiers to Botha, 29 September 1916.
43. D.C. 768/40/1917, Secretary of Defence to T. Orr, 26 September 1916.
44. *Het Volksblad*, 13 October 1916 ('Vergadering O.V.S. Nationale Partij Kongres'). Translation.
45. E. Stember, *Sexual Racism*, p.199.
46. C. van Onselen, *Studies in the Social and Economic History of the Witwatersrand, 1886-1914, 2, New Nineveh*, pp.45-54.
47. *Sunday Times*, 10 September 1916 ('Imperial impi'). See also Chapter 6 below.
48. *Natal Advertiser*, 13 September 1916 ('Sir Liege Hulett's views'). See also *Natal Mercury*, 10 October 1916 ('Natives for war work').
49. *Natal Mercury*, 12 September 1916 ('Native contingent, local opinion').
50. W. Long papers, 947/602/65, Buxton to Long, 5 June 1917.
51. *Cape Times*, 21 March 1917 ('Parliamentary debates').
52. *The Christian Express*, 2 October 1916 ('The native labour contingent').
53. *Ibid.*
54. W.W.I. I.S.D. 36/1595, B. Buchan Brown to Smuts, 22 November 1916.
55. Plaatje, *Native Life*, p.263.
56. *Ilanga Lase Natal*, 8 January 1915 ('The South African native as a soldier'). See also *Tsala ea Batho*, 17 October 1914 ('Return of native deputation').
57. *Tsala ea Batho*, 26 September 1914 ('Champion fighters to go to war'); *Tsala ea Batho*, 24 October 1914 ('France's sepoy army'); *Tsala ea Batho*, 7 November 1914 ('Black forces of the Empire'); *Imvo Zabantsundu*, 22 September 1914 ('Natives and the war'); *Ilanga Lase Natal*, 16 October 1914 ('Natives and the war'); *Ilanga Lase Natal*, 10 September 1915 ('Natives at arms').
58. *Imvo Zabantsundu*, 17 May 1917 (Letter from R.M. Tunzi).
59. *Ilanga Lase Natal*, 30 April 1915 ('South African Native National Congress'). Emphasis in original.
60. *Ilanga Lase Natal*, 12 November 1915 (Letter from A.Z. Twala).
61. *Ilanga Lase Natal*, 30 April 1915 ('South African Native National Congress').
62. *Izwe Lase Afrika*, 5 December 1941 ('South African Natives in World War One').

63. *Ilanga Lase Natal*, 3 November 1916 ('The Native Contingent').
64. *East London Daily Dispatch*, 13 September 1916 (Letter from L. Ndondela).
65. *Ilanga Lase Natal*, 3 November 1916 ('The native contingent').
66. *Natal Mercury*, 11 October 1916 (Letter from 'H.N.').
67. *Ilanga Lase Natal*, 3 November 1916 ('The native contingent').

CHAPTER 3

'You Have to Go Over the Water': Recruitment of Blacks for Military Service

During the war approximately 74 000 Africans were recruited for service in South-West Africa, East Africa and France.[1] This chapter analyzes the methods used to induce these blacks to enroll, the tensions the recruitment campaign caused, and the considerations which actually prompted them to enlist.

Africans were first drawn into the war through the demand for railway workers and transport drivers during the South-West African campaign. The Government Native Labour Bureau (GNLB), under the auspices of the Native Affairs Department, was responsible for providing the Defence Force with the necessary recruits and the bureau in turn depended on local magistrates and native commissioners to initiate the recruiting drive. Furthermore, local white notables deemed by the authorities to possess influence amongst the African population were also called on to assist.[2]

However, more than official and semi-official white channels were needed to complete the recruiting network. S.M. Pritchard, director of the GNLB, regarded it as imperative to gain the support of the black elite. To this end he organized a meeting with delegates of the SANNC in Johannesburg, inviting their comments on the conditions of service and emphasizing the need to obtain the cooperation of Congress. The delegates were suitably impressed by these overtures. As President, J.L. Dube expressed his satisfaction that Pritchard was 'the one official of the Government who was administering Native Affairs in the right direction — namely, by consulting the Natives in matters in which they were interested and for not hesitating to take them into their confidence'.[3] Congress was clearly not concerned with the motive for consultation, which was not to confide in them or accord them any form of recognition, but merely to obtain their help in a time of need. However, from their point of view some consultation — even if there was an ulterior motive — was better than none, and they optimistically chose to regard the meeting as 'but a stepping stone to still closer co-operation between the Government and the Natives'. In addition, Congress used this opportunity to demonstrate their assumed influence and importance amongst blacks to the authorities. Dube, for example, claimed that 'the people looked to them for advice and if they approved of this scheme and they explained it to the people, men would soon be forthcoming to volunteer for service in German S.W. Africa.'[4]

In the event it proved to be more difficult to find recruits than the SANNC had anticipated. Dube was instrumental in arranging numerous recruiting meetings on behalf of the government in Natal, but neither he nor the officials who addressed those present were able to make much headway. Those who attended the meetings suspected the government's motives in sending them to South-West Africa, arguing that on arrival in the war zone they would be 'put in front of the Troops to explode mines which had been laid by the Germans'. Dube's assurances to the contrary had no effect; he was regarded as a mere 'catspaw', being paid by the government and therefore not to be trusted.[5]

Outside Natal, Africans were equally wary and expressed similar doubts about the government's intentions. A dismayed magistrate from the Mount Ayliff district in the Transkei reported that the 'Natives will not go to German Africa. Could not get a single man or driver or leader. They will have it we are beaten and simply want to put them in front of the firing line'.[6] Magistrates and other recruiting agents, however, did not relax their efforts and the constant demands for recruits became an increasingly discordant element in African social life. Thus J. Sipika, a migrant worker from the Witwatersrand mines, resented official harassment during his spell at home in the Matatiele district. Sipika regretted being home 'on account of these recruiting meetings' and he, along with other Africans in a similar position, therefore decided to choose the lesser of two evils and to return to the goldfields instead of running the risk of being pressurized into military service.[7]

And indeed, confronted with African apathy, government officials soon started to exert pressure. In the Mahlabatini and Harding districts of Natal the magistrates threatened to arrest and fine headmen who failed to produce a certain number of recruits. Under duress they complied, even though it meant some alienation between them and the commoners.[8] Similar tactics were employed in parts of the Transkei and caused an anonymous African to comment: 'war methods are bad out here' and 'Natives are made by force to join for the front'.[9] Under such circumstances African enlistment can hardly be described as voluntary. This happened despite Pritchard's assurances to the SANNC that 'the system of obtaining labourers . . . would not be compulsory [and] no pressure or other influence would be exercised in order to induce Natives . . . . *The system would be voluntary*'.[10] So far as Africans were concerned, there was clearly a wide gulf between government principles and their practical application. Coercive recruiting methods coincided with an increasing need for labourers in South-West Africa and in January 1915 the demand assumed critical proportions. Anxiously Smuts wired from the front:

> Very gravely concerned about the serious position created by formidable shortage of transport natives which threatens virtual suspension [of] real progress [in the] campaign.[11]

H.R.M. Bourne, the Secretary for Defence, was also perturbed and feared that if the supply of labourers did not improve, 'a breakdown with lamentable results is inevitable'. Bourne even considered the drastic step of conscripting Africans under martial law regulations.[12] However, as far as can be ascertained, this suggested solution was not implemented.

Instead, the government turned for help to the largest employer of Africans in Southern Africa, the Chamber of Mines. Since the gold-mining industry was in the unusual position of having a surplus of labourers, the request to aid the government's war effort was not incompatible with the interests of the Chamber. It was therefore agreed that African labourers recruited from Mozambique to work on the goldfields would be employed for the first three months of their annual contract on railway construction in South-West Africa. The approval of the Portuguese governor-general was obtained before the decision was acted upon.[13] In addition, a considerable number of Africans engaged by the railway administration in the Union were summarily transferred to South-West Africa, for similar service in that territory.[14] It would appear that these arrangements eased the labour situation and satisfied the demands of the South African military. By the end of the campaign approximately 35 000 labourers (mostly Africans, but also some 'coloureds') had served in South-West Africa.[15]

Besides assisting in South-West Africa, Africans were also required as labourers for the South African military expedition to East Africa. Information on the recruiting aspects of this campaign is very scant, but it can be assumed that the authorities also experienced difficulties in securing African recruits for this venture. Indeed, some recruiting agents became so desperate that, to the annoyance of the military authorities in East Africa, even children aged fifteen or sixteen and physically infirm Africans were signed up.[16] In total, 18 000 South African blacks served in East Africa during 1916 and until April of the following year.[17] The gold mines did not provide labourers for this campaign. However, after Portugal had abandoned its neutrality in 1916, the staff of the Witwatersrand Native Labour Association (WNLA) in Mozambique was expanded to recruit not only workers for the gold mines, but also labourers for war purposes in East Africa.[18] This was done independently of recruiting in South Africa.

Africans constituted almost one third of the total number of South Africans (161 000 men) involved in the South-West African and East African campaigns.[19] In terms of manpower it certainly was a significant contribution — one which received no recognition at the time and has subsequently remained largely ignored in South African historiography.

Nor were these the only war theatres in which South African blacks served. The demand for African manpower increased dramatically with the decision to send labourers to France and resulted in the most intensive recruiting drive conducted during the war. For different reasons, the formation of the SANLC was a controversial issue for whites and blacks alike which compounded the problem of raising recruits in sufficient numbers. Moreover, the Chamber of Mines declined to assist; it was not prepared to allow black workers to leave the country for a period which would extend the annual contractual terms.[20] For some Africans, as will become clear, the renewed demand for labour meant an additional burden. Their structural vulnerability as an oppressed class was exploited to the hilt; firstly by the on-going general labour needs of a developing capitalist economy, secondly by the military demands for labour in South-West Africa and East Africa, and now thirdly, they were expected to serve the white man's cause even in Europe. The scheme to mobilize Africans for service abroad thus generated a wide range of issues, reflecting conflicting ideological and material interests.

Once again, as in the case of the South-West African campaign, the authorities tried to obtain the support of the SANNC. This time, however, Congress was not prepared to render unqualified support. In return for its cooperation it expected the authorities to abolish the projected closed compound system in France and also requested the appointment of more black non-commissioned officers. The Native Affairs Department replied that the arrangements for the SANLC had already been finalized and that the demands made by Congress were received too late for consideration.[21] It is, however, inconceivable that the authorities would even have considered abolishing the compound system; as shown earlier, Botha had only agreed to the imperial request for a black labour contingent on the clear understanding that compounds would be provided.

Despite this rebuff and its initial reservations, Congress nevertheless decided to cooperate with the government. In line with their thinking at the outbreak of war and their response to the announcement of the scheme, its leaders persisted in the view that support for the war effort could increase their bargaining power and ultimately exert more pressure on the government. 'It would be folly not to comply', it was argued, 'for surely if we do not, then our future . . . and general welfare cannot be assured'.[22] In addition, Sol Plaatje, according to his biographer, reasoned that it was important for Congress to support the scheme since 'recruitment for the Native Labour Contingent would bring the war to a swifter conclusion and thus make it possible to attend to their grievances'.[23] Clearly, for Congress the possible further advantages of such cooperation outweighed the fact that their demands had been rejected by the Native Affairs Department.

Not surprisingly, then, some of the leading members of Congress became actively involved in the recruiting campaign. In Kimberley, for example, Sol Plaatje organized and addressed meetings, while in Natal John Dube sought to fire the Zulu with enthusiasm for the white man's war.[24] Other educated blacks followed their example and publicly declared their support for the venture. Thus F.Z.S. Peregrino — a flamboyant Capetonian, and at the turn of the century editor of the newspaper, *South African Spectator* — published a special brochure, painting the contingent in glamorous colours. To serve in it was the ideal way for Africans to demonstrate their loyalty to Britain.[25] And in a somewhat similar vein, an anonymous African clergyman from East London issued a general appeal to his 'countrymen' urging them to 'give heed to the call of duty'.[26]

In government circles the recruiting drive was considered to be of such paramount importance that Botha as prime minister and Buxton as governor-general became personally involved. During September 1916 Botha visited the Transkei and, at every meeting he held in the territory, encouraged support for the contingent.[27] Similarly, Buxton went on a tour of the Transkei and Zululand in July 1917, ostensibly making a routine official visit but with the actual intent of stimulating recruitment. In order to demonstrate to the Africans the solemnity and importance of this aim, Buxton wore his Privy Council uniform with ribbons and medals during meetings with prospective recruits. Buxton's attempt to cast himself in the role of the 'great white chief' was based on the assumption that African tribesmen were used to their own chiefs appearing in their regalia, and were easily overawed by a symbolic display of power. With only a superficial knowledge of the dynamics of African societies and a certain degree of cultural arrogance Buxton confidently claimed that it was undoubtedly the 'right thing to wear uniform at these gatherings' since it 'enables the Native to distinguish the Inkosi and also impresses them'.[28]

At grassroots levels in densely populated black areas it was the local magistrates, native commissioners and chiefs, aided by merchants and individual recruiters, who were primarily responsible for recruitment. In addition, the English churches were approached for assistance through their missionaries and other church members in close contact with the African population.[29] The churches readily offered their help. Besides patriotic considerations, they also visualized the scheme as an ideal opportunity for concentrated missionary work — a captive African audience, its members uprooted from their normal cultural environment and under military discipline in a foreign country, constituted conditions which any missionary might envy in furthering his own objectives. No wonder that after a visit to Rosebank in Cape Town where the recruits were encamped before leaving for France, the Anglican bishop of Zululand was convinced that 'a large number of the men belonging to the battalion who were heathens to-day, would come back Christians'.[30]

Three basic themes, with some variations, were stressed in the call for black recruits. In the first place, an appeal was made to the loyalty and patriotism of the Africans. The educated African class regarded and depicted service abroad as a joint enterprise between black and white and also couched their appeal in the general terms familiar to the public in war-time Britain and South Africa:

> The present war is a world war. Every nation must take part in it. Even we Bantu ought to play our part in this war. Some of you have done a great deal in German East Africa and South West Africa already. You

are still expected, even across the seas, to go and help. Without you, your white comrades cannot do anything, because they cannot fight and provide labour at the same time. So you must go and do the labour while your white fellows are doing the fighting. Please everyone who loves his country and respects the British government, join this war without hesitation. Forward! Forward![31]

The same patriotic theme, but couched in a more paternalistic tone, is also evident in the attempts by government officials to convince Africans that they were privileged to enjoy the benefit of British rule and therefore they should show their gratitude by assisting the British in times of need. In overbearing terms Africans were often reminded of their 'duty' towards King and Country. 'I have laid matters to Natal Natives in such a way', reported C.A. Wheelwright, Chief Native Commissioner of Natal, 'that they have the entire responsibility of the finger of scorn being pointed at them should they fail to come forward'.[32] Secondly, the harshness of German colonial rule was enlarged upon to create the impression amongst Africans that it was in their own interest to prevent Germany from winning the war and eventually ruling South Africa to the detriment of black and white alike. 'German rule is hell rule', F.Z.S. Peregrino pointed out, and for blacks it would only mean 'slavery, oppression and cruelty'.[33] Thirdly, the practical advantages of enlistment were emphasized: free food, a free uniform and a wage of 60/- per month as opposed to the average wage of approximately 50/- paid on the mines.[34] Plaatje, in his attempts to raise recruits, varied the pattern somewhat. For those not to be swayed by the stock arguments of patriotism and financial benefits, he played on the notion, common amongst the aspiring black class in South Africa, that their advancement depended in part on education and that service abroad presented an ideal 'educational' opportunity. Thus he told his audience on the diamond fields 'that six months in France would teach them more than ten months in Kimberley; it was just like a great educational institution without having to pay the fees'.[35]

In an attempt to move away from the somewhat rarefied nature of some of these appeals, the authorities obtained for propaganda purposes appropriate letters from Africans who had joined and were already serving in France. Such letters, heavily censored to create a favourable impression of conditions in France, were widely distributed in African communities in the hope that the information from fellow blacks would carry more weight than official efforts. However, it was none too easy to lend credibility to the venture as an African concern. 'These letters are regarded with some suspicion as coming through officials', it was reported.[36] The authorities were nevertheless undeterred; if the letters were not convincing enough, then perhaps the presence of the authors themselves would be. 'The best way to counteract sinister rumour, and to give confidence', Buxton argued, 'is that some of those who have been with the Contingent should return and disseminate the actual truth'.[37] This plan was duly put into practice and 20 carefully selected members returned to the Union and were sent to their home districts. There they dutifully organized meetings and generally followed the official line by relating tales of loyal and contented African labourers abroad, only too grateful to serve the Empire in the 'great white war'.[38] Some, however, felt the need to embroider on the official version, and without the knowledge or approval of the authorities, introduced a new element — more appealing to basic human nature — in their call for service abroad. 'In France you will find magnificent entertainment, you will be going out with ladies of high standard and you will be eating nice food', was D.S. Makohliso's way of tempting prospective recruits.[39] In a similar vein other enterprising recruiters created the impression that those who enlisted had 'a lazy, happy life . . . to look forward to: load and offload ships and trains — that is all, and the most important item — to have your meal and a rest, or go out for a stroll . . . and for this you get paid £3 per month'.[40]

The authorities, only because they were mindful of the controversial nature of the scheme and the possible damaging effect of appeals which promised Africans the 'good life' abroad, clamped down on representations which overstepped the official mark. However, regardless of the contents of the appeals, the plan to raise recruits through returned members of the contingent failed miserably. 'It was a great frost', a disappointed Buxton reported.[41]

For those officials who were burdened with the task of supplying recruits, it became increasingly apparent that the strategies hitherto employed would not produce the desired results. 'Our recruiting methods need to be more imaginative and elastic', urged W. Carmichael, the magistrate from Tsolo in the Transkei. 'At present they take no account of human nature and . . . unless we abandon our wooden methods we have not hope . . . .' Carmichael thought it essential that recruiting agents should be paid a *per capita* grant, over and above their fixed wage, for every labourer recruited.[42] D.L. Smit, the magistrate's clerk in East London who was intimately involved in recruiting, also advocated such a departure 'as the fact is undeniable that the average native expects an occasional "swazi" or tip, and the amount of zeal thrown into the work too often depends on this consideration'.[43] Even the chief magistrate of the Transkei favoured this proposal since 'every other means of inducing Natives to go overseas has been tried with small success'.[44] The Native Affairs Department declined to condone such perquisites, but since the magistrates who generally supported the idea were hard pressed to obtain recruits, it is more likely that such a system did operate unofficially. Other inducements were readily sanctioned; thus African recruiters who enrolled sufficient recruits were officially promised that they would be entitled to non-commissioned ranks in the contingent.[45]

As an additional strategy the government deliberately tried to appease those sections of the African population whom they considered most likely to provide recruits for the contingent. This policy was followed in Zululand, where the government officials were sorely disappointed that the Zulu, whom they generally regarded as the martial race *par excellence*, only provided 300 recruits after seven months of intensive recruiting.[46] In an attempt to redress the situation the government decided to appoint Solomon, son of the revered Dinuzulu, as chief of the Usuthu 'tribe' in Zululand. Dinuzulu's trial and imprisonment after the 1906 rebellion was a controversial issue and deeply resented by the Zulu.[47] By appointing the direct successor of Dinuzulu the authorities hoped that they could heal old wounds and gain the goodwill of the Zulu. The Chief Native Commissioner, C.A. Wheelwright, explained in a confidential letter 'that the government feels rather that the Chiefs, in acting independently as they have done, have failed to come up to scratch in . . . assisting the Government to obtain labour for the Overseas Contingent, and that it is a question as to what extent Solomon's influence in Zululand might . . . be availed of'.[48] Buxton also mentioned in this respect that the 'reinstatement of Solomon . . . was carried through . . . with the hope that that might assist in recruiting'.[49]

The Zulu, however, were not to be swayed by Solomon's appointment. During a meeting organized by Solomon and attended by almost 12 000 Zulu, it was reported that the appeal to join the contingent met with the following unambiguous rejection:

One man raised a shout of 'We are no longer free agents. We belong body and soul to the Gold Mining Companies and the Government'. This declaration seemed to be a straw for which the men had been waiting, as the whole concourse took it up in one shout of 'Electu, Electu'. (It is our word).

The meeting then came to an abrupt and disorderly end as those present rapidly dispersed.[50] They clearly perceived that Solomon had been coopted and as the magistrate at Estcourt declared from his particular perspective, 'disloyalty to the government is at the root of the matter and as Solomon has identified himself with the government he is . . . also a casualty of the same disloyalty. . . .'[51] Given the general attitude of the Zulu, it is not surprising that they formed a distinct minority in the contingent; up to June 1917 only 629 men from the whole of Natal enrolled.[52]

Attempts to manipulate 'tribal' attitudes were not restricted to Zululand. In the Transkei certain magistrates played on traditional rivalries between 'tribes' in an effort to rouse enthusiasm and a spirit of competition as to which 'tribe' could proclaim the most recruits. To their dismay, however, the magistrates found that such contrived 'games' were not at all popular.[53]

As in most wartime recruiting campaigns, inflated promises were also made to lure the unsuspecting into the recruiting net. In this respect Major H. Dales, the officer commanding the contingent's transit and demobilization depot in Cape Town, complained that 'many of the upcountry Commissioners and other authorities made promises to the natives which in numerous instances it was found impossible to carry out'.[54] The contents and nature of these promises are difficult to ascertain because they were often made verbally by enterprising recruiters with no official authority to employ such methods. There is sufficient evidence, however, to discern some of the more extravagant promises made; certain recruits were *inter alia* informed that they would be relieved from paying poll tax, be exempted from the pass laws and be given free grants of land as well as cattle.[55] These promises were of course never kept. While securing the enlistment of some Africans, such deception also contained the seeds of possible future resentment amongst members of the contingent.

After wilful misinterpretation, possibly the most popular recruiting tactic was the intimidation of African chiefs and headmen. Thus in the Transkei certain headmen were told that they would be deposed if they failed to enlist men and in some cases their subsidies were suspended for not complying with these orders.[56] 'Often', as A.K. Xabanisa, a Transkeian member of the contingent testified, it was 'only the fear that the government may deprive them of their Chieftainship or Headmanship' that induced them to cooperate.[57]

From intimidation to forceful commandeering was but a short step. Some magistrates in fact argued that a drastic approach was the only one which offered any hope of success. G. Cauvin, the magistrate at Port Shepstone, was in no doubt on this point:

> It will take years to train and instruct the native mind to a proper sense of duty they owe to King and Country. The only thing they understand at present is brute force. Short of compulsion you will get no recruits.

In line with this thinking Cauvin dropped all pretence of persuasion and decided 'to order them out for labour overseas'.[58] Certain chiefs, under pressure from the authorities, also resorted to coercion. Thus it was reported that Solomon, in an effort to demonstrate that he still exercised control over his subjects, was 'press ganging Natives into the Overseas Corps, and a large number of these people were being forced to go whether they liked it or not'.[59] Similar tactics were also used in the Transvaal and caused the Transvaal Native Congress to complain that the 'Natives were treated like sheep and driven overseas'.[60] Despite such compulsion, it would be wrong to assume that Africans were completely at the mercy of recruiters; as will be shown later, they displayed considerable resourcefulness to avoid being impressed into military service. Nevertheless, it is clear that questionable methods abounded and that some blacks did not, in the true sense of the word, volunteer for the contingent. Although the government officially disapproved of conscription,[61] in practice they turned a blind eye to the way in which recruiting was conducted. As a consequence, through the pressures emanating from magistrates, native commissioners, individual recruiters and chiefs beholden to the authorities, some blacks found themselves enmeshed in a system which was geared to the whittling away of personal choice. In certain instances, the crucial decision to enlist was taken for them. An anonymous African tellingly described how the recruiting system operated on the ground: the recruiters 'come to you, ask your name, they write it down, they tell you to prepare, you have to go over the water'.[62] Thus although official and systematic conscription was not resorted to, informal labour compulsion served much the same purpose.

Despite the variety of carrot and stick methods employed, the government was unable to find sufficient recruits. Initially, in September 1916, the Imperial authorities requested 10 000 labourers, but in January 1917 the Union government was urgently requested to send 40 000 men abroad.[63] They failed to reach this target by a considerable margin; in total 25 000 recruits were secured, but after weeding out the sick and infirm 21 000 were eventually sent to France.[64] To make up the shortfall, it was at one stage even contemplated at ministerial level to release selected black prisoners from gaol to supplement the numbers. However, after consultation with the British War Office it was decided not to adopt this contentious and risky policy.[65]

Dismayed at the disappointing response, the authorities, whose attitude in this matter was distinctly paternalistic, accused the Africans of ingratitude towards the Union and Imperial governments. Botha, in particular, was distressed that the 'natives did not recognise more fully, by joining the Corps, all that the Imperial Government and Union Government had done for them in the past'.[66] There were, however, much more cogent reasons for African apathy than that suggested by Botha's bland observation. At this juncture then, we have to look more closely at the nature of black resistance and apathy.

Black resistance has assumed a multitude of historical forms, but its consistent object has been 'the avoidance, disturbance, or destruction of one aspect or another of the system of domination'.[67] For numerous blacks, the call to serve in a white man's struggle amounted to yet another attempt to dominate and control their lives. However, as is evident from the failure to raise sufficient recruits, blacks managed with a considerable degree of success to withstand the pressures exerted during the recruiting campaign. In particular they were concerned to exercise the right to choose, within limits, the working conditions which offered them the best comparative benefits. Working for the government under war circumstances was clearly not an attractive option. During a recruitment meeting in a township near East London the blacks present demonstrated explicitly that they were not prepared to tolerate the unfettered exploitation of their labour. In a remarkable expression of working class consciousness they challenged W.R. Ellis, the local superintendent of Native Affairs:

Who is working the Gold Mines, the Diamond Mines, Coal Mines; what labour laid the Railway to G.W. Africa? Numbers of us have proceeded both to G.E. and G.W. Africa whilst a big contingent is overseas. We have our places to which we will proceed to labour where and when we like.[68]

The most common form of resistance was simply to stay clear of recruiters. 'I am aware of instances where, [when] recruiting meetings were in the air, they [the Natives] have deliberately absented themselves and made into the bush', the hapless Ellis of East London reported.[69] A number of Sotho also fled across the border to the Free State where they looked for employment with white farmers in order to avoid being pressed into service.[70] Such tactics were of course the most effective way of resisting unacceptable demands. Once recruited, however, another strategy, desertion, remained. Some deserted a day or two after they had been attested, or if that was impossible, during the train journey to Cape Town. In time though, recruiting agents discovered that the number of recruits despatched did not tally with those arriving at the mobilization camp in Cape Town. In order to prevent desertion, all recruits were then placed under stricter supervision immediately after they had been enrolled.[71]

A further form of resistance is revealed in the tactics of chiefs and headmen who were not prepared to cooperate with the authorities. In order to diminish official pressure, they feigned an interest in recruiting. 'Hence you get the familiar impasse, common enough in native territories', one frustrated recruiting officer reported, 'of the chiefs' polite disdain, sultry indifference, cordial but insincere promises, or even underground thwarting of the Government's proposals'.[72] Of course the pretence could not be kept up indefinitely since the authorities would soon press for tangible results, but in the short term such a delaying strategy was certainly effective.

As well as evoking passive resistance, the recruiting drive also led to the consideration of more drastic action over a wide front. From the Lydenburg district in the Eastern Transvaal it was reported that Africans were stocking up on 'assegais and if the Government wants to send them . . . to Europe they will use the assegais and make an attack'.[73] Likewise, in Griqualand East and Natal some Africans threatened to resist violently any efforts to force them to join the contingent.[74] Furthermore, in the black township of East London a protest meeting was held and a motion accepted 'that any persons sent by the Government to recruit for the Contingent should be assaulted'.[75] As far as can be ascertained these threats were not carried out, but they nevertheless demonstrate the unpopularity of wartime recruitment and the intensity with which certain blacks were prepared to resist being dragooned into military service.

Recruitment also generated divisive tensions within black communities, as one speaker at a recruitment meeting in Pretoria revealed:

> When we speak of joining the overseas contingent our women curse and spit at us, asking us whether the Government, for whom we propose to risk our lives, is not the one which sends the police to our houses at night to pull us and our daughters out of bed and trample upon us.[76]

Similarly, in the Bulwer district in Natal it was reported that certain women 'made a terrible row' upon learning that their husbands contemplated supporting the Union war effort.[77] It is evident that those who were prepared to consider enlistment ran the risk of being branded collaborators, and it would also appear that women played a pivotal role in dissuading men from enrolling. Although the intransigence of these women may have been prompted by the possible detrimental financial effects of an absent breadwinner, the evidence from the meeting in Pretoria certainly suggests that their opposition was also politically inspired.

The recruiting drive caused tension not only between men and women, but also between chiefs and commoners. Those chiefs who cooperated with the authorities, and often formed the cutting edge of the campaign, found that they did so at the expense of alienating their followers. In one particular case the Pedi chief, Sekhukhune II, was openly confronted by a group of tribesmen who refused to proceed to war after they discovered that he had enlisted them under false pretences. They had already arrived at Germiston station when they learnt that they were about to entrain for war service and not, as the chief had made them believe, for road construction in Mozambique. The authorities tried in vain to persuade them and in desperation Sekhukhune II was called to Germiston to convince them. Even this had no effect. Upon his arrival the chief was told in no uncertain terms by Mpsamaleka, one of the ringleaders,

> that he was teaching him, the chief, a lesson, a lesson to tell the truth . . . [and] that in future, when whites tell you something, do not

connive with them. We are the tribe, tell us the truth. We should not be herded like goats, that is not right. I am not afraid to go to war, I am not afraid to die. What I want is that you tell us the truth in future. You must tell whites that our people want to be told the truth. We are not going to war.[78]

Clearly, the conduct of the Pedi chief infuriated these tribesmen and they did not hesitate to resist his devious recruiting tactics.

Turning from black resistance to the reasons for African apathy, a whole range of considerations unfolds. At one level the government failed to make the war a live issue to Africans, for many of whom the European conflict was a remote event which did not threaten them in any immediate way. Under such circumstances it certainly was a formidable task to convey a convincing appeal to a largely illiterate people. This problem was compounded by the government's refusal to adapt and relate Allied war propaganda in such a way that it might have some relevance for the African population. This is not surprising: the oft-repeated claim that the war was being fought for the rights of oppressed nations could hardly have been conveyed to subject people without arousing in them expectations of greater freedom. The price of the government's necessary silence on this topic was that Africans could identify themselves positively with neither the war aims nor the war propaganda. Indeed the government's silence spoke volubly to some Africans who, as a prerequisite for participation, insisted on drastic change within South African society. Thus Chief Mangala of Western Pondoland declared during a recruiting meeting (though he must have realized the futility of his demand) that 'the Union Government should do away with the colour bar before we go overseas'.[79]

Recruitment was further hampered by the fact that the subordinate position of blacks in South African society was reproduced in the wartime role allocated to them by the government's defence policy. Certain blacks argued that since the authorities refused to grant them combatant status and the equality with whites that implied, they were not prepared to participate in a lesser capacity as labourers. This attitude is reflected in the stance of certain educated blacks from the Eastern Cape that if the government 'distrusts us so much that it cannot put rifles into our hands when we ask for them in order to fight for the Empire; well then, we are a disloyal, dangerous people; we cannot do anything; we might be a danger to the army in France'.[80] This does not, however, imply that blacks would necessarily have enrolled in greater numbers had the government decided to arm them; the perceived inferior role assigned to them was only one of a wider range of objections which account for African apathy.

The main reasons why blacks declined to serve are all traceable to one underlying theme: basic mistrust of the white man. The pervasive nature of black misgivings are perhaps best illustrated by the following conversation between two Africans as reported by a white Natalian who called the speakers A and B:

A: How are things your way?
B: Oh, all right, but there is a lot of talk about the natives the Government wants to go and work over the sea. . . .
A: Yes? . . . Why do they want our young men to go and help them?
B: I don't know. I don't know what to think.
A: I thought the white people could not be beaten. Why then do they call upon us to help them?
B: I don't know what to think. Why do the white people want to take them . . .?
A: I won't go and our people won't go.
B: I hear that the white people will . . . take our boys if they don't go.
A: Yes, then if they do that, there is going to be trouble . . . .
B: The white people will humbug us about this.
A: Yes, they are a clever people.

According to the farmer this was the prevailing attitude amongst a considerable number of Africans he had been in contact with: 'they all appear to have the same idea that the white man is "humbugging" them in some way'.[81]

The general lack of trust in the white man found more specific expression in a refusal to cooperate with those governmental institutions which were responsible for controlling the lives of Africans in peacetime and now, in time of war, were utilized to obtain their goodwill and support. In particular the recruiting drive suffered from its association with the Native Affairs Department. For many Africans the Department was a symbol of oppression. 'Nine cases out of ten a native goes to Native Affairs Department office and comes out of it fully convinced that it is the Native Oppression and Persecution Department', ran a black newspaper's summary of the general attitude towards the department.[82] Not surprisingly, then, objections were raised because recruitment for the contingent — 'an essentially Imperial Native business' — was conducted by 'a narrow-minded set of officials whose outlook and methods in Native matters . . . are selfish and shortsighted'.[83] Blacks who involved themselves in recruitment were also confronted with this dilemma; Sol Plaatje found that his own efforts to raise recruits were hampered by the 'Union's methods of administering native affairs'.[84] It was on the basis of their day-to-day encounters with unsympathetic and overbearing officials that certain Africans formed their concept of the Union government. While in a vague, somewhat utopian way, some Africans might still have considered the British government to be more liberal and therefore worthy of their support, the attitude of the Union government was often perceived to be harsh and despotic. At a recruiting meeting held in Pretoria, a speaker clearly revealed how the arbitrary conduct of officials, in this case the police, shaped African perceptions and ultimately influenced their attitude towards the war effort:

> We are not against the King of England; in fact he is our only hope. But as for the Union Government, it has thrown us away like filthy rags. We are loyal, but what about those police who kick us and shove us out of the way?'[85]

Moreover, certain individuals, selected as recruiting agents, were most unlikely to secure African cooperation. In Natal the choice of Sir George Leuchars, who was well remembered for his severe suppression of the Zulu rebellion in 1906, was generally unpopular. 'That fact alone will contribute to militate against the success of recruiting natives in this province and Zululand', an African observer noted.[86] And so it did: Leuchars subsequently admitted to Botha that he was unable to raise recruits in any considerable number but, understandably, he failed to mention that his lack of standing had any bearing on the matter.[87] Like Leuchars, other officials in Natal were also frustrated in their recruiting efforts because their past conduct in quelling the 1906 rebellion counted against them.[88]

A further and important reason for the prevailing apathy relates to African reservations and apprehensions about the government's land policy. The 1913 Land Act, in particular, had generated considerable resentment and the subsequent 1917 Native Administration Bill, which the government was considering at the time of the onset of war, increased African fears that they might be dispossessed of their land. Even Buxton, who was a staunch supporter of the Union's policy in this respect, had to admit that it had a negative effect on recruitment:

The feeling of unrest which has undoubtedly followed the introduction and discussion of the Native Land Bill . . . has made the natives very suspicious, and made many of them believe that they will be consequently dispossessed of their land. This makes them afraid to go away just now in case they may find when they come back that their homes have been removed.[89]

However, it was not only the implications of official policy which alarmed Africans. Certain white farmers, anxious to retain their labour, undermined the recruiting drive by intimidating those Africans who considered enlistment. Threats that their families would be evicted were a powerful deterrent. 'How can a Native join the colours if he is fully aware of the fact that his house might be destroyed after his departure?' asked Daniel Hafe from Natal.[90]

In addition, some Africans were not impressed by the conditions of service in the contingent. The somewhat higher than average wage to be earned by joining was not sufficient to induce them to proceed to an unknown and strange country for the purpose of labouring under risky wartime circumstances. As one African explained: 'the wage of £3 per month was not enough in France where bullets were flying about, seeing that a similar wage was obtainable on the mines in Johannesburg without the fear of bullets'.[91] Moreover, the closed compound system was criticized and certain educated Africans also argued that the opportunities for black advancement in the contingent were too limited. Initially blacks could be promoted to the rank of sergeant — called 'chief induna' so as not to embarrass white sergeants — but as these appointments were in terms of authority on par with those of their white counterparts, they soon ceased and blacks were restricted to the rank of lance-corporal. This had a detrimental effect particularly on those educated blacks who might have aspired to higher positions.[92] Finally, African reluctance to proceed to France increased with the news that the SS Mendi — a transport ship carrying members of the contingent — had sunk on 21 February 1917 with the loss of 615 African lives after being rammed by the SS Darro off the Isle of Wight.[93]

In the overall evaluation, it is clear that the main reasons for African apathy were directly related to the structurally subordinate position of blacks in South African society. Precisely because of this, the white man's enemy was not necessarily the enemy of his black compatriots, who consequently did not feel obliged to support the war effort.

Indeed, for many Africans the battle was at home rather than abroad. However, there were of course also those who did join and it now remains to explain their reasons for doing so.

In assessing the motives of African recruits, the emphasis will be placed on those who joined the SANLC for service in France. Those who had enlisted for the South-West African and East African campaigns are excluded, partly because of a lack of information on their reasons for doing so, but also because a considerable number of those sent to South-West were either transferred from the South African Railways or seconded by the Chamber of Mines and had little or no choice in the matter. Those who enrolled for France had, albeit only comparatively, a greater degree of choice.

It is of considerable interest that a disproportionately large number of recruits were drawn from the Northern Transvaal. Buxton estimated that this area contributed 66 per cent of the total number, whilst Lieutenant-Colonel H.P. Wolff, a senior officer in the contingent, calculated that the region produced 60 per cent of the recruits.[94] Such a high percentage is surprising. In the first place the combined African population in other regions such as Zululand, the Transkei, Basutoland, and the Eastern Cape far exceeded that of the Northern Transvaal, and secondly, Africans in these areas had been exposed to British values over a fairly long period and would conceivably have been more receptive to recruiting appeals emphasizing 'loyalty and duty' to the Empire. Although Africans in these parts were not necessarily enthusiastic about the British connection, it has to be explained why their contribution to the contingent was eclipsed by the comparatively less populous northern Transvaal, where British influence was weaker.

Botha claimed it was because Africans were better treated in the Transvaal than elsewhere and therefore showed greater willingness to support the SANLC.[95] This is an unconvincingly idealistic explanation, even if one is prepared to accept the very dubious proposition that they were in fact better treated. H. Lambert, a senior official in the Colonial Office, made a more perceptive comment on the uneven regional distribution of recruits: 'I think it was simply because . . . conditions in the Transvaal were less satisfactory than in the native territories that the natives were readier to leave their homes'.[96]

Indeed, conditions in the Northern Transvaal do provide the key to understanding why this area produced such a large percentage of recruits. At the time of the recruiting drive the region experienced an intense drought. In April 1917 the native commissioner in the Soutpansberg district commented that because of the very bad drought 'we expect the natives to be asking for assistance shortly'.[97] This was in fact the worst drought in 26 years,[98] and severely undermined the self-sufficiency of African peasants dependent on agriculture. Moreover, other avenues of employment were restricted.[99] Consequently, military service became an option worth considering. Joining the SANLC meant that poverty-stricken Africans were at least assured of an income, part of which could be remitted to their destitute families. 'To keep the wolf from the door', was, according to the local native commissioner, an important reason why a considerable number of Africans from the northern Tranvaal decided to enroll.[100]

It was not only the prevailing drought in this area which helped to swell the ranks of the SANLC, however. It would also appear that more pressure was exerted on the African population in this region than in other parts, as Buxton suggests:

> The natives there [the northern Transvaal] no doubt are somewhat more under the control of their Chiefs, and the Chiefs there are more under control of the Government than elsewhere, . . . [and] the legitimate pressure by Officials has produced a greater result than it has produced elsewhere.[101]

Whether such pressures were indeed 'legitimate' is open to doubt, but the importance of Buxton's statement lies in his explanation of the regional discrepancy in numbers. In an article in *The Christian Express*, essentially the same point was made in somewhat more euphemistic terms. The African response was generally disappointing, it reported, 'except in the Transvaal where General Louis Botha has been able to apply administrative pressure'.[102]

Although the drought and official harassment in the northern Transvaal propelled Africans into service, there were also other reasons why Africans from various regions of the Union enlisted. One important aspect to be considered in this respect is the representation of the black elite in the contingent. 'Educated natives of all kinds have volunteered', noted the Rev. John Lennox of Lovedale, who accompanied the contingent as a chaplain. 'They have left their schools, their businesses, their congregations to serve the King'.[103] Likewise, C.A. Wheelwright, chief native commissioner of Natal, mentioned that 'a great proportion of Natives who have gone Overseas is of the more or less educated type'.[104] The black elite was obviously well represented; missionaries who went with the SANLC calculated that they constituted 25 per cent of the total[105] — a significant proportion when considered in relation to their relatively small size in the population as a whole. There is insufficient evidence to provide a statistical breakdown of the different professions practised by the educated Africans in the contingent, but from various scattered sources it appears that teachers were in the majority.[106]

Educated blacks formed a clearly defined aspiring class in South African society. They were, in the main, products of English mission schools and had integrated the values of a Christian-British education with their own, African consciousness. They shared a common ideological outlook and at the time of the First World War the effects of their socialization were discernible in their support of the British Empire — a symbolic embodiment of 'justice and fairness' — and the perception that their own future was linked to that of the Empire. Moreover, integral to this world-view was the belief in 'progress' and that recognition depended in part on their unflagging efforts to develop and improve their own abilities. 'Progress' and 'improvement' were vital concepts in these African circles.[107]

The value system of this class is of central importance in determining why they joined the contingent. It made them generally more responsive to the idea of serving the Empire in a time of need, while the recruiting appeals which emphasized 'loyalty and patriotism', and the notion that service abroad was an educative experience, also struck a particularly sensitive chord. J. Mtemba expressed the sentiments of his class when he wrote in a letter from France: 'It is ambition that comes first when a man thinks of coming here, and then extension of knowledge and last comes patriotism and loyalty'.[108] Similarly, for R.M. Tunzi enrolment in the SANLC was 'a splendid chance' of 'learning about the world and becoming well informed men'.[109] Just how widespread the idea was that military service in France presented a chance to acquire a broader educative experience, is evident from the comment of the resident-commissioner in Basutoland that 'most' of the 1 397 Sotho who had joined 'were men who had passed through school and were anxious to see the world'.[110] Closely allied to the preceding notion was the self-perception of this class as standard-bearers of a new breed of 'civilized' Africans; they considered it as a self-imposed task to induce others to follow their example in the quest for 'improvement'. Thus, F.H. Kumalo, a Natal teacher who had joined the contingent, declared: 'Although our schools needed us, we felt that it was our duty to lead the way . . . .'[111]

The manner in which patriotic and loyal considerations surfaced as motives for enlistment is clear from the following interview between a newspaper reporter and W.B. Yiba, a member of the SANLC:

> 'Was it the pay that attracted you?'
> 'No Sir', was the prompt reply. 'When I volunteered I was a compositor at the "Imvo" office at King[williamstown], and I was getting the same pay as I was offered by the British government'.
> 'What then induced you to leave your wife and family to go to France?'
> Pulling himself together and looking as if such a question were quite unnecessary, he promptly replied, 'I answered the call of my King'.[112]

It can be argued, and with considerable force, that such a rhetorical patriotic declaration is meaningless and only serves to mask the real motives of the recruit. However, it assumes greater validity if it is placed in the context of the wider ideology expounded by members of the aspiring African class. As indicated, they had, through their education, internalized certain British values; hence, by joining the contingent they could provide tangible proof of their sincere desire to uphold these values and, perhaps ultimately, prove that they were worthy to be considered as full British citizens on a par with the whites, and with the same rights.

In contrast to the 'lofty' motives of this class, there were also criminals serving with the SANLC who had joined to cover their tracks and evade arrest and punishment. H. Bulaweni, for instance, was wanted in connection with a murder case in the Engcobo district in the Transkei. However he enrolled in the contingent under an assumed name and was only apprehended on his return from France. In the subsequent court case Bulaweni was condemned to death after he had confessed his guilt; he also admitted that he had enlisted 'with the idea of trying to escape the consequences of the stabbing'.[113] In another case the authorities were informed of 'a Native who had offered his services and after enlistment was found to be wanted by the police in connection with a charge of murder'. This man was then arrested in the mobilization camp in Cape Town.[114] Blacks who had committed other crimes also perceived the contingent to be a relatively safe haven where they could establish a new identity and prevent police detection. Thus, as it transpired later, 'several Natives who belonged to the Johannesburg criminal class' had joined the contingent.[115] The 'criminal class' referred to by the authorities was in all probability made up of members of the Ninevite gang on the Witwatersrand — an extensive criminal organization which, significantly, was increasingly being pressurized by the police at the time of the First World War.[116]

Highly personal and individual reasons — as opposed to those of a particular group — also prompted some Africans to join. Jason Jingoes, for one, was disconsolate and depressed after an unrequited romantic entanglement; war service seemed to offer a dramatic escape from the turmoil of his personal life. 'But it was because of Jemina that I wanted to die in France without a wife', he explained.[117] Others, young and perhaps bored with their daily existence and the narrow confines of everyday life, considered war service as an eventful and exciting new experience. S. Phala, for example, recalled that 'we were driven by adventure as young men'.[118]

Finally it should be emphasized that the reasons why Africans decided to join the contingent cannot be categorized in watertight compartments. The preceding exposition is merely an indication of the various considerations which induced blacks to enlist; more than one reason or a combination of reasons could obviously have influenced an individual's decision. It is therefore difficult to determine which particular set of reasons was of overriding significance. Nevertheless, when it is taken into account that the majority of recruits were drawn from the drought- and poverty-stricken Northern Transvaal it can be assumed that for a considerable number material considerations were of crucial importance.

Notes

1. This figure is based on O.C. Records, 93/139/2, Recruiting Statistics, 1914-1918; G.N.L.B. 187/1217/14/D110, undated memorandum by Col. S.M. Pritchard, probably 1918. The statistics which appear in the *Official History of the Union of South Africa and the Great War*, pp.218-19 are incomplete.
2. D.C. 625/67/205/9199, Pritchard to Native Labour Bureau, 20 and 22 March 1915.

3. *Ilanga Lase Natal*, 22 January 1915 ('South African Native National Congress').

4. *Ilanga Lase Natal*, 22 January 1915 ('South African Native National Congress'). See also *The Christian Express*, 1 February 1915 ('Natives and the war'); B. Willan, 'South African Native Labour Contingent, 1916-1918', p.65.

5. D.C. 626/205/2441, Report by H.M. Taberer, 2 February 1915.

6. G.N.L.B. 192/1329/14/D48, Magistrate Mount Ayliff to Secretary of Native Affairs, 27 November 1914.

7. G.N.L.B. 192/1329/14/D48, Intercepted and translated letter from J. Sipika, 30 October 1914.

8. S.N.A. 1/4/25/L5/1915, State of Native feeling in the Mahlabatini district, report by Chief Native Commissioner in Natal; S.A.P. file 6/245/14/308, Report by Sub-inspector J.H. Jones, 3 April 1915.

9. G.N.L.B. 192/1329/14/D48, Anonymous intercepted letter, 27 October 1914.

10. *Ilanga Lase Natal*, 22 January 1915 ('South African Native National Congress'). Emphasis in original.

11. D.C. 46/15/993, Smuts to Defence Headquarters, 23 January 1915.

12. D.C. 625/205/9199, Bourne to Secretary of Native Affairs, 2 November 1914.

13. D.C. 625/205/9199, Governor-General Pretoria to Governor-General Lourenzo Marques, 22 January 1915, and Secretary of Native Affairs to Pritchard, 25 January 1915; P.M. 1/1/35, Governor-General Lourenzo Marques to Governor-General Pretoria, 28 January 1915 (copy).

14. D.C. 625/205/9199, General circular, 10 December 1914.

15. O.C. Records, 93/139/2, Recruiting statistics, 1914-1918.

16. B.L. 4/3/25, General circular, 26 February 1917.

17. O.C. Records, 93/139/2, Recruiting statistics, 1914-1918; D.C. 851/219/22714, Statistics on South African blacks in East Africa, 1916.

18. T.H. Henriksen, *Mozambique: A History*, p.107; A.G. 205/412, General scheme of recruiting natives for East African campaign, 1917.

19. *Official History*, pp.218-19.

20. *Sunday Times*, 10 September 1916 ('Imperial impi').

21. *Natal Mercury*, 9 October 1916 ('Native contingent for Europe'); *Ilanga Lase Natal*, 20 October 1916 ('Native contingent').

22. *Ilanga Lase Natal*, 27 October 1916 ('The 10 000 for France').

23. B. Willan, 'The role of Solomon T. Plaatje (1876-1932) in South African society' (D.Phil. thesis, University of London, 1979), p.195. An expanded and revised version of the thesis was published in 1984 under the title *Sol Plaatje: A Biography*.

24. *Diamond Fields Advertiser*, 28 June 1917 (Native Recruiting Meeting); Willan, 'South African Native Labour Contingent, 1916-1918',

pp.66-67; *Natal Mercury*, 19 October 1916 ('Arise ye Zulu'). A Zulu version of Dube's article also appeared in *Ilanga Lase Natal*, 20 October 1916.

25. F.Z.S. Peregrino, 'His Majesty's black labourers: a treatise on the camp life of the SANLC', p.40. For biographical details on Peregrino see C.C. Saunders, 'F.Z.S. Peregrino and the South African Spectator' in *Quarterly Bulletin of the South African Public Library*, XXXII, 3 March 1978, pp.81-89.

26. *East London Daily Despatch*, 6 October 1916 (Letter from a 'Native Minister').

27. *Territorial News*, 7 September 1916 ('General Botha's visit'); *Territorial News*, 21 September 1916 ('General Botha's tour'); *Territorial News*, 28 September 1916 ('General Botha's tour'); *Imvo Zabantsundu*, 26 September 1916 ('General Botha at Umtata').

28. *Long Papers*, 947/602/84, Buxton to Long, 15 April 1917.

29. G.G. 545/9/93/56, Botha to Buxton, 25 May 1917; *Rand Daily Mail*, 9 September ('Natives wanted for France'); I/T.B.U. 25/66/1, Circular from Botha to English churches, 11 June 1917; P.M. 1/1/480, Botha to Anglican Bishop of Cape Town, 6 June 1917; *Ilanga Lase Natal*, 13 July 1917 ('Botha's appeal').

30. *Cape Times*, 17 November 1916 ('Mission development after the war'). See also P.M. 1/1/480, Anglican Bishop of Cape Town to Botha, 20 July 1917.

31. Quoted in Perry (eds.), *Jingoes*, p.72.

32. D.C. 768/40/1997/9199, Wheelwright to Secretary of Native Affairs, 3 October 1916 (copy).

33. Peregrino, 'His Majesty's black labourers', pp.3, 40. See also Willan, 'South African Native Labour Contingent, 1916-1918', p.66.

34. *Cape Times*, 28 March 1917 ('Natives for France'); Long Papers 947/602/84, Buxton to Long, 15 April 1917; *Diamond Fields Advertiser*, 28 June 1917 ('Native recruiting meeting'). For the average wage rate on the gold mines see S. van der Horst, *Native Labour in South Africa*, p.205.

35. *Diamond Fields Advertiser*, 28 June 1917 ('Native recruiting meeting').

36. Long Papers 947/602/84, Buxton to Long, 15 April 1917. For copies of these letters see C.M.T. 3/930/778/2, A.K. Xabanisa to Chief Magistrate, 25 May 1917; M. Mbanye to Magistrate Elliotdale, 15 May 1917 and G. Nomvele to Magistrate Matatiele, 17 June 1917.

37. Long Papers 947/602/84, Buxton to Long, 15 April 1917.

38. G.G. 545/9/93/56, Botha to Buxton, 2 July 1917; *Alice Times*, 15 November 1917 ('Returned Native labourers'); *Alice Times*, 18 October 1917 ('The native contingent').

39. *Imvo Zabantsundu*, 11 December 1917 (France). Translation from Xhosa.

82 Fighting Their Own War

40. D.C. 768/119/9199, Secretary of Native Affairs to Secretary of Defence, 19 January 1917.
41. Buxton Papers, unsorted, Buxton to Long, 4 November 1917 (copy).
42. C.M.T. 3/92/778/2, W. Carmichael to Chief Magistrate, 10 March 1917.
43. Smit Papers 35/17, D.L. Smit to Magistrate East London, 26 July 1917.
44. C.M.T. 3/930/778/2, Chief Magistrate Transkei to Secretary of Native Affairs, 10 August 1917.
45. S.3/13/1/2, Resident Commissioner Maseru to Assistant Commissioner Mafeteng, 11 March 1918; 1/T.B.U. 25/66/1, Circular of the Department of Native Affairs, 9 November 1916; C.M.T. 3/930/778/2, Chief Magistrate Transkei to Magistrate Tsolo, 5 September 1916.
46. S.N.A. 1/4/26/1/1917, C.A. Wheelwright to R. Fyfe King, 26 March 1917.
47. S. Marks, *Reluctant Rebellion*, pp.249-303; 338-65.
48. S.N.A. 1/4/26/1/1917, Wheelwright to Shepstone, 17 November 1916.
49. Long Papers 947/602/65, Buxton to Long, 5 June 1917.
50. C.M.T. 3/930/778/2, Report by O. Fynney, 9 July 1917 (copy). See also *Zululand Times*, 8 July 1917 ('Solomon's meeting'); *Natal Mercury*, 25 July 1917 ('The Nongoma meeting'); *Natal Advertiser*, 25 September 1917 ('Natives for overseas'); *Ilanga Lase Natal*, 14 September 1917 ('Solomon ka Dinuzulu').
51. S.N.A. 1/4/26/1/1917, Magistrate Estcourt to Wheelwright, 19 July 1917.
52. *Ilanga Lase Natal*, 15 June 1917 ('Native contingent').
53. C.M.T. 3/926/778/2, Magistrate Matatiele to Chief Magistrate Transkei, 3, 26 November and 4 December 1917.
54. O.C. Records 44/22/81, Report on SANLC, 12 April 1918.
55. Eddie Roux, *Time Longer than Rope: A history of the black man's struggle for freedom in South Africa*, p.113; J.318/3/754/21, Native Congress meeting at Pietersburg, 7 September 1921; S.N.A. 1/4/26/1/1917, Capt. A.P. Graham (from France) to C.A. Wheelwright, 8 May 1917 and Wheelwright to Graham, 26 July 1917; Stanford Papers B.C.293/F4/23, Sworn declaration by P. Seroke, 7 August 1923; C.M.T. 3/927/778/2, Report of a meeting with headmen in the Mount Fletcher District, 23 November 1922.
56. C.M.T. 3/925/778/2, Magistrate Tsomo to Chief Magistrate Transkei, 8 and 28 November 1917; C.M.T. 3/925/778/2, Magistrate Kentani to Chief Magistrate Transkei, 27 July 1917.
57. G.G. 549/9/93/179, A.K. Xabanisa to Buxton, 12 January 1918.

58. S.N.A. 1/4/26/1/1917, G. Cauvin to C.A. Wheelwright, 21 September 1917.
59. S.N.A. 1/4/26/1/1917, W.N. Angus to C.A. Wheelwright, 1 October 1917.
60. G.N.L.B. 192/1329/14/48, Transvaal Native Congress meeting, 17 October 1916. See also J. 318/3/754/21, Native Congress meeting, 7 September 1921.
61. S.N.A. 1/4/26/1/1917, C.A. Wheelwright to G. Cauvin, 26 September 1916.
62. *De Burger*, 7 May 1917 ('Opinies uit de Vrijstaat'). Translation.
63. P.M. 1/1/20, British Secretary of State to Governor-General, 18 January 1917 (copy).
64. W.O. 107/37, Appendix F, History of the SANLC, 1918.
65. G.G. 549/9/93/167, F.S. Malan to Buxton, 4 October 1917; G.G. 545/9/93/56, British Secretary of State to Governor-General, 29 November 1917.
66. Buxton, *General Botha*, p.288.
67. B. Bozzoli, 'History, experience and culture', in B. Bozzoli (ed.), *Town and Countryside in the Transvaal*, p.28.
68. 1/E.L.N. 71/16/16, W.R. Ellis to Magistrate East London, 26 June 1917.
69. *Ibid.*
70. *De Burger*, 7 May 1917 ('Opinies uit de Vrijstaat').
71. S.N.A. 1/4/26/1/1917, Magistrate Port Shepstone to Wheelwright, 21 September 1917; D.C. 851/253/22714, Magistrate East London to Quartermaster-General, 21 June 1917; *Natal Mercury*, 25 July 1917 ('An obstinate native').
72. S. 3/13/1/1, Lt. J.N. Fraser to Government Secretary Basutoland, 15 October 1917.
73. J. 255/3/527/17, Commissioner of Police to Secretary of Justice, 24 October 1917.
74. S.A.P. file 6/496/17, Lt. C.F. Bluett to Commanding Officer Durban, 11 June 1917; S.N.A. 1/4/26/1/1917, Magistrate Nongoma to Wheelwright, 10 September 1917.
75. Smit Papers 36/17, D.L. Smit to State Prosecutor East London, 26 July 1917.
76. Quoted in W.C. Scully, 'The colour problem in South Africa' in *The Edinburgh Review or Critical Journal*, July 1919, p.85.
77. N.A. 9130/69/363, Sworn declaration by Chief Ntshibela, 1 August 1917.
78. African Studies Institute, University of the Witwatersrand, Oral History Project, Transcript of an interview with S. Phala, a member of the SANLC, 20 November 1979.

79. C.M.T. 3/925/778/2, Report of a meeting with Chief Mangala, 10 November 1916.
80. *The Christian Express*, 2 July 1917 ('Native recruiting').
81. *Natal Mercury*, 3 October 1916 (Letter from 'A colonist of 35 years standing').
82. *Tsala ea Batho*, 15 August 1914 ('The administration of our native affairs').
83. *Imvo Zabantsundu*, 28 November 1916 (Letter from 'A Native').
84. *Diamond Fields Advertiser*, 22 August 1917 ('Native grievances').
85. Quoted in Scully, 'The colour problem in South Africa', p.85.
86. *Ilanga Lase Natal*, 15 June 1917 (Letter from J. Mampumulo).
87. P.M. 1/1/482, Leuchars to Botha, 21 August 1917.
88. N.A. 9130/69/363, M. Ndabaco to Wheelwright, 6 September 1917.
89. Long Papers, 947/602/80, Buxton to Long, 28 July 1917.
90. *Ilanga Lase Natal*, 26 October 1917 (Letter from Daniel Hafe).
91. *Cape Times*, 28 March 1917 ('Native Labour for France').
92. O.C. Records 447/22/81, Report on the SANLC, 12 April 1918; G.G. 545/9/93/56, Botha to Buxton, 23 July 1917; C.M.T. 3/930/778/2, Magistrate Tsolo to Chief Magistrate Transkei, 5 September 1917.
93. C.M.T. 3/926/778/2, Report of a meeting in the Matatiele district, 17 March 1917; Long Papers, 947/602/84, Buxton to Long, 15 April 1917; Willan, 'South African Native Labour Contingent, 1916-1918', p.70.
94. Long Papers, 947/602/80, Buxton to Long, 28 July 1917; U.W.H. 89/34, Report on the SANLC by Lt.-Col. H.P. Wolff, 8 March 1919.
95. *Cape Times*, 21 April 1917 ('Parliamentary debates').
96. C.O. 551/123/35976, Marginal note by H. Lambert, 16 June 1919 on correspondence between Botha and Colonial Office, 1 June 1919.
97. S.N.A. 1/4/26/1/1917, Native Commissioner Pietersburg to C.A. Wheelwright, 19 April 1917.
98. C.J.J. Blignault, 'Die reënval van die Pietersburg-plato' (unpublished M.A. thesis, University of Pretoria, 1952), p.106.
99. N.A. 99/568, Director of Native Labour to Secretary of Native Affairs, 22 March 1917.
100. N.A. 99/568, Native Commissioner Pietersburg to Secretary Native Affairs, 24 October 1917.
101. Long Papers, 947/602/80, Buxton to Long, 28 July 1917.
102. *The Christian Express*, 2 July 1917 ('Recruiting for the Native Labour Contingent').
103. *Alice Times*, 24 May 1917 (Letter from Rev. John Lennox).
104. S.N.A. 1/4/26/1/1917 (A. Wheelwright to Magistrate Nongoma, 27 September 1917).
105. *The Christian Express*, 1 November 1917 ('The SANLC'); *Ilanga Lase*

Natal, 9 November 1917 (Letter from L. Hertslet).

106. *Ilanga Lase Natal*, 10 May 1918 (Letter from 'A Native'); G.G. 549/9/93/179, A.K. Xabanisa — Buxton, 10 December 1917; C.M.T. 3/930/778/2, M.J.C. Matheson to Chief Magistrate Transkei, 29 January 1918; S.N.A. 1/4/26/1/1917, A.E. Le Roy to E. Crosse, 30 August 1917; *Native Teachers Journal*, October 1920 (Letter from F.H. Kumalo).

107. See for instance the analysis by Willan, 'Plaatje', p.36.

108. *Ilanga Lase Natal*, 7 December 1917 (Letter from J. Mtembu).

109. *Imvo Zabantsundu*, 22 May 1917 (Letter from R.M. Tunzi).

110. S.3/13/2/3, Report of Resident Commissioner Maseru, 15 August 1917.

111. *Native Teachers Journal*, October 1920 (Letter from F.H. Kumalo).

112. *Alice Times*, 20 December 1917 ('Interview with returned corporal').

113. J.256/3/527/17/, Rex vs. H. Bulaweni, July 1918.

114. G.G. 545/9/93/56, Botha to Buxton, 23 June 1917.

115. G.G. 545/9/93/56, Maj. H. Dales to British Staff Officer, 28 June 1917.

116. C. van Onselen, *Studies in the Social and Economic History of the Witwatersrand, 1886-1914, 2, New Nineveh*, p.192.

117. Perry (eds.), *Jingoes*, p.75.

118. African Studies Institute, University of the Witwatersrand, Oral History Project, Transcript of an interview with S. Phala, 20 November 1979.

CHAPTER 4

In the Crucible:
The Nature of Military Service for Blacks

This chapter explores the war-time experience of those Africans who had enrolled for service in South West Africa, East Africa and France. In particular, attention is paid to the work they performed, the conditions under which they laboured (and died), the nature of the disciplinary measures to which they were subjected, and their immediate responses to the often harsh set of circumstances that participation in a 'white man's war' inflicted upon them. Finally, the reasons why the contingent in France was disbanded before the end of the war will be examined.

As far as South-West Africa was concerned approximately 500 blacks worked as stevedores in Walvis Bay where they assisted in unloading war supplies, while a considerable number were responsible for all the animal transport and served as drivers of ammunition and supply wagons. Most, however, were employed to repair rail links destroyed by the retreating Germans and particularly in the construction of new railways, linking the northern South African station, Prieska, to the southern station in the war zone, Kalkfontein (modern Karasburg), some 490 kilometres distant.[1]

The strategic importance of the railways to the South African war effort made their speedy completion imperative, and to this end relay teams of black workers toiled day and night. Although the white personnel were highly praised in official reports for their part in the project, no mention was made of the important role of black labourers. The official omission, despite the undoubted contribution of African labour in terms of manpower and output to the eventual success of the Union's forces, is hardly surprising. The work-force, after all, was taken for granted unless it caused problems; if it performed satisfactorily it could be ignored. And there was, of course, also the possibility that official praise might raise unwanted expectations. Therefore, as Sol Plaatje explained, 'lest their behaviour merit recognition, their deeds and acts must, on account of their colour, not be recorded'.[2]

Although blacks served as non-combatants, this did not imply that they were not exposed to the dangers of warfare. In the course of their duties a number of transport riders came under German fire at Sandfontein (in the southern part of South-West) and were captured in September 1914. There is limited, but telling, evidence available on the manner in which the Germans treated black prisoners-of-war; at least some of them were tortured and mutilated. Allegedly this happened because the Germans had warned them not to become involved in hostilities between the 'white races'. Since the Germans themselves employed blacks in their colonial forces, this injunction must not be taken at face value. Rather, the Germans were trying to deter blacks from joining their enemies. Nevertheless, whatever the precise motive, certain black South African prisoners-of-war suffered badly. An anonymous African later testified that those who had managed to escape and had found their way back to the Union 'tell piteous stories and bear marks of their treatment by the Germans. Some had one eye scooped out, some had their ears cut off, and others were castrated'.[3] It is highly unlikely that this was an exaggeration. In 1916 a South African commission of enquiry, though concerned with the German treatment of white prisoners-of-war, remarked in passing that the way in which the Germans treated their black captives showed 'instances of hardship and in one or two instances of what would be according to our ideas cruelty'.[4] Although somewhat of an understatement, it bears out the undoubted brutality experienced by some of those unfortunate enough to fall into German hands.

During the East African campaign, as in South-West, South African blacks served as transport drivers and as dock and railway workers. The climate and terrain, however, differed markedly, and in East Africa blacks also acted as porters and carriers in areas difficult to traverse by animal and wagon transport. A South African missionary who had visited the contingent was impressed by the part played by transport workers on the supply lines in conveying food, ammunition, material for bridges, wireless apparatus, telegraph wire, and medical stores. This prompted him to ask: 'Who shall say that they are not doing their bit?'[5]

The nature of the work in East Africa was arduous, and it was also performed under adverse tropical conditions. Moreover. the workers had to contend with the ravages of disease, particularly malaria. For the blacks this was probably one of the worst features of an exceptionally difficult campaign. Those who were stationed in unhealthy areas and had contracted the disease had no better than a slim chance of survival. During the first four months of 1917, when a section of the force was quartered along the coast in an area heavily infested with malaria, fully 1 600 of the 2 000 men (80 per cent) succumbed, while those that survived were often broken in health for the remainder of their lives. The fatalities did not end in East Africa; of the 700 men on board the ship *Aragon*, 135 died before it reached Durban. For the contingent as a whole (18 000 men) the monthly mortality rate shot up from 5,4 per 1 000 to 22,2 per 1 000. After a visit to the war zone, a South African official recorded that many black labourers 'became saturated with fever which sapped all their energy, enterprise and morale. Self-help and self-respect almost disappeared. Men lay down to die rather than combat the difficulties in the field'.[6] Clearly, the human dimension behind the statistics is one of profound misery. 'The suffering of these men defies description', the commanding officer, Major T.E. Liefeldt recalled later.[7]

Disease, of course, made no distinction between Allied or German troops, or between black and white. All the troops in East Africa suffered from malaria, but blacks and whites did not suffer equally. Although there are no comparable statistics for white South African troops during the height of the disease between January and April 1917, their average monthly mortality was considerably lower than that of blacks and did not exceed 2,9 per 1 000.[8] Major-General R.A. Ewart, the South African quartermaster-general in East Africa, ascribed the sudden increase in black mortality during the first four months of 1917 to the inclement rainy season, and the discrepancy between the number of white and black deaths to the different kinds of work and conditions experienced during the campaign. He explained:

> During this period the European troops have been practically stationary owing to the heavy rains and, although they have suffered considerably owing to their retention in unhealthy areas . . . they have not been exposed to the same hardships as the native transport personnel and porters who have had to work day after day in pouring rain over incredibly bad roads, delivering or carrying the bare requirements of the Force.[9]

In South Africa, news of the disconcerting number of deaths amongst blacks caused uneasiness in government circles. Botha, in particular, expressed his doubts whether sufficient care had been taken about the welfare of the contingent:

However bad Malaria may be in East Africa, I am unable to believe that the death rate amongst the Native labourers can be so much higher than amongst the European and Coloured troops, unless there is much that is lamentably lacking in the military arrangements for rationing and medical and hospital treatment.[10]

In response to this situation Botha instructed H.S. Cooke, assistant director of native labour in South Africa, to conduct an enquiry into the circumstances that had led to the appalling death rate amongst South African blacks in East Africa. Cooke interviewed 41 whites associated with the contingent as well as some of the black members. He concluded that, although the mortality rate was particularly high, it was inevitable in view of the nature of the campaign. Inadequate hospital and medical facilities, poor organization and negligence did not, he claimed, aggravate the situation.[11] To say the least, this conclusion is surprising; one cannot but suspect that the report was designed to exonerate military and other officials from blame. True, it was a difficult campaign conducted under adverse conditions, but that is hardly the full explanation. Fourteen years after the war Major T.E. Liefeldt acknowledged that the hospital facilities for South African blacks were woefully inadequate and disorganized.[12] Moreover, Lieutenant-Colonel O.F. Watkins, director of the labour bureau for all military labour in East Africa, stated at the end of the war: 'Where a Medical Officer had to deal with white and with black patients in times of stress, the latter suffered. In a word, the condition of the patient was apt to be a consideration subordinate to his colour . . . .'[13] In contrast to the conclusion in Cooke's report, then, it seems clear that the lives of many South African blacks in East Africa were lost through the prevalence of discriminatory practices. More generally, such practices were of course built into the repressive and exploitative structure of colonial and South African societies. In war-time these were transferred to the military setting: fatally so, for many blacks serving in East Africa. Whereas class and colour mainly determined wealth and poverty in times of peace, in war-time these were often the arbiters of life or death.

The soaring death rate amongst South African blacks in East Africa forced Botha to act before he had received Cooke's flawed report. Despite protests from the military authorities, in April 1917 he ordered the cessation of recruitment for East Africa. Although the general policies of the Botha government towards Africans could by no stretch of the imagination be described as humanitarian or philanthropic,

Botha appears to have been genuinely concerned about the fate of South African blacks in East Africa. 'Nothing has grieved me more', he claimed in a private letter, 'because apart from the dictates of humanity, if there is one thing I have insisted upon during this war it is that the treatment and well being of our Natives who have responded to the call for labourers should be properly provided for in every possible way'.[14] It is unlikely though that this was the only reason for Botha's decision to stop the recruitment for East Africa. He was keen that recruitment for the labour contingent in France should be speeded up and given first priority, and this consideration also seems to have played a part in his decision to call off competing recruitment for East Africa.[15]

It was not only malaria and neglect that made war services for South African blacks a particularly traumatic experience. In East Africa, as well as in South-West, they were subjected to harsh discipline. Of course, it must be borne in mind that by its very nature military discipline is strict and especially so on active service. However, the system of military justice and discipline in a 'white man's army' was weighted against Africans and left them more vulnerable.

Although the authorities did try with the advent of the South-West African campaign to codify the procedures to be followed, and decreed that officers should deal with minor transgressions and a provost-marshal or magistrate with more serious cases,[16] these regulations were honoured more in the breach than in the observance. In fact, the white 'gang-bosses' who directly supervised black labourers were a law unto themselves and frequently resorted to corporal punishment as a means of coercion or retribution. E. Dower, secretary for native affairs, stated that he 'has received constant complaints from all parts as to the indiscriminate punishment and flogging of natives, being inflicted without any proper enquiring and by conductors and other persons in no responsible positions'.[17] Similarly, the commanding officer of the labour depot at De Aar where the blacks assembled before and after service in South-West, reported that 'from complaints received from various parts it would appear that the men directly in charge of Natives resort to unlimited chastisement and that the Natives are subject to severe ill-treatment'.[18] In this respect the treatment of South African blacks did not differ much from that in other colonial armies in Africa where flogging was a common form of punishment. It was thought to be the most effective way of disciplining African soldiers and was only finally abolished by the British in 1946.[19] This demeaning and callous form of punishment was of course also discriminatory; it only applied to blacks and was never inflicted on white troops during the First World War. Indeed, the flogging of white troops in the British army had been ended decades before, in 1881.[20]

The South African authorities approved of flogging as an established form of punishment, but considered it prudent to issue directives that the 'flogging of natives should be restricted to punishment for very grave offences and should only be sanctioned by quite senior and responsible officers and proper steps should be taken to see that it is properly carried out without undue severity'.[21] Apart from decidely vague formulations like 'proper steps' and 'undue severity', this regulation was not primarily designed to ameliorate the lot of the labour force in South-West; on the contrary, it reflected the concern of the authorities that reports of the ill-treatment of labourers might filter through to the Union and discourage other Africans from enlisting.[22] In any case, such regulations, like those that went before them, were empty gestures and doomed to failure in an environment where there were more pressing matters for officers to attend to, and often little real concern. Even in cases where Africans were actually brought to trial, it was often not for the purpose of dispensing justice. For example, in one incident in Walvis Bay, three black dock workers refused to work after their contracts had expired. A month before the time they had informed their supervisors that they did not intend to renew their contracts. They were nevertheless arrested and had to stand trial before the assistant provost-marshall who summarily dismissed the case and sentenced the workers to be horsewhipped. The commanding officer, Lieutenant A.W. Biddell, fearing that the punishment might lead to general discontent, felt obliged to make an obvious point to the officer concerned:

> Do you think the sentence was rather severe? In cases like these where there appears to be a *bona fide* grievance as far as the natives are concerned, I think it would be better if you first of all enquired into that grievance before trying and sentencing to corporal punishment.[23]

Not surprisingly, South African blacks had to endure the same punishments and arbitrary justice in East Africa. Major T.E. Liefeldt himself admitted that he was unable to exert any effective control:

> Though indiscriminate flogging of natives . . . is prohibited, I have reason to know that the practice is indulged in to a considerable extent by transport conductors and other subordinates who unfortunately are supported by their officers, thus depriving the native of any possibility

of redress . . . . Flogging would seem to be the only recognized method of punishing the native who receives his 25 cuts with a sjambok for the most trivial offence, in most cases without any pretence of a trial, proving his guilt or otherwise.[24]

This practice was so wide-spread and so brutally carried out, that it stirred some Christian consciences in South Africa. During a session of the Anglican Church synod in Johannesburg, Rev. E. Paget raised the issue. Perceptively he realized that the punishment meted out to South African blacks did not primarily stem from military procedures or demands, but that 'the treatment that went on there was very largely due to the accepted attitude of the white people towards the natives in South Africa, and that they were almost treated as being of less importance than the mule or oxen'. Indeed the wider values of society were crucial in determining the nature of military punishment and therefore Paget could argue convincingly that the 'whole thing is due to the brutal, callous and absolutely ungodly and beastly attitude of the average white person towards the natives'.[25]

This value system also permeated other forms of punishment meted out to Africans. For the most trivial offences 'gang-bosses' in South-West-Africa arbitrarily inflicted fines ranging from £1 to £2, a heavy penalty considering that the average wage of African labourers was about £3 per month. Moreover, to add insult to injury, 'gang-bosses' often pocketed the money themselves. Punishing and fining Africans thus became a lucrative way for 'gang-bosses' to supplement their own incomes. The authorities did try to stop such corruption by insisting that only the paymaster could dock African wages, but since the 'gang-bosses' themselves were the ultimate authority in the day-to-day work situation it is highly unlikely that these malpractices were rooted out. As a matter of fact, senior officers with the force admitted that there was little they could do to remedy the position.[26]

It stands to reason that these circumstances must have provoked profound African resentment. However, the very nature of the system to which they were subjected ensured, officially at least, that the African voice remained inaudible. Thus a labourer known as John, who was upset about a fine he had to pay, 'was threatened with being put in the stocks when he wanted to make representation'.[27] Moreover, in cases where Africans did manage to make their grievances known, the authorities, despite ample corroborating evidence, showed no inclination to believe information emanating from blacks and even less willingness to act upon their requests. When headman Malokoane of the Pietersburg district approached the Defence Force for permission to investigate the situation, after he had been informed by some returning members of the treatment meted out to labourers in South-West, the request was turned down with the following comment: 'Natives are prone to magnify and publish their grievances, and it is doubtful if Malokoane's impression would be of value to Defence Force interests'.[28] Clearly, black opinions were unwelcome in a 'white man's war'.

However, as several strikes which occurred in South-West show, Africans did express their discontent more forcibly and directly. These strikes were usually of short duration and often ended in the arrest of the ringleaders, with the others being cajoled or forced back to work. But on one occasion, marked by the solidarity of some 365 workers who persistently refused to return to work, the authorities were forced to accede to their demand to be sent back to South Africa.[29] Desertion was another way in which blacks manifested their dissatisfaction. The vastness and inhospitality of the terrain in South-West did not deter prospective deserters; they hid in empty goods trains bound for the Union. At times desertion assumed considerable proportions, as is evident from a telegram despatched by a distressed officer in command of large numbers of transport workers: 'Very short of Natives owing to many deserting'.[30] There can be little doubt that for many workers the problems involved in deserting were of lesser importance than the treatment they had to endure in military service.

The experiences of some members of the SANLC in the French theatre of war were no less harrowing than those of their counterparts serving in Africa. One of the most dramatic episodes in the whole history of black South African participation was the collision involving the troopship, *Mendi*, on its way to France with members of the contingent on board. Near the Isle of Wight and in the early morning hours of 21 February 1917, with visibility reduced by fog over the English channel, the transport ship, *Darro*, rammed into the starboard side of the *Mendi* and left a gaping hole of 20 metres long and 20 metres wide. The damage was severe; the *Mendi* tilted almost immediately, took in a flood of water through the hull, and began to sink after 25 minutes. There was barely enough time to order the men on deck and launch a number of life boats.[31]

Captain L.E. Hertslet, who survived the accident, later recollected how hundreds of Africans came 'up quickly and quietly from below, and each man finding his own appointed place on the deck, notwithstanding the blackness of the night. There is no panic; they put on their clothes and lifebelts as they fall into position'.[32] This account cannot be regarded as a wholly accurate description of the behaviour of the men, unaccustomed to the sea, and on board a sinking ship. Perhaps, in part at least, Hertslet's account was influenced by his own notions of how well the officers had trained their men. An African survivor later gave a somewhat different version. He recalled that he had heard 'a terrific bang which shook the ship, putting lights out and had everybody scrambling around. There was great panic and confusion . . . . Below there was a sea of darkness, but the men plunged into the rough, cold water, singing, praying and crying'.[33] Despite the obvious contradictions in these two accounts, they can be regarded as complementary. Immediately after the *Mendi* had been struck, some men at least might have followed the prescribed drill; but it is also more than likely that many others blindly followed their own instincts.

In the icy water of the English Channel, about 38°F at the time of the collision, hundreds were involved in an unequal battle against death. Many drowned almost immediately, others died of exposure, while some clung desperately to pieces of wreckage. Under these circumstances the men had to rely on their own efforts and luck to stay alive. Nevertheless, there were instances in which some further endangered their lives in attempting to drag exhausted and struggling men into already overcrowded lifeboats.[34] An officer who had survived the dramatic night later claimed: 'Could everything that occurred that night be told, it would be a record of undying fame for our South African natives'.[35] Whatever the extent of such heroic deeds, relatively few men survived the disaster: of the 882 men on board the *Mendi* a mere 267 were saved, while 615 lost their lives.[36]

Subsequent to the collision a Court of Inquiry was convened in England and in August 1917 it found the Captain of the *Darro*, H.W. Stump, guilty of gross negligence. In the foggy weather he had failed to transmit the relevant warning signals and he had also exceeded the speed limit laid down for such conditions. Moreover, in an even more serious breach of regulations, Stump had made no more than feeble attempts to assist the floundering men in the water. The court was convinced that had Stump 'got the boats out as soon as he knew his vessel was safe, more lives would, in all reasonable probability have been saved'. In delivering the verdict the court declared that Stump's inaction was 'inexcusable', and as a disciplinary measure his licence as a ship's captain was suspended for a year.[37]

Given the explicit finding of the court, the disciplinary action was surprisingly lenient. One of the British officers associated with the case, Captain A.H. Young, was of the opinion that Stump's licence should have been cancelled. He argued that either Stump was

> utterly callous to all sentiments of humanity or, as a result of the collision, his nerve deserted him to such an extent as to render him incapable of rational thought and action at a time when every instinct of the trained seaman should have been brought into play. In either case it points to the necessity for a prosecution with a view to cancellation of certificate for gross incompetence or criminal neglect and so prevent him from again becoming a common danger. I consider that if inhumanity be proved he should be punished by cancellation; if incompetence through loss of nerve be the judgement then he is not a fit person to again have command of any ship.[38]

The case remained closed, but Young was not alone in condemning Stump. In South Africa some blacks maintained that for Stump's share in the 'never-to-be-forgotten *Mendi* holocaust, he should not be permitted to enjoy liberty for another twenty-four hours'.[39] It is furthermore of interest that despite a wide-ranging inquiry, once the court had established Stump's negligence, it did not in any systematic manner attempt to assess the reasons for his misconduct. The absence of any reliable evidence makes it impossible to provide an answer, but in view of Stump's blatant disregard for the plight of the *Mendi*'s passengers, one is certainly justified in raising the question that the court failed to probe in any depth: was Stump's indifference entirely unrelated to the fact that the *Mendi* carried black troops?

Be that as it may, the circumstances surrounding the *Mendi* disaster and a subsequent administrative delay on the part of the South African government to release full details gave rise to unconfirmed suspicions amongst certain blacks that there was 'more behind it than has been revealed'.[40] More specifically, from New Brighton, near Port Elizabeth, an Anglican missionary reported that 'some mischief-makers had created unrest by hinting that the same care was not taken in the case of natives as with white troops'.[41] Even if these rumours were baseless, they are significant in as far as they reflected deep-seated African suspicions of the white authorities. In general, Africans had been deluded so often in dealing with whites that they had more than ample reason to believe the worst.

Botha was aware of these rumours and in his official announcements in parliament about the collision he claimed that such 'idle and mischievous stories' were unjustified. He then expressed the government's sincere regret at the loss of life and extended his deepest sympathy to the relatives of those who had died in the disaster. T. Smartt, leader of the Unionist Party, and John X. Merriman made similar speeches and a motion of sympathy was unanimously passed. The adoption of this motion witnessed the unusual sight of an all-white parliament rising to pay respect to deceased blacks.[42] The government furthermore undertook to assist the next-of-kin financially through a gratuity of £50 each.[43] For the authorities this was the end of the matter, but as will be shown in the following chapter, for many blacks the memory of the *Mendi* disaster lived on to be embedded in African political consciousness.

At this juncture, however, the activities of those who had arrived safely in France remain to be discussed. The 21 000 men formed part of an ever increasing general labour force in France (consisting of Chinese, Japanese, Indian, Egyptian, French, Canadian, and British labourers, as well as German prisoners-of-war) who had to provide the necessary infrastructure for the soldiers fighting in the trenches. In December 1916 there was a total of 42 000 military labourers; a year later in December 1917 the number had increased to 91 097 and at the end of the war it stood at 124 299.[44] Thus in December 1917, shortly before its withdrawal from France, the SANLC constituted 23 per cent or almost a quarter of the total labour force. Clearly, in terms of numbers they contributed significantly to the combined Allied workforce.

The contingent was divided into 42 companies of about 500 men each. Some companies were employed in laying and repairing railway lines and roads, and in lumbering in the French forests to provide the Allied forces with timber for construction work. Other companies worked in stone quarries. Most, however, were employed in the French harbours, Le Havre, Rouen, and Dieppe where they unloaded ammunition, food supplies and timber, and transferred these to trains bound for the front.[45] A military chaplain, Rev. R. Keable, has graphically described the nature of their work in the dockyard areas. They worked in 'great, gaunt, enormous sheds of iron and steel. Trains run into these and are dwarfed to insignificance. Ships of three or four thousand tons stretch in a line outside.' The moment a ship had anchored, the men sprang into action: 'As fast as the stores are built up into monstrous heaps in the hangar, those heaps are eaten away on the other side by boys who load the stuff into railway-trucks — night and day, week in and week out, for the Army in France must be fed.' With more than a touch of imperialistic fervour Keable concluded that the 'sons of Chaka and Moshesh have come six thousand miles to feed men from every land and island in our wide-flung Empire who make up the army in France.'[46]

Only a few men were used for work which could be classified as 'semi-skilled' or 'skilled'. In the quarries some blacks who had experience on the Witwatersrand mines were entrusted to do the blasting. They took the place of German prisoners-of-war because the authorities were reluctant to trust captured enemy soldiers with explosives. Furthermore, a small number served as clerks and inter-preters, or as orderlies in the two SANLC hospitals.[47] On the question of skilled labour an officer remarked after the war 'that possibly better use might have been made of the more educated and intelligent Natives by employing more of them on semi-skilled work, even if it had entailed a certain amount of training, the time and trouble would have been well repaid by the results'.[48] However, mindful of the likely political ramifications that such a step might have in South Africa and the further possibility that it might encourage African material and political aspirations, the authorities declined to use this option.[49]

Similar considerations also ensured that the companies were stationed well clear of the actual war zone. The authorities were not concerned merely about the possible loss of life. As the commanding officer, Col. S.M. Pritchard, explained, 'there would be considerable trouble politically if the South African natives were reported to be near the fighting'.[50] Although not employed in the vicinity of the battle front, some Africans were nevertheless exposed to German air raids and occasional shelling. In a private letter an officer mentioned that 'one poor fellow got a direct hit, he was blown to a pulp and we had to bury him in his clothes'.[51] There were several air raids over Rouen and some members claimed that apart from the harbour and dockyard areas, the German aeroplanes singled out SANLC compounds as targets. This is probably somewhat of an exaggeration, but apparently the Germans, to alarm Africans, did drop propaganda leaflets which read: 'In this war I hate black people the most. I do not know what they want in this European war. Where I find them, I will smash them.'[52]

The contingent furthermore worked in extremely cold and inclement weather. One member wrote that 'it has been admitted that such a winter has not been experienced for the last thirty years'.[53] Those companies who had to work out in the open suffered particularly. It is possible to form an idea of what they had to endure in the cold, muddy and soggy conditions by reading the first-hand account of an officer:

> The dampness and cold of the slush first got through your boots, then through your flesh, then through your bones and when it got to your marrow you went on because you had no more to get wet, and when the snow, sleet and freezing arrived, it was really terrible. The natives . . . simply had to go on. If we had stopped for one day and allowed ourselves to get stiff, I believe we would have given in.[54]

The South African government, concerned about the effect of the climatic conditions because it did not want a repetition of the high fatality rate in East Africa, called for regular reports on the health of the contingent.[55] Moreover, it insisted on suitable precautions being taken in France and, although there were occasional problems in obtaining medical supplies, the workers were regularly injected and vaccinated. The Aborigines Protection Society in England also provided additional warm clothing. A few members did lose limbs as a result of frost-bite, but they were the unfortunate exceptions. Given the conditions under which they worked, the mortality rate of the contingent was not particularly high. Out of a total of 21 000 men 331 (or 1,5 per cent) died in France, mainly from pulmonary diseases.[56]

All the reports on the SANLC indicated that the contingent had performed exceptionally well under difficult conditions. For example, an engineering firm in La Havre, commenting on the work-rate of the South Africans, stated: 'We believe that the discharge of . . . a cargo of grain in sacks at such a pace, viz: nearly 170 tons per hour, is an absolutely unique achievement and in spite of a great deal of experience of what can be done in handling sacks, we were ourselves utterly astonished at the result'.[57] In several instances, platoons and companies were responsible for the loading and unloading of war material in a record time, and some of the British officers who witnessed this believed that the records were broken only through the efforts of the labourers themselves.[58] This impression was further confirmed by H. Sloley of the Aborigines Protection Society who claimed that he 'had the advantage of hearing the opinions of officers of the Royal

Engineers, Army Service Corps, Commisariat, Transport and Ordnance Departments, and the general estimate of the African native as a labourer appears to have been that, man for man, he is equal to any other class of labourer employed behind our lines'.[59] Not surprisingly, such favourable comments met with the approval of a South African government anxious to present the venture as a success.[60]

Although the officers and others concerned were not likely to mention cases where the contingent did not meet expectations, there is no reason to doubt the general veracity of the reports. It is of greater importance though to establish the context in which the SANLC performed these feats of labour. On one level one can accept that being in a foreign country and working under difficult, sometimes risky war conditions, might have posed a challenge to some members and appealed to a spirit of adventure. To a certain extent, at least, they might have experienced a sense of exhilaration, camaraderie and achievement in excelling at their work and demonstrating their capabilities. This was probably true of F.H. Kumalo who stated after the war: 'I was pleased to be in the SANLC and did my best'.[61] However, this can hardly be a full explanation. It is also of particular relevance in this respect to consider the discipline and control exercised over the SANLC, a matter touched on in a pamphlet dealing with the contingent:

> Colonel Pritchard and his colleagues have adopted and insisted upon a general recognition of certain excellent methods of administration. First in order is that of getting the very best of their men, and letting them know that . . . as regards the discharge of their duties . . . the Africans are expected to be no less diligent in their work . . . than the European subjects of the King.[62]

In practical terms this meant that the black workers were given very little leeway or respite. Indeed, the formal disciplinary regulations were formulated in such a way that they could be punished for virtually anything except satisfactory work.[63] One worker summed it up when he said that the 'golden rule was to do as you are told'.[64] Of course, such discipline is not uncommon in the army, particularly during wartime; the point here is that it certainly contributed in no small measure to the labour output demanded of and achieved by some SANLC companies.

Moreover, it was insisted on that the contingent should work only under the supervision of South African staff. The reason given was that the British officers did not realize 'that considerable moral deterioration resulted from failure to obtain a full day's work from the South African Natives, who were perfectly aware of the labour output of which they are capable'. Pritchard maintained that the men did one third less work if they were not under the supervision of South African personnel.[65] In addition, every effort was made to prevent members of the SANLC from working with groups of other labourers, particularly those from the French, British and Canadian contingents. These white workers were considered as 'being of a low physical category, work at a different pace and to a different standard output; and the native working alongside has his ideas of the white man disturbed, in addition to the natural tendency to slacken to the white man's pace.' It was, in fact, firmly believed by the authorities that a largely successful policy of separation in the workplace had enabled them to 'obtain the best possible results.'[66]

The South African officers were not only concerned about the possible effect of white workers on the labour output of the contingent, but were also acutely aware that a common workplace and common conditions of labour might transcend racial differences and forge bonds of class. Thus Lt.-Col. H.P. Wolff pointed out that 'the average man in the White Labour Companies had no knowledge of the Native or the conditions in South Africa, and was inclined to treat him with familiarity and on terms of equality. The native was quick to take advantage of this fact'.[67] Even when allowance is made for Wolff's stereotyping, the way in which Africans responded to this situation is certainly revealing. However, this was cause for considerable alarm amongst the white staff since it raised the spectre of a less tractable workforce, who might assert their position not only in France but perhaps later in South Africa as well. The policy of separation was therefore also, and probably essentially, designed to stifle any signs of incipient class consciousness, and to eliminate, as one officer indicated, possible exposure to 'socialist' ideas.[68]

Indeed, a central feature of the contingent's sojourn in France was the extent to which attempts were made to control the socio-political perceptions of members. By their very nature military establishments often exert a high degree of social control to ensure conformity and, depending on the particular circumstances, the level of control is often such that the military environment can approximate that of total institutions. But in the case of the SANLC, even the standard measures of control were deemed inadequate; they had to be elaborated and refashioned not only in order to meet military demands but also to provide a guarantee that the socio-political ramifications of black war service in a European country would not be detrimental to white South African interests.

It is furthermore important to note that, although the concept of 'social control' has its critics amongst scholars who argue that it can be (mis)used to direct attention away from underclass initiatives, it nevertheless remains a useful analytical tool. The concept does not necessarily exclude such class action, and is valuable in that it emphasizes the complex and often subtle nature of control over the subordinate classes. As one historian has explained, 'many social control mechanisms operate independently of any conscious manipulative process; thus control will not always be overt, and may or may not be recognized as such by controller or controlled.'[69]

Perhaps the best example of the way in which black aspirations were implicitly and tacitly controlled by the authorities, can be found in an apparently insignificant matter such as the type of uniform issued to the contingent. While many recruits attached particular value to a uniform as a symbol of their newly acquired status as troops in the service of the British Empire, they received a uniform that was described 'as the most atrocious, vile-smelling cotton velveteen; brown, sloppy and shoddy looking.'[70] The authorities did not explain the reason for this, but such a uniform could certainly not have created the impression amongst members of the contingent that they were in any way equal to white soldiers dressed in the standard and widely recognized khaki uniform. On the contrary, the unattractive uniform of poor quality visually confirmed the inferior status of the SANLC. Whereas the authorities in all likelihood acted subconsciously, reflecting the way in which African 'inferiority' was taken for granted, some blacks were acutely aware that the uniform actually served a degrading purpose. On receipt of his clothing an offended member remarked: 'This is only fit for convicts!' Another asked: 'Why do we have to wear *this*?'[71] And yet another member went to the heart of the matter: 'The suit of brown corduroy certainly lowered the status of the Native labourers in the eyes of the other troops.'[72]

A particularly crucial aspect in the process of control was the appointment of the white staff to accompany the contingent. Those appyling for officer rank had to be familiar with 'the mentality and customs' of blacks, and had to have a 'combined knowledge of the Native, Military Procedure and Labour.'[73] Similar qualifications were sought in non-commissioned officers; they must have had previous experience in supervising African workers and had to be 'men of the right stamp.'[74] Even more explicitly it was reported in the press that the officers were 'specifically selected by the Union Government with the view to ensuring that the natives should be kept in their proper sphere whilst away.' In effect this meant, *inter alia*, that 'they were the right sort of South Africans to appreciate the danger of allowing the natives to come into contact with white women.'[75] Not surprisingly, applications for posts in the contingent were carefully screened. Botha as prime minister even took it upon himself to make the final appointments. 'We are sifting with utmost care the many hundred applications,' H.R.M. Bourne, Secretary for Defence, informed Botha, 'so that you will have the best possible facilities for deciding on the selection of the best among the really suitable candidates for every class of appointment.'[76] Clearly, the matter of control was far too weighty to be left to chance.

The background typical of the white staff who had been appointed after such careful scrutiny is well illustrated by the career of the commanding officer of the contingent, Col. S.M. Pritchard. He had come from England in 1894 and joined the Basutoland Mounted Police. After serving for four years, he was appointed private secretary to Sir Godfrey Lagden, then Resident Commissioner in Basutoland. When in 1901 Lagden became Secretary for Native Affairs in the Transvaal, Pritchard joined him as Chief Inspector of Native Labour in that colony. In 1903 he was promoted to Assistant-Director of the Native Labour Bureau of which he became Director in 1914. Shortly afterwards, during August and September 1915, Pritchard was sent to Ovamboland to report on the possible incorporation of the area into the newly acquired South-West African territory and to investigate the potential for securing labour from the Ovambo.[77] Here, then, was a man with impeccable credentials — well versed in 'native administration', with ample experience in dealing with black labour and a commendable military background — that made him eminently suitable to take command of the contingent and to ensure from the South African government's point of view that the undertaking would have no negative consequences.

Other members of the white staff had also held positions in civilian life which gave them considerable control over Africans. Most of them were attached to the Native Affairs Department and some were mine compound managers; a sprinkling of magistrates completed the complement.[78] Furthermore, to make assurance doubly sure, it was impressed upon everyone appointed that 'he has a heavy responsibility placed upon his shoulders. It will be his duty as a representative of the Union not merely to discharge the duties of military commanders, but for the sake of our country to see that no ill effects arise from this undertaking.'[79]

Of course, it may be argued that men who had experience in 'native affairs' were obvious choices for such an enterprise. Who else, after all, could be appointed? However, the important point is that the selection was dictated by the specific social and political concerns of the South African government. Viewed from the vantage point of the rank-and-file of the SANLC, it meant that they were to be continually under the control of men intimately involved in the implementation of South African race policies; men who could be relied upon to minimize, if not completely eliminate, any influences construed as detrimental to the interests of white South Africa. In short, the social and political environment of South Africa had to be kept intact in war-torn France; members of the contingent had to be shielded from influences at variance with the prevailing orthodoxies in the Union.

In France the white staff did not hesitate to demonstrate the qualities for which they were appointed. Upon learning that French women, involved in providing refreshments for those engaged in the war effort, had also served tea to some black dock workers at Rouen, an officer immediately told the Africans concerned: 'When you people get back to South Africa again, don't start thinking that you are whites just because this place has spoilt you. You are black and you will stay black.'[80] One veteran also recalled later that they soon learnt 'to recognize two distinct factors — namely the Government who had laid down the rules and regulations, and the officers who administered them.'[81] Moreover, some officers certainly enforced their authority with more than sweet persuasion or mild cajolement. As some members stated after their return to the Union, 'the fact was that the treatment of labourers in France by the European officers and non-commissioned officers was brutal and barbarous.'[82] While the situation could, and probably did, vary from company to company and within companies, it is most unlikely, given the basis of selection of the white staff, that individual SANLC officers strayed outside the authoritarian (at best, paternalistic) approach of the officer corps as a whole.

The selection of those in control of the contingent drew some criticism from blacks in South Africa, mainly on account of the preponderance of officials from the Native Affairs Department and also because Africans were excluded from positions of real authority.[83] The government did not even contemplate making such appointments but instead, after careful screening, selected twelve African chaplains whom it regarded as the highest representatives of the rank-and-file of the contingent. Whereas the white chaplains were ranked as captains, their African counterparts were given no military rank or status.[84] Neither, as Rev. R. Keable disclosed, were they accorded much respect or standing by the white staff:

> We found ourselves, in the great majority of cases, up against white officers who disliked 'educated natives' and who particularly disliked natives in clerical dress. Their whole attitude was an attempt to deny all privileges. Black was black, and a boy was a boy, however dressed, educated or entitled.[85]

Despite the fact that the black chaplains were the victims of discrimination, they in turn perceived themselves to be superior to the ordinary labourers and they consciously strove to set them apart as a separate class.[86] Their self-perception was vital in determining their ultimate function in the contingent. They failed to act as committed spokesmen for the labourers and did not even assume the role of 'honest brokers' between the staff and the workers, but were, in fact, co-opted to strengthen the network of control. Thus, as stated in a general report on the chaplaincy, they supported their white colleagues in preventing 'that contact with new social conditions in France should complicate the social question on the return of the Natives to South Africa'.[87] Revealingly, one officer also found it commendable that 'the Native parsons were always willing to assist in the cause of discipline, patriotism and good order'.[88] In particular Rev. J.J. Xaba was singled out for praise, since 'his influence was at all times used to maintain discipline and keep the natives straight'.[89]

As a reward for their contribution, and also to effect an even closer identification of the African chaplains with the white power structure, four chaplains, along with a white colleague, were allowed to visit London where the blacks were placed under the watchful care of J.H. Harris of the Aborigines Protection Society. The purpose of the visit, as Harris indicated, was of a 'political nature', and he welcomed the opportunity of impressing on his guests the achievements and values of British civilization and assured the military authorities that the visit 'will be judiciously controlled'.[90] The exercise was considered an unqualified success. The black chaplains, it was reported, had been 'profoundly impressed by the greatness of Britain and the vast resources at her disposal':

> Britain, British life and character, British industry and ingenuity, British cheerfulness and kindness, and the amazing wealth . . . have excited their deepest admiration and wonder, and the scheme has produced nothing but good to the men themselves, and for the future of . . . South Africa.[91]

The report might have been an overstatement of the actual African response, but given the role played by the chaplains in the contingent, one can readily assume that it contained more than a grain of truth. Viewed from a somewhat broader perspective, it is clear that the chaplains found themselves, wittingly or unwittingly, in the classical collaborationist position of some of the aspiring black bourgeoisie of the time. They were carefully and selectively exposed to some of the values of the dominant system (even the films which the chaplains were allowed to see were vetted before the time and were described as an 'admirality official film' and 'a quite good story film, nothing objectionable or even comic'),[92] and were expected to internalize those values so that they in turn could become effective agents for extending ideological control over the subordinate classes. Generally, through this process hegemonic control could be facilitated with the ultimate aim of reinforcing the social and political system of the ruling classes.

Certainly the clearest manifestation of control over the contingent was to be found in the insistence of the South African government that the companies must be housed in closed compounds. The closed compound system had originated on the Kimberley diamond fields in the 1870s and, with certain modifications, it was later extended to the Witwatersrand and Rhodesian mines. As one historian has noted, in the development of mining capitalism the compound was a crucial institution in the depersonalization of Africans and in ensuring a servile workforce:

> Everywhere in southern Africa, the compounds served to isolate, regiment and exploit the . . . black working class . . . . It was the

compound, acting as the college of colonialism, that did much to rob Africans of their dignity and help mould servile black personalities.[93]

The authorities thus decided to transplant an exceptionally well-refined system of control from the mining to the military context to fulfill a similar function in France as it did in southern Africa.

Of all the Allied labour contingents in France — both white and 'non-European' — the SANLC was the only one to be housed in compounds. Only the German prisoners-of-war, who were regarded as a source of forced labour, were likewise confined. 'The conditions of service for our men in France as regards freedom of movement', reported Lt.-Col. G.A. Godley, second-in-command of the contingent, 'are similar to those applying to prisoners-of-war, and the camps occupied by our men and the prisoners-of-war are identical in every respect, except that as regards locality those occupied by the prisoners are in the majority of cases more favourably situated'.[94] It is certainly ironic that German captives, enemies of the British Empire, were somewhat better off than South African blacks who, as subjects of the Empire, had been sent to France in support of the Allied cause against Germany.

The instructions regarding the construction of the compounds were elaborate as were the regulations governing the conditions under which the inhabitants were to live. The members of the contingent had to be confined to an area surrounded by a stout barbed-wire or corrugated-iron fence or a wall which had to be at least six feet high with 'a wire netting or barbed wire along the top of the screen to prevent the natives climbing over.' To prevent fraternization it was stipulated that all the exits had to be guarded. The possibility of Africans leaving the compounds and meeting local whites was not the only danger which the authorities had in mind. The reverse, that whites might enter the compounds, was also possible. Hence it was emphasized that

> care should be taken to prevent unauthorized persons from entering the camp or conversing with Natives and especially to prevent all familiarity between Europeans and Natives, as this is subversive to discipline and calculated to impair their efficiency as working units.

Moreover, Africans could only leave the compounds under very exceptional circumstances and then only if they were accompanied by a non-commissioned or senior officer. The staff had to ensure that they did not obtain alcohol and that they were not entertained in the homes of local residents. Under no circumstances was a member of the SANLC, unattended by a white man, allowed outside the compounds. 'Under the conditions under which they are living in France,' it was explained, 'they are not to be trusted with white women, and any Native found wandering about . . . and not under the escort of a white N.C.O., should be returned to his unit under guard, or failing this, handed over to the Military Police'.[95] Limitations on the freedom of movement of troops are, of course, normal and generally accepted procedure in any military environment, but it is abundantly clear that in the case of the SANLC the regulations were unrelated to military concerns and were formulated with explicit socio-political objectives in mind.

The rationale behind the closed compound system did not go unremarked upon by certain blacks in South Africa. At a meeting of the SANLC in Natal J.J. Dube explained that 'the reason for closed compounds was that if allowed out the Natives would enjoy the same privileges as the white man,' and the audience stridently voiced their disapproval of the system: 'It's slavery! They want to make us prisoners!'[96] While Congress had hoped that one result of the contingent will be 'the opening of their minds to what the world is like outside South Africa', it now realized that 'cooped up as they are, all this may not be possible.'[97] The vast majority of white South Africans understandably approved of the compound system, but surprisingly, there was one lone voice of criticism. G.K. Hemming, an Umtata attorney who was destined to become a Native Representative in the House of Assembly in 1937, raised the issue in the press and asked: 'Is it right that thousands of robust men should be herded for so long a period?' He pointed out that the 'conditions surrounding them will preclude the giving of leave of absence' and commented scathingly that 'they are placed on conditions which even an animal is not expected to support.' This led Hemming to conclude that the 'spectacle of these men herded together for so long was one of the most terrible indictments against the ruling race ever framed.'[98] In contrast to Hemming's criticism, a philanthropic body like the Aborigines Protection Society in London merely accepted and approved of the compound system as a necessary measure for the welfare of Africans in a foreign environment. Without questioning the assumptions underlying the compound system, members of the organization, after a visit to the compounds, reported in the best traditions of paternalism that they were impressed by the way in which Africans were cared for. The only role the organization could see for itself in this respect was to provide the contingent with additional warm clothing, sporting equipment and school books.[99]

For the effective functioning of the system, the authorities realized that they had to provide some form of outlet for those cloistered in the confines of the compounds. Tensions within the compounds had to be regulated and potentially explosive situations had to be defused. This meant that the off-duty hours of the workers had to be spent in 'healthy relaxation'. 'To this end', an officer explained, 'periodical sports were arranged at which they ran races, jumped, threw the cricket ball, pulled "tug-o'-war" against one another, and altogether used up their superfluous energy.'[100] On one level it can perhaps be argued that such activities at least provided the labourers with some relief from their dreary existence in the compounds and the monotony of their work. As W.R. Nasson has pointed out in a study of black transport riders during the Anglo-Boer War,

> Recreation and entertainment flourished, and came to occupy an extremely important space in transport riders' lives, lending vibrancy and rich colour to war experiences, and offering ritual consolation from, and defence against, the hazards, tensions, and uncertainties of wartime living. It is arguable that recreational pastimes did not simply mushroom as a safety valve. They were a way of rolling with the punch: wartime disorder provided new spaces and opportunities for conviviality, ceremony, and displays of skill.[101]

However, in the restricted and regulated environment of the SANLC compounds, sport was not a spontaneous activity initiated by the workers themselves; it was an organized and a structural affair, dictated from above and intended to function as a mechanism of control. Traditional African war dances, organized by the authorities and attended by large numbers of invited guests, served much the same purpose. Moreover, taking their cue from the mining compounds in southern Africa where such dances had become part of an early publicity programme for the mines, the military realized that the propaganda value of these performances was an added bonus. It was an opportunity to display the stereotyped view of 'happy' and 'exuberant' black 'warriors', obviously 'contented' with the conditions and circumstances which the authorities had created for them. This view was also processed for wider consumption; twelve out of the fifteen minutes of a contemporary war film about the SANLC dealt with traditional dances performed before the numerous white spectators.[102] Despite the enthusiasm of the authorities in organizing sports meetings and traditional dances, these forms of entertainment were not really popular amongst the workers and only a small minority participated. An officer indicated that 'the majority preferred to be left to their own devices and sat around their fires, talking and smoking after their work was done.'[103] Perhaps they suspected the motives of the organizers, or more prosaically they were just too exhausted after long hours of manual labour to participate in any further physical activity.

However, educational classes arranged for the workers in the evenings were far more popular and were well-attended. The classes were mainly conducted by black chaplains and the teachers who had joined the contingent, and the labourers were instructed in reading, writing, translation, arithmetic and geography. These classes were preferred to the other organized activities partly because no physical exertion was required, but also because they provided the workers with an opportunity for self-improvement and the acquisition of certain basic educational skills which Africans might have hoped would benefit them once they returned to South Africa. The primary motive of the authorities was not to provide an educational service for the betterment of the labourers; like the organization of sport and traditional dances, education was seen as a means of exercising control. 'These schools,' it was officially reported, 'assisted in no small measure to keep the Natives content in mind and employed profitably during their leisure hours in the compounds.'[104]

The bulk of the evidence relating to the way in which Africans responded to their controlled environment in France gives the impression that if they did not actually welcome the disciplinary measures and various restrictions, they certainly accepted these passively.[105] It is true that many Africans, outwardly at least, might have acquiesced; but that does not imply compliance. It is also pertinent to note that all correspondence was subjected to military censorship and, moreover, that most of the letters and other available documents were written by officers or other whites with a vested interest in the undertaking. Furthermore, it was of course only the educated blacks in the contingent who recorded their experiences. Their letters often reflected their class bias and, in any case, they had little option but to report favourably. Indeed, after their return some contradicted their previous correspondence and explained that 'they couldn't write otherwise', and were now prepared to 'corroborate the statements of those who complain of ill-treatment.'[106]

Although much of the documentation is either skewed or silent on African responses, there are scattered pieces of information which suggest that black workers were not as placid and docile as the authorities had wished to portray them. Occasionally, occurrences of 'minor strikes' were (understandably only fleetingly) mentioned in reports.[107] While the demands of the workplace and the harsh discipline might have precipitated strike action, these factors probably also ensured that such protests were shortlived. Whether the strikes were well-planned and calculated or an immediate and spontaneous expression of discontent, it was most unlikely, given the imperatives of the war effort and the nature of control over the contingent, that the authorities would have acceded to any strike demands. However, Africans also attempted in less dramatic ways to regulate and modify working conditions. Thus certain companies insisted on doing piece work — completing a specific task instead of working long stipulated hours.[108] In some instances this was allowed, and the workers themselves could then, in some measure, determine the time they had to spend at work.

The relationship between the white supervisory staff and the workers was furthermore one of considerable friction. Bearing in mind that the personnel were specifically chosen for their ability to 'control and handle Natives' or, less euphemistically and more accurately, for their willingness to use physical force in dealing with them, it is not surprising that several clashes occurred. Many Africans were not prepared to tolerate the heavy-handed treatment meted out to them by bullying supervisors and retaliated in kind. Reports on the SANLC were often punctuated by references to Africans who had 'resisted authority' or who had 'offered violence to superior officers.' In fact, the war diary of one battalion reveals that over a three month period such incidents were an almost daily occurrence.[109] Such acts of resistance and retribution were not restricted to the workplace or the compounds. On their return voyage to South Africa ten members on board the *Militiades* were accused of 'gross insubordination' in a heated exchange with Commanding Officer E. Farrar. Mutual antagonisms flared up in the open and soon developed into a particularly violent confrontation during which Aaron Monliba was shot dead, another African wounded, and the others confined to their bunks under armed guard. On arrival in Cape Town they had to stand trial for 'mutiny on the high seas', and despite their shrewd argument that their contracts had expired and that they were therefore no longer subject to military law, the judge decided to 'show the Natives their position' by passing severe prison sentences which ranged from ten to twelve years. However, Buxton, the governor-general, as well as Botha realized that the sentences were inappropriate and would serve no real purpose as a deterrent in the closing stages of the war, and the men were released after only a limited time in prison.[110]

Complaints about food served as another indicator of African discontent and resentment. It is generally true that troops often complain about the quality of their fare, but in the case of the contingent, food became a focal point for registering protests of much wider import. Thus one company refused to accept the rations given to it and insisted on receiving exactly the same as white troops.[111] The concern clearly went beyond food as such and reflected their demand to be treated on an equal footing.

Although the regulations limiting freedom of movement in France were strictly enforced, the network of control was not infallible. In a few instances some members, in search of either women or drink, or perhaps simply to experience ordinary life in a foreign country, did manage to abscond from the compounds.[112] For a necessarily brief and probably somewhat uneasy period, they thus had the opportunity of savouring what France had to offer and what was permitted to other troops but denied to them. Furthermore, some Africans also tried to entice women to come and visit them in their quarters. Obviously, it must have been as difficult to arrange such meetings as to abscond from the compounds. Nevertheless, it is revealing to note the attempts which were made shortly before one battalion embarked for their return voyage, and while they were stationed in a transit camp at St. Budeaux in Devonport, England, where in the absence of a closed compound it was somewhat more difficult for the officers to exercise control. Marching through the streets on their arrival they were, along with other troops, enthusiastically welcomed by the local residents, including women, who cheered and greeted the 'gallant' forces of the Empire. Certain members carefully noted the addresses of some of the houses of those women who had waved at them, and once in camp tried to establish contact by means of letters delivered by children. Unfortunately for one African and perhaps also for the woman concerned, the attempt failed when the letter was intercepted by the military authorities. Fortunately for the historian, however, the letter has survived and reads as follows:

> Dear Lady — I am so pleased that I can't even tell anybody, and I am much anxious if this note could be received by you. Then I am kindly asking you, if possible you will be so kind to do me a favour and call round our camp tonight at 8.30. I am in the first hut by the second gate as you go down; and I will be found just on the right-hand when you get in the camp. If you too late, do cleverly come, approach the door and give a small knock. I will hear you. And I will then explain to you about my notion concerning you. I beg to remain with best greetings of love to you. God be with you till I meet you. Respectfully yours. R.V.

In response to this incident, Brig.-Genl. F.C. Stone, commanding officer of the Devonport area, warned the women of St. Budeaux in terms that must have gladdened the hearts of South African officers:

> It is absolutely essential that the Kaffir should regard white women as unapproachable; the mischief that can be done by merely good-natured familiarity — apart from anything worse — is incalculable: and the people who will suffer from this levity on the part of white women at home, are the wives and daughters of our settlers in South Africa.[113]

There were also persistent rumours that large numbers of Africans refused to embark for South Africa, had married British women, went to Wales as coal miners and eventually 'became absorbed in the motley population settled in the dockyard areas of Cardiff'. This, however, seems rather far-fetched. The rumours about black and white marriages abroad emanated from the National Party in South Africa to embarrass the government and were consistently denied by the authorities. Without any corroborating evidence these rumours must then be dismissed as untrue.[114]

Not surprisingly, the main thrust of black resistance in France was directed at the closed compound system. It was seen for what it was: a blatant discriminatory measure which applied to South African blacks only. It also left a deep impression: 'The compounds where our people were housed in, cannot be forgotten as they were like prisons', certain veterans remarked on their return to the Union.[115] For some resistance against the system took the form of petitions, even one to the King of England, but predictably this had no effect.[116] Others took more direct action. On Christmas Eve 1917 Rev. R. Keable awoke to find a commotion on foot, for a party of drunken white soldiers had called to the boys over the barbed wire and asked them why they did not come out and enjoy themselves like the rest. When these had moved on, the sergeants had to deal with an excited camp, ready for anything, and arguing against the compound system heart and soul.[117]

This was not an isolated outburst during the festive season. Some officers, in letters to the South African press, referred obliquely but significantly to cases of 'riotous behaviour' in the compounds, and somewhat more explicitly in private letters it was revealed that 'many companies' were giving 'problems' because of the compound system.[118] One particularly violent incident took place on 23 July 1917 when a labourer, known as Charlie, was arrested for attempting to do his washing in a nearby stream outside the compound. This sparked off pent-up tension and an agitated crowd soon rallied to his assistance. While some tried to free Charlie by force, others succeeded in breaking the lock of the compound gate with a pick axe. When they emerged from the compound, they were fired on immediately and without warning by the armed guard. Four members were killed and eleven wounded. The South African authorities kept the matter strictly confidential, but they could not stop certain members from relating the affair on their return to South Africa.[119]

Despite this bloody confrontation, or perhaps because of it, black resistance against the compound system continued unabated and even intensified. Incidents of 'unruly behaviour' became so frequent that the authorities had considerable cause for alarm. It was a perturbed Lt.-Col. Godley who admitted in a confidential letter towards the end of 1917 that 'the temper of a large proportion of the men is distinctly nasty' and that there was an 'ever constant undercurrent of feeling amongst the Natives that they of all the King's soldiers are singled out for differential treatment'.[120] In fact, it had become increasingly difficult for the military to maintain the closed compound system, which was on the verge of collapsing in the face of persistent and effective black resistance.

This development led to the decision to disband the contingent. In December 1917 it was Godley's 'deliberate opinion' that they were running

a grave risk of finding it impossible to effectively carry out the Government's strict instructions in regard to close compounding and control, and that it is unfair to ask, or even allow men to bind themselves down indefinitely under conditions which are unique, as all other units in France, both *white and black* are free to move about.

Should the South African government wish to keep the contingent in France, Godley concluded, it had seriously to consider abandoning the compound system.[121] Instead, however, the cabinet decided in January 1918 to disband the SANLC. 'Having regard to the difficulties which can be anticipated in maintaining the closed compound system', Botha wrote confidentially, 'Ministers are of the opinion that it will not be advisable to continue recruiting'.[122] The government, increasingly under pressure at the time from the Nationalist opposition for allowing the undertaking at all, did not make the true reason for the decision public. Officially it was only announced that there was a shortage of ships, and that the contracts of members of the contingent were too short to justify the continuation of the scheme.[123] Many blacks in South Africa refused to believe this explanation. Rev. Z.R. Mahabane, prominent in the Cape branch of Congress, declared 'that as far as the Natives are concerned, the dramatic cancelling of a pact already signed and entered into, will give rise to feelings of suspicion that the reasons for this cancellation are more of a political than of a military nature'.[124] These suspicions were indeed well-founded: the government could not allow the contingent to stay in France, for fear of the possible political and social ramifications.

Thus it was that the black members of the SANLC, though they failed to better their conditions of service, had by their sustained opposition confronted South African officialdom with a major dilemma. Realizing that the restrictive practices which had always been a *sine qua non* for allowing the SANLC to serve in France could no longer be upheld without risking further disturbances, the South African government had little option but to abandon the whole enterprise. Inasmuch as it had raised the political risks of their continued employment in France to unacceptable heights, the opposition of SANLC members was not without effect. It now remains to consider whether war-time service also stimulated black resistance and political consciousness on a wider front.

Notes

1. *Ilanga Lase Natal*, 22 January 1914 ('German South-West African campaign'); G.N.L.B.190/1300/14/D78, Lt. A.W. Biddell to Director of Native Labour, 18 November 1914; N.A. 9111/36/363, Mendi Memorial Addresses, 1932.

2. S. Plaatje, *Native Life in South Africa*, p.267. See also U.G. 24-16, *Report of the Board of the South African Railways and Harbours, 1915*, pp.2-3; A.J. Beaton, 'Railway construction during the campaign of 1914-15 in German South-West Africa' in *Transactions of the South African Society of Civil Engineers*, July 1916, pp.1-11.

3. G.N.L.B. 192/1329/14/D48, Anonymous intercepted letter, 27 October 1914. See also *Tsala ea Batho*, 14 November 1914 ('German South-West campaign').

4. U.G. 13-1916, *Report of the Commission of Enquiry into the Treatment of Prisoners-of-War by the German Protectorate Authorities During the Late Hostilities*, p.8.

5. *The Christian Express*, 1 July 1916 ('Sidelights on the campaign in East Africa'). See also G.G. 480/9/57/19, Report on the Union Natives on Military Service in East Africa, 27 June 1917.

6. G.G. 480/9/57/19, Report on the Union Natives on Military Service in East Africa, 27 June 1917. See also D.C. 769/1997/9199, Botha to Buxton, 30 April 1917 (copy).

7. N.A. 9111/36/363, Mendi Memorial Addresses, 1932.

8. *Cape Times*, 21 February 1917 ('Parliamentary debates'); Merriman Papers, 246, Botha to Merriman, 27 April 1917; D.C. 769/185/9199, Genl.-Maj. R.A. Ewart to Secretary of Defence, 28 May 1917.

9. D.C. 769/185/9199, Genl.-Maj. R.A. Ewart to Secretary of Defence, 28 May 1917.

10. Merriman Papers, 246, Botha to Merriman, 27 April 1917.

11. G.G. 480/9/57/19, Report on the Union Natives on Military Service in East Africa, 27 June 1917.

12. N.A. 9111/36/363, Mendi Memorial Addresses, 1932.

13. C.O. 533/216/4603, Report on Military Labour in East Africa, 31 December 1919.

14. Merriman Papers, 246, Botha to Merriman, 27 April 1917.

15. D.C. 851/219/2274, Maj. Leifeldt to Director Native Labour, undated; Smuts Collection, CXV/100, Bourne to Staff Officer German East Africa, 2 December 1916; D.C. 768/129/1997, Bourne to Staff Officer German East Africa, 23 February 1917.

16. D.C. 625/205/9199, Director of Transport to Officer Commanding Transport, German South-West Africa, 18 December 1914.

17. D.C. 625/205/9199, Secretary of Native Affairs to Secretary of

Defence, 24 February 1915.

18. D.C. 625/205/9199, Commanding Officer De Aar to Director of Native Labour, 21 January 1915.

19. D. Killingray, 'The colonial army in the Gold Coast: Official policy and local response, 1890-1947', unpublished D.Phil. thesis, University of London, 1982, p.243.

20. E.M. Spiers, *The Army and Society, 1815-1914,* p.90.

21. D.C. 625/205/9199, Secretary of Native Affairs to Secretary of Defence, 24 February 1915.

22. C.S.O. 50/75, Secretary of Native Affairs to Secretary of Defence, 5 January 1917; D.C. 625/205/9199, Secretary of Native Affairs to Secretary of Defence, 24 February 1915.

23. D.C. 626/108/9199, Lt. A.W. Biddell to Officer Commanding Walvis Bay, 3 March 1915 and Biddell to Assistant Provost-Marshal, 5 March 1915.

24. D.C. 850/104/22714, Maj. Liefeldt to Director Native Labour, 3 February 1917 (copy).

25. *Rand Daily Mail,* 20 September 1917 ('How the natives are treated').

26. D.C. 625/205/9199, Quartermaster-General to Director of Native Labour, 29 January 1915 (copy); U.G. 14-1916, *Report on the work done by the Inspection Staff on War Expenditure in connection with the Rebellion and the German South-West Campaign to the end of October 1915,* p.20.

27. C.M.T. 3/926/772/8, H. Lowry on behalf of 'John' to Director of Native Labour, 24 August 1915.

28. D.C. 625/67/9199, Magistrate Pietersburg to Secretary of Defence, 15 June 1915, and Secretary of Defence to Magistrate Pietersburg, 12 July 1915.

29. D.C. 625/108/9199, Officer Commanding Walvis Bay to Headquarters Swakopmund, 3 March 1915 and Secretary of Defence to Director of Native Labour, 27 November 1914 (copy); D.C. 625/205/9199, Quartermaster Central Force to Quartermaster-General Pretoria, 21 March 1915.

30. D.C. 626/108/9199, Secretary of Defence to Director Native Labour, 27 November 1914 (copy) and Officer Commanding Transport Depot to Headquarters Pretoria, 9 April 1915.

31. G.G. 565/9/124/45, Report of the Board of Inquiry into the Mendi accident, 8 August 1917 (copy).

32. S.M. Bennet Ncwana, *Souvenir of the Mendi Disaster,* p.20 (Recollections of Capt. L.E. Hertslet).

33. *The Star,* 27 February 1967 ('Mendi Disaster Survivor').

34. Ncwana, *Souvenir of the Mendi Disaster,* p.21 (Recollections of Capt. L.E. Hertslet).

35. *The Christian Express*, 2 July 1917 (Letter from an anonymous officer).
36. G.G. 565/9/124/45, Report of the Board of Inquiry into the Mendi Accident, 8 August 1917 (copy).
37. T.9/1115/6590, Finding of the Court of Inquiry, 8 August 1917.
38. T.9/1115/6590, Statement by Capt. A.H. Young, 15 August 1917.
39. *Imvo Zabantsundu*, 16 October 1917 ('The deplorable disaster').
40. Long Papers, 947/601/42, Buxton to Long, 10 March 1917.
41. P.M. 1/1/483, A.T. Wijmans to Botha, 15 March 1917. See also Merriman Papers, 166, A.T. Wijmans to Merriman, 17 March 1917.
42. *Cape Times*, 10 March 1917 ('Parliamentary debates').
43. G.G. 545/9/93/56, Botha to Buxton, 8 June 1917.
44. W.O. 107/37, Report on the Work of Labour during the War, December 1918.
45. W.O. 107/37, History of the SANLC, 1918; *Ilanga Lase Natal*, 9 November 1917 (Letter from Capt. L.E. Hertslet).
46. R. Keable, *Standing By.*, pp.124-26.
47. A.P.S. Pamphlet, *British Africans in Europe and the Work of the Welfare Committee*, p.5
48. U.W.H. 89/34, Report on the SANLC, 8 March 1919.
49. W.O. 107/37, History of the SANLC, 1918.
50. *Ibid*.
51. N.A. 9107/8/363, H. Astouken to E. Dower, 11 August 1917.
52. *Native Teachers Journal*, October 1920 (Letter from F.H. Kumalo); Perry, J. and Perry, C. (eds.), *A Chief is a Chief by the People: The Autobiography of Stimela Jason Jingoes*, 1985, pp.88-89; B.P. Willan, 'The South African Labour Contingent, 1916-1918' in *Journal of African History*, XIX, 1, 1978, p.73.
53. 1/T.B.U. 25/66/1, A.K. Xabanisa to Chief Magistrate Transkei, 25 May 1917.
54. N.A. 9107/8/363, H. Astouken to E. Dower, 11 August 1917.
55. These reports are in G.G. 545/9/93/56 and run from January 1917 to July 1918.
56. G.G. 545/9/93/56, Health reports SANLC, January 1917 to July 1918; A.P.S. Pamphlet, *British Africans in Europe and the Work of the Welfare Committee*, pp.6, 9-14; W.O. 107/37, History of the SANLC, 1918; Willan, 'The South African Native Labour Contingent, 1916-1918', pp.76-77.
57. W.O. 107/37, Appendix H, Henry Simon Ltd. to Directorate of Labour, 19 June 1917.
58. W.O. 107/37, History of the SANLC, 1918; *Imvo Zabantsundu*, 27 November 1917 (Letter from Capt. L.E. Hertslet).
59. Sloley, 'The African Native Labour Contingent and the Welfare Committee', p.205.

60. *Cape Times*, 27 June 1917 ('Parliamentary debates').
61. *Native Teachers Journal*, October 1920 (letter from F.H. Kumalo).
62. A.P.S. Pamphlet, *British Africans in Europe and the Work of the Welfare Committee*, pp.7-8.
63. G.G. 545/9/93/56, Memorandum on the SANLC, September 1916.
64. *Ilanga Lase Natal*, 7 December 1917 (Letter from J.A. Mtembu).
65. W.O. 107/37 History of the SANLC, 1918 and Pritchard to Directorate of Labour, 5 July 1918.
66. W.O. 107/37, History of the SANLC, 1918.
67. U.W.H. 89/34, Report on the SANLC, 8 March 1919.
68. W.O. 107/37, History of the SANLC, 1918.
69. A.P. Donajgrodzki (ed.), *Social Control in Nineteenth Century Britain*, p.11. The concept has been criticized by, amongst others, G. Stedman Jones, 'Class expression versus social control? A critique of recent trends in the social history of "leisure" ', *History Workshop*, 4, Autumn, 1977.
70. *Cape Times Annual*, 1919 (Article by Lt. F.C. Cornell, 'The SA Native Labour Contingent'). According to Cornell the uniform caused them a great deal of trouble.
71. *Ibid*.
72. *Ilanga Lase Natal*, 10 May 1918 (Letter from 'A Native').
73. W.O. 107/37, History of the SANLC, 1918. See also Willan, 'The South African Native Labour Contingent, 1916-1918', p.72.
74. G.G. 545/9/93/56, Lt.-Col. J. Jacobsz to Col. S.M. Pritchard, 20 May 1917.
75. *The South African Review*, 4 January 1918 ('White Women and Blacks').
76. D.C. 768/31/1997, Bourne to Botha, 20 September 1916.
77. *South Africa*, 18 November 1916 (Colonel S.M. Pritchard); K. Donaldson (ed.), *South African Who's Who, 1919-1920*, p.162; Long Papers, 947/603/133, Buxton to Long, 8 January 1917.
78. *Pretoria News*, 14 September 1916 ('Names of the elect'); *Cape Times Annual*, 1919 (Article by Lt. F.C. Cornell, 'The SA Native Labour Contingent').
79. D.C. 768/64/1997, Letter of Appointment, undated.
80. Perry (eds.), *Jingoes*, p.92.
81. Ilanga Lase Natal, 10 May 1918 (Letter from 'A Native').
82. *Abantu-Batho*, 18 April 1918 ('The labour contingent'). The authorities also intercepted letters in which Africans complained of 'brutal treatment'. (D.C. 1136/2/1197, Chief Censor to Acting Secretary of Defence, 4 June 1918). Furthermore, Jason Jingoes declared: 'We bantu are often treated like dogs here by the white people from home, yet they forget that we are all here at war against a common enemy'. (Perry (eds.), *Jingoes*, p.83).

83. *East London Daily Dispatch,* 30 September 1916 (Letter from H. Ziduli); *East London Daily Dispatch,* 2 October 1916 (Letter from 'A Native'); G.N.L.B. 192/1329/14/48, Transvaal Native Congress General Meeting, 11 October 1916.

84. G.G. 545/9/93/56, General report on the chaplaincy and welfare work of the South African Native Labour Corps, 31 July 1918; *Imvo Zabantsundu,* 9 July 1918 (Letter from Capt. L.E. Hertslet); D.C. 768/46/1997, Bourne to Dower, 25 September 1916.

85. R. Keable, 'African Priests in France' in *The East and West,* January 1918, p.54.

86. *Ibid,* p.56.

87. G.G. 545/9/93/56, General report on the chaplaincy and welfare work of the South African Native Labour Corps, 31 July 1918.

88. U.W.H. 89/34, Report on the SANLC, 8 March 1919.

89. O.C. Records 44/22/81, Report on the SANLC, 12 April 1918.

90. A.P.S. Papers S 23 H 2/3, Harris to Buxton, 10 September 1917 and Harris to A. Loring, 14 September 1917 (copies).

91. A.P.S. Papers S 23 H 2/3, Report by the Rev. J.W.W. Owen on the tour of native chaplains, 10 October 1917.

92. A.P.S. Papers S 23 H 2/3. Chapman to Harris, 1 October 1917.

93. C. van Onselen, *Chibaro: African Mine Labour in Southern Rhodesia, 1900-1933,* p.157.

94. G.G. 545/9/93/56. Godley to Dower, 8 December 1917.

95. W.O. 107/37, Appendix G. Notes on South African Labour. See also Willan, 'The South African Labour Contingent, 1916-1918', p.72.

96. G.N.L.B. 192/1329/14/48, Report on a meeting of Natal Natives, 27 September 1916.

97. *Ilanga Lase Natal,* 31 August 1917 ('General notes').

98. *East London Daily Dispatch*, 2 October 1916 (Letter from G.K. Hemming).

99. A.P.S. Papers S 23 H 2/1, Memorandum for the information of the Committee, 13 April 1917 and J.H. Harris to A. Steel-Maitland, 18 December 1917. It is also pertinent to note that in general the Aborigines Protection Society had very little criticism on the direction of 'native policy' in the Union. See B.P. Willan, 'The Anti-Slavery and Aborigines Protection Society and the South African Natives' Land Act of 1913' in *Journal of African History,* XX, 1, 1979, pp.183-202.

100. *Cape Times Annual,* 1919 (Article by Lt. F.C. Cornell, 'The S.A. Native Labour Contingent'). See also U.W.H. 89/34. Report on the SANLC, 8 March 1919.

101. W.R. Nasson, 'Moving Lord Kitchener: Black military transport and supply work in the South African War, 1899-1902, with particular reference to the Cape Colony' in *Journal of Southern African Studies,*

11, 1, October 1984, p.40.

102. *Rand Daily Mail*, 8 September 1917 ('Interview with Native Soldiers'); Imperial War Museum, London, Archival film on the SANLC, 1917. For the function of these dances in the mining context see Van Onselen, *Chibaro*, p.188.

103. U.W.H. 89/34, Report on the SANLC, 8 March 1919.

104. W.O. 107/37, History of the SANLC, 1918. See also G.G. 545/9/93/56, General report on the chaplaincy and welfare work of the South African Native Labour Corps, 31 July 1918.

105. For examples see *Cape Times*, 1 February 1918 (Letter from a white SANLC sergeant); *Cape Times*, 22 March 1917 (Letter from A. Shabane); *Alice Times*, 24 May 1917 (Letter from Rev. J. Lennox); *Cape Times*, 22 October 1917 (Letter from Capt. L.E. Hertslet); *Sunday Times*, 22 July 1917 (Letter from A.K. Xabanisa).

106. *Abantu-Batho*, 14 February 1918 ('Natives and the war').

107. U.W.H. 89/34, Report on the SANLC, 8 March 1919; W.O. 107/37, History of the SANLC, 1918.

108. W.O. 107/37, History of the SANLC, 1918.

109. D.C. 1136/2/1197, List of SANLC transgressions, undated; G.G. 1282/51/49/56, Incomplete list of SANLC military prisoners with commentaries on their transgressions, 9 December 1918; G.G. 1275/51/45/56, Botha to Buxton, 11 March 1918; W.O. 95/267, War Diary of 2nd Battalion SANLC, 2 January 1917 to 31 March 1917.

110. G.G. 545/9/93/56, Brig.-Genl. A. Cavendish to Buxton, 20 December 1917; G.G. 545/9/93/175, Botha to Buxton, 27 December 1917; *Juta's Daily Reporter: Decisions of the Cape Provincial Division of the Supreme Court of South Africa*, 27 February 1918, p.1; G.G. 1275/51/45/56, Botha to Buxton, 11 March 1918.

111. W.O. 95/267, War Diary 2nd Company SANLC, 13 December 1916.

112. Transcription of an oral interview with P. Mabathoana at Maseru, 22 April 1980; D.C. 1136/2/1997, Chief Censor to Acting Secretary of Defence, 23 April 1918, and Acting Secretary of Defence to Chief Censor, 17 January 1918; W.O. 95/4115, SANLC General Hospital Diary, 1917 (venereal disease cases).

113. A.P.S. Papers S 23 H 2/1, Cutting from the *Western Morning News*, 22 October 1917 ('White women and black men').

114. *Sunday Express*, 27 February 1938 ('They refused to return'); N.A. 9108/22/903, Secretary of Defence to Secretary of Native Affairs, 2 March 1938; *De Volkstem*, 4 October 1917 ('De Honderd Huweliken per week agitasie'); *Imvo Zabantsundu*, 16 October 1917 ('Nationalists and the natives'); F.S. Malan Collection 15/41, Malan to Buxton, 9 October 1917 (copy).

115. *Abantu-Batho*, 14 February 1918 ('Natives and the War').
116. M.D.W. Jeffreys, 'The *Mendi* and after: recollections of Jacob Matli' in *Africana Notes and News*, 15, 5, March 1963, p.187.
117. Keable, *Standing By*, p.134.
118. *Ilanga Lase Natal*, 9 November 1917 (Letter from Capt. L.E. Hertslet); N.A. 9107/8/363, H. Astouken — E. Dower, 11 August 1917.
119. N.A. 9107/12/863, Confidential letter from Godley to Pritchard, 28 July 1917; J. 248/5/242/16, Police report of SANNC meeting on 29 March 1918 containing statements by D. Modiakgotla; *Abantu-Batho*, 14 February 1918 ('Natives and the War'); SANLC attestation forms, names of the diseased killed in the incident; Willan, 'The South African Native Labour Contingent, 1916-1918, p.79. Although returning members claimed that 13 people had died, Godley established after an enquiry that 11 were wounded and four killed.
120. G.G. 549/9/93/56, Godley to Dower, 8 December 1917.
121. *Ibid.* (Emphasis in original.)
122. G.G. 549/9/93/56, Botha to Buxton, 18 December 1917.
123. *Cape Times*, 29 June 1917 ('Parliamentary debates'); *Cape Times*, 18 January 1918 ('Native Labour Corps'); 1/LSK 13/9/2, Circular from Botha to all chiefs and headmen, 18 January 1918.
124. *Cape Times*, 2 February 1918 (Letter from Z.R. Mahabane).

CHAPTER 5

Military Service, the War, and Black Political Consciousness

Military service often leaves its mark on those who undergo it. Some of the effects of this experience may be enduring and substantial, others ephemeral and transient. Thus attitudes, values and political behaviour may be shaped and informed by war-time experiences or, depending on various factors, military service may fail to have an appreciable effect.[1] This chapter evaluates the impact of war-time service on black participants and determines whether veterans acted as catalysts for change on their return to the Union. The wider impact of the war on African political thinking is also considered.

As far as can be ascertained, the political outlook of those Africans who served in South-West and East Africa was not influenced critically by their war-time service. Although many might have resented the harsh treatment meted out to them, it must be borne in mind that they served for a relatively short period only and, perhaps more importantly, that the ideological climate in these colonial territories differed little from what blacks were accustomed to in South Africa. Thus they were not exposed to a markedly new environment.

The SANLC, of course, completed its service in a somewhat different milieu. Nevertheless, the reports of the white officers accompanying the contingent reflect an almost obsessional tendency to present the venture as an unqualified 'success'. In this view those who served returned to South Africa 'uncontaminated' and 'unspoilt' and 'more useful to the state in every way'.[2] However, because of their own prejudices and vested interests in the matter, the impressions of the officers are heavily biased towards a sanitized version and the African voice is audible only when we have decoded it; even then it is rarely heard.

There can be little doubt that service overseas did present Africans with an opportunity to contrast the crass or, at best, paternalistic racism prevailing in South Africa, to the way in which whites abroad behaved towards them. Although the officers tried to ensure that members of the contingent had limited contact with the civilian population, some of them did on the odd occasion manage to acquaint themselves with life outside the compounds. Such encounters with French civilians gave them sufficient reason to question in a more searching manner the rigidity of South African society. 'Coming from South Africa, we had fixed ideas about black/white relationships, so we were surprised that some of the French would mix freely with us', declared R. Mohapeloa. Similarly, P. Mabatoana was impressed that 'we were treated with dignity by white people'.[3] Moreover, Jason Jingoes drew a fine distinction between paternalistic racial attitudes and involvement on the basis of equality. The way in which white women received them with tea and other refreshments when they stopped at Liverpool in England before embarking again for France, caused him to remark: 'They were so friendly and we warmed to their concern for us . . . . Although white women had served us with tea in Cape Town, we know they were only doing it because we were going to war. These girls were different'.[4]

As pointed out earlier, the South African authorities were particularly concerned about the possibility that members of the contingent might establish intimate relationships with French women; in fact, this was one of the main reasons for the compound system. However, some Africans devised resourceful plans to abscond from the compounds and a few were involved with French prostitutes who frequented the dockyard areas. The very nature of such affairs made them momentary and superficial, but there is also evidence to suggest that certain members formed somewhat more enduring relationships with French women that went beyond the casual sexual flirtation. It is instructive to note that after the return of the SANLC to South Africa, the chief censor, J.M. Weaver, intercepted and destroyed ten letters from French women to members of the contingent. Weaver argued that such letters 'will give the natives a wrong impression as to their relative position with regard to Europeans'.[5] The fact that such correspondence actually took place reflects a certain degree of commitment between the parties and Weaver's concern is a clear indication that colour became a minor consideration in such relationships. Liaisons between black males and white females were not completely uncommon in South Africa; however, white public 'morality' ensured that they were often clandestine, and when revealed such relationships met with near hysteria as a dangerous aberration that threatened the *status quo.*[6] In war-torn France a relatively more permissive atmosphere prevailed amongst the civilian population,[7] and it can be surmised that particularly those members of the SANLC who were involved in black/white affairs became more acutely aware of the discrepancy and less inclined to view the racist ideology in South Africa as an immutable force.

Through the exigencies of war-time service certain companies of the SANLC also came into occasional contact with white labour battalions engaged in exactly the same manual work as blacks. This exposure, which was in sharp contrast to the position in South Africa where whites left most of the hard labour for Africans to perform, did not fail to leave an imprint. What impressed some blacks even more, though, was that the whites in labour battalions displayed little colour prejudice and treated them as equals.[8] Jason Jingoes even struck up a friendship with a British labourer, named William Johnstone, and it was in this respect that he noted: 'It was our first experience of living in a society without a colour bar'.[9] The implications of black labourers identifying with their white counterparts, as has been seen, caused considerable distress amongst the white officers in the contingent — those ever watchful custodians of vested South African interests who were so concerned to prevent Africans from being 'indoctrinated' by 'socialist' ideas.

In one respect the carefully controlled labour regimentation of the SANLC in France differed from the standard procedures usually followed in South Africa. Whereas it was normal practice on the South African mines to divide the black labour force along ethnic lines, in France it was decided to integrate various 'tribes'. Practical considerations dictated this course of action, and it was also argued that such an arrangement would prevent the possibility of sympathetic strikes amongst members of the same ethnic group.[10] This had an unintended consequence. The continuous contact between workers from the different 'tribes' in the work situation and the fact that they were all exposed to the same conditions in a white man's war, meant that at least for some Africans the ethnic affiliations became distinctly blurred. In an unambiguous statement Z.F. Zibi revealed:

> We are not here as Mfengu, Xhosa and other tribes. We are conscious of the fact that we Blacks are united in staying together . . . . Therefore we shall never be deceived . . . . Otherwise it would mean that we are like people who share a mat but quarrel — in such cases one never sleeps well.[11]

The exact degree and intensity of solidarity is difficult to determine, but it seems clear that to some extent a common consciousness of their position as workers, as opposed to members of an ethnic group, began to develop in France.

In a more general sense the war-time experiences of some members also meant an expansion of their world view. On the way to France several troopships called at Sierra Leone, where M. Mokwena was particularly impressed by the fact that he met 'some pure black negroes of very high educational attainments equal to that of the best Europeans . . . .'[12] Similarly, certain Africans regarded the sea voyage and that which they were allowed to witness abroad as formative influences. Thus D.S. Makoliso, who came from a small Transkeian village, Cala, wrote: 'I am glad to say that my experiences are more than any man's in Cala . . . . My head is full up with new things and the wonders of the world'.[13] Likewise, for an anonymous member of the contingent an astonishing aspect of his experiences in France was 'to see the different kinds of human races from all parts of the world'.[14] Others again, were impressed by the agriculture and 'cultivation seen in an old and settled country'.[15] Despite the hardships and restrictions they had to endure, some members were convinced that they had gained by the general experience of visiting a foreign European country. E. Mdlombo, for one, did not regret his decision to enlist and he viewed the period spent in France as 'an education' which provided him with new insights and knowledge.[16] This exposure to a world so different from their own clearly opened up new horizons for at least some members of the contingent.

One event in France left a very marked impression. On 10 July 1917 the British King, George V, inspected and addressed the contingent. For many of the educated Africans it was an unforgettable experience to see the king in person — the supreme symbol of imperial power and British 'justice' which loomed so largely in their imagination. 'We saw him, George V, our king, with our own eyes . . . . To us it is a dream, something to wonder at', mused M.L. Posholi.[17] What made this visit even more memorable, was that the king in his address not only praised them for their labour, but also assured them: 'You are also part of my great armies fighting for the liberty and freedom of my subjects of all races and creeds throughout the empire'.[18] The implications of these words were not lost on Posholi. 'We are indeed in the midst of great wonders', he wrote, 'because we personally heard that we blacks too are British subjects, children of the father of the great Nation, trusted ones and helpers, and that we are cared for and loved'.[19]

A similar noteworthy occasion was the visit by a group of French parliamentarians and other dignitaries which included a black man — in all probability Blaise Diagne, commissioner of recruitment in the French colony of Senegal and a deputy in the French assembly. His presence in such eminent white company was of considerable interest to some members. At first they had thought that he was 'simply there to accompany his white masters', but after enquiries they realized that he was an important official in his own right. The significance of this fired their political imaginations and inevitably raised pertinent questions as to their own position in South Africa. 'One of us asked', it was subsequently related, '"Would such a thing ever happen in our country?" Some replied, "Who knows?" But others said quietly, "It might . . . ."'[20]

For some Africans at least, the cumulative effect of their war-time experience — what they saw as well as their hope that something might yet come of their assistance to the white man in troubled times — found expression in greater self-esteem and a less deferential attitude towards whites. Jason Jingoes strikingly revealed that 'we were aware, when we returned that we were different from the other people at home. Our behaviour, as we showed the South Africans, was something more than they expected from a Native, more like what was expected among them of a white man'.[21] Jingoes was not the only one to experience a change in outlook and to adopt a more assertive attitude. The commanding officer at the demobilization depot in Cape Town, Major H. Dales, who was in a unique position to witness the demeanour of time-expired Africans returning from France, testified from a white point of view that 'the conduct of these natives left much to be desired, great laxity of discipline being apparent, and their behaviour in general being a great contrast to that of recruits in training for overseas'.[22]

Although the period spent in France undoubtedly sensitized certain members, one should also consider those factors which counteracted the development of increased militancy. Apart from the fact that the impact of military service differed according to individual circumstances, temperament, personality and pre-existing degree of socio-political awareness, members of the contingent were also exposed to influences which undermined their confidence. In this respect they had occasion to witness the almost inexhaustible armed resources of the white man and the techniques of modern warfare in France. This caused some of them to realize that in the face of the ever increasing military potential of the white, an African uprising in South Africa stood even less chance than before of succeeding. One veteran summed up the situation succinctly when he said: 'Our assegais are no good now; they could not reach an aeroplane'.[23]

Moreover, it was the avowed policy of the South African authorities to stifle the potential 'harmful' effects of war-time service; virtually all the factors in overseas service which had the potential to broaden the social and political perceptions of black members were consciously emasculated. Central to this policy was the closed compound system and although it was not completely successful, it nevertheless severely limited the intensity of exposure to new conditions in a foreign country. Colonel S.M. Pritchard, commanding officer of the contingent, probably had sufficient reason to declare in a self-congratulatory statement in November 1919:

> Knowing as he did the conditions under which they [the Africans] were employed, knowing the restrictions placed on their movements, and the strict discipline enforced, it would be a remarkable thing if these natives came back any the worse.[24]

From a different perspective, what is indeed remarkable under these circumstances is that at least some Africans, as has been indicated, used the restricted opportunities in the way they did.

This analysis points to the need to maintain a fine balance in evaluating the effect of participation in a white man's war. For every participant who returned from France with a changed outlook, there may have been another who was less affected. Indeed, from Sibasa in the northern Transvaal, an area which yielded a considerable number of recruits, C.L. Harries, an official of the Native Affairs Department, reported:

> I . . . find all those who went overseas most respectful and law-abiding and in no single instance have I found that the experiences gained abroad have reacted to the moral detriment of the individual. My own cook was 18 months in France and he is still the quiet respectful and unsophisticated native that he was before he went.[25]

Clearly, in as far as Harries's evidence can be accepted, service in France had little, if any visible effect on the perceptions of these Africans. In general, then, the experience of military service abroad

---

had an uneven impact: the black veterans ranged from those who arrived back in South Africa with an increased and more explicitly defined individual and social consciousness to those who returned with their established views on the political and social order in South Africa apparently intact.

Related to the war-time exposure of SANLC members were grievances about the callous treatment meted out to them by South African officers in France, and resentment about the paucity of post-war recognition. Despite frequent protests, veterans received no war medals or gratuities, solely because the authorities considered it politically imprudent to acknowledge publicly that whites had required the services of blacks during war-time.[26] Furthermore, the inflated promises made to lure the unsuspecting into the recruiting net during 1916-17 were simply brushed aside; promises that they would be relieved from paying poll tax, be exempted from pass laws and be given free grants of land as well as cattle remained unfulfilled. To add insult to injury, former members were even expected to pay poll tax for the period they had been absent from South Africa.[27] For a considerable time these slights and injustices rankled among former members of the contingent. Even 20 years after the war an anonymous veteran was still aggrieved and resentful. On the eve of the Second World War he wrote:

> It takes my memory back to the days of the Great War in 1914-1918, when the Government of South Africa said it would do all sorts of good things for us if only we would help them in the fight against Germany. Some of us were so foolish as to give belief to what they said. We went with the Native Labour Corps . . . . We were a help in overcoming the Germans. But when we came back we still had to have passes and we even had to make payment of Poll Tax for the time we were away.[28]

Not surprisingly, many veterans felt misled, deflated and discarded, particularly in the immediate post-war period. 'The beliefs we entertained have proved to be absolutely worthless as the Government has done and is doing nothing for us', complained E.Q. Madayi in 1921.[29] For S.T. Zondani and E. Ntusi the calculated indifference of the government was a vindication of their suspicion that blacks in South Africa were totally expendable. In bitter terms they wrote two years after the war:

> The fact that . . . after we returned from France, having sacrificed our

lives, no recognition whatsoever has been shown us, assures us and confirms the fact that the natives of this country, in spite of their loyalty, are a nonentity, and are only called upon when the Government are in dire straits, and are then not recognised when their services are finished with.[30]

In a similar vein A.K. Xabanisa echoed the sentiments of a considerable number of veterans when he explained succinctly: 'I am just like a stone which after killing a bird, nobody bothers about, nor cares to see where it falls'.[31] To their chagrin these ex-members discovered that the promises made and expectations raised by whites in the turbulent and uncertain times of war meant nothing in the more placid and tranquil times of peace. Undoubtedly, numerous veterans nurtured a real and intense sense of grievance.

The complete abandonment of the interests of the veterans created the potential for increased militancy. Edward Roux, in his seminal work on black resistance in South Africa, drew attention to this post-war disillusionment amongst ex-members of the contingent. 'After 1918', he claimed, ' there were thousands of black men in the country who were prepared to stir up their fellow Africans to revolt against the system'.[32] In 1920 D.D.T. Jabavu was also convinced that

the Native Labour Contingent . . . has imported into this country a new sense of racial unity and amity quite unknown heretofore among our Bantu races. Common hardships in a common camp have brought them into close relation. They had a glimpse at Europe and even from the closed compounds they got to discover that the white man overseas still loves the black man as his own child, while on the contrary some of their white officers . . . made themselves notorious by their harsh treatment and slanderous repression of them when French people befriended them. All this was carefully noted . . . in this country when they returned. The result is that there is amongst the diversified Bantu tribes of this land a tendency towards complete mutual respect and love founded upon the unhealthy basis of an anti-white sentiment.[33]

How valid were those generalizations and did the veterans, in fact, act as political catalysts? We now turn to explore the links between military service in France and tangible, perceptible opposition to white rule in South Africa. The fact that some members of the SANLC returned from France with a sharper awareness of their relative deprivation and were discontented over their post-war treatment, does not necessarily mean that their feelings and insights were actually translated into active resistance. It is therefore essential to consider whether the stimuli of service abroad, and all that accompanied it, were sufficient to galvanize veterans into action directed against the system of white domination.

On a personal and individual level some veterans did not hesitate to demonstrate their sharper perception and increased self-confidence in everyday South African situations. In the Pietersburg district in the Northern Transvaal an anonymous ex-member refused to accept passively what he regarded as exorbitant prices in the local trading store. He confronted the shopkeeper, named Williams, and a subsequent police report on the incident strikingly reveals the way in which this particular veteran asserted himself:

> A native who had recently returned from France came to his [Williams's] store and stated that the Europeans were responsible for the high prices of foodstuffs. He then asked Williams to whom the ground on which he was trading belonged, on receiving a reply that the ground belonged to Williams, the Native replied, 'the ground belongs to the Natives and we will show you'.[34]

In another incident certain members on their train journey home had an altercation with the station master at Christiana in the western Transvaal. They entered his office 'in an insolent manner and used abusive language which was levelled at white people in general'. Some of them were also less than deferential to white women. As the train left they shouted at the local ganger's wife, '*Wil jy saam gaan?*' ('Would you like to come along?')[35] Rowdy behaviour is of course common amongst returning soldiers, but in this case there was obviously an added socio-political dimension.

Certain veterans furthermore attempted to shape the perceptions of rural black communities. Shortly after his return from France, L. Molife addressed peasants in the Rustenburg district in the western Transvaal and assured them in the following terms that their plight would soon be relieved: 'The Germans were building powerful airships, capable of moving an army — they must not worry, that shortly a German army would be in Africa and would help them gain their freedom'. This message, endorsed by similar statements from other ex-members, was received with considerable acclamation.[36] The factual accuracy of Molife's account is of course beside the point; what is important is its strong millenarian element and that veterans were involved in the dissemination of such ideas. However, the significance must not be exaggerated and it appears to have been an isolated incident. There were no large-scale post-war millenarian movements in the Transvaal, nor is there evidence to suggest that ex-members were in any sustained way politically active in the rural areas.

In contrast with the Transvaal, millenarianism was an outstanding characteristic of rural resistance in the eastern Cape and Transkei during the twenties. Here America featured prominently as the country which would deliver Africans from bondage.[37] There is some tantalizing evidence to suggest that a few former members of the contingent were involved in these movements; however, it seems as if they could only have played a very marginal role.[38]

On a more formal level some ex-members did become active in organized black politics. Shortly after the war Doyle Modiakgotla and Ben Nyombolo joined the Industrial and Commercial Workers' Union of Africa (ICU) and Modiakgotla later became secretary of the Griqualand West branch. In 1920 S.M. Bennet Ncwana also became a member of the ICU and in addition initiated a short-lived publication, *The Black Man*.[39] Although it is significant that they became overtly involved in · politics, there is no firm evidence that their war experiences were the prime motivating force. It can only be surmised that to some extent their exposure in France must have had a contributing influence.

Veterans were also involved in working class action in Port Elizabeth during October 1920. During a campaign for higher wages the police arrested one of the leaders, S.M. Masabalala, whereupon a crowd of approximately 3 000 gathered outside the local gaol and demanded his release. When the police refused to consider their appeal, the demonstrators attacked with sticks and stones. Retaliation was swift and bloody; after a few warning shots the police fired indiscriminately into the retreating crowd — wounding 81 and killing 22. Amongst the victims of police violence were a number of former SANLC members.[40] The participation of veterans in this protest indicates post-war dissatisfaction and militancy amongst some ex-members, but their precise role in these events remains hazy and there is no suggestion in the documentation that they spearheaded the unrest or that their war service was a decisive consideration in their action. Like the other participants they might have been swayed by more immediate concerns, unconnected with their earlier experiences.

There is certainly no justification for claiming on the basis of this incident, as one historian has done recently, that the veterans 'constituted
the vanguard of the emerging black working class movement and of
radical black nationalism in South Africa'.[41] The conspicuous absence
of ex-members in the endemic and large-scale labour unrest on the
Witwatersrand between 1918 and 1920 can only make the point that
such an assertion is far-fetched.[42]

There is thus no satisfactory evidence that veterans were in the
forefront of sustained black resistance to white domination in the
post-war years. Nor does it appear that ex-members acted as 'modern-
izers' in rural societies. Immediately after his return, Jason Jingoes
(and one can readily assume that his was not an isolated case) found
that 'he was thrown back into the old traditional ways'.[43]

The relative passivity on the part of ex-members in the sphere of
overt resistance seems to prove that, for the reasons already mentioned,
war service was not sufficient to jolt veterans into revolt or to spur
them to encourage resistance in others. However, it must be borne in
mind that even those who possibly contemplated such action had to
consider the formidable power of the state. It is nevertheless clear that
in the South African case the general assumption that service in a
'white man's' war is a catalyst for vigorous black resistance cannot be
taken for granted. When Africans did resist, as on the Witwatersrand
between 1918 and 1920, it was not because they were influenced by
new ideas emanating from abroad, but because of the fundamental
oppression built into the South African system of white domination —
and they did not have to go to France to become aware of that.

The impact of the war was not restricted to those who actually participated. It is therefore important to delineate the wider effect of the
war as it was manifested in African political thinking.

It will be remembered that the loyal stance of the SANNC at the
outbreak of the war was based on the hope that such a policy would
increase its bargaining power and also render the authorities more
sympathetic to black aspirations. During and immediately after the
war the SANNC maintained its faith in this belief, which was further
strengthened by the contribution of the labour contingent to the Allied
war effort. These expectations were clearly expressed by R.V. Selope
Thema, Secretary-General of the SANNC, in May 1917:

We . . . are now facing the enemies of our King-Emperor on the battle-fields of France. When that mighty Army of Sir Douglas Haig, which is now slowly but surely marching on Berlin, shall enter that City of Destruction, it will do so through the energetic efforts of our men at the front who are building railways, making roads and unloading ships . . . . On such a high tide are we afloat, and we must take the current . . . . Never before did the Bantu people stand on such a high tide . . . as today.[44]

Towards the closing stages of the war black participation in the hostilities had further raised the level of expectancy amongst African political leaders and they became more strident in their demands. 'We expect to be rewarded for our work after the war when prizes are distributed to the brave who were in battle', insisted D.S. Letanka, an influential SANNC member, in February 1918.[45] A month later S.M. Makgatho, then chairman of the SANNC, openly declared at the organization's annual conference that 'the blood of these sons of ours, spilled on behalf of the Empire, entitled us to claim a say . . . in the Parliament.'[46] Another member, L.T. Mvabaza, made a similar point in April 1918 and furthermore located African aspirations in the context of freedom and democracy — the oft proclaimed war aims of the Allied forces. Unambiguously he stated:

That in consideration of the sacrifices the Bantu have made during this war which we are continually being told is for democracy and freedom, the British and white people of this land should redress our grievances and give the freedom for which we lost thousands of men in this struggle.[47]

Black expectations were also stimulated by the pronouncements of Allied statesmen and other dignitaries. H.S. Msimang recalled 42 years after the war that he found the address of King George V, in which the king recognized the work of the labour contingent, particularly encouraging.[48] In addition, David Lloyd George, the British Prime Minister, and Woodrow Wilson, the American President, propagated the idea from 1918 onwards that sufficient allowance should be made in the post-war dispensation for the self-determination of smaller and oppressed nations. This was interpreted as yet another hopeful sign. 'We look upon Mr Lloyd George's declaration as a message of hope that the dawn of freedom is at last breaking forth', commented D.S. Letanka. This view was not as naive as it may at first appear. Letanka was well aware that the policy was not formulated with South Africa in mind, but for him the post-war credibility of Britain was at stake in this matter. 'It may be argued that Lloyd George's doctrine of self-determination does not apply to South Africa', he continued. 'Against this, we argue that if this doctrine is not applicable to the native inhabitants of this country, then the case of the British Government falls to the ground'.[49] Closer to home the Governor-General, Lord Buxton, futher impressed the SANNC when he addressed a mass meeting of Africans during the peace celebrations in December 1918 and declared that 'the war has proved to you that your loyalty was well placed; and I can assure you that it will not be forgotten'.[50]

Visions of a new world order in which Africans would be elevated to their rightful place were not restricted to the educated elite. British, but particularly American pronouncements on the self-determination of oppressed nations were absorbed in a somewhat distorted form by Transkeian peasants and exerted an influence on the millenarian movements which surfaced during the twenties. In 1927 W.D. Cingo, a Transkeian journalist, graphically explained this strand in millenarianism and its relation to the war:

> The Great European War also had its contribution to these illusions. The moral and military power of America came into prominence. Her declaration for the 'Self determination of smaller nations' . . . caught the tender ears of the unsophisticated natives in these parts. They regard the voice of America as that of a mighty race of black people overseas, dreaded by all Europeans. . . . Hopes for political and economic emancipation were revived and today the word America (iMelika) is a household word symbolic of nothing but Bantu National freedom and liberty.[51]

Whereas the hopes engendered by an optimistic post-war mood contributed to the millenarian movements in the Transkei, increased expectations led the SANNC to consider yet another deputation to Britain. The perceived need for such a deputation was further reinforced by the refusal of the Union Government to include an African in the official delegation under Botha and Smuts to the Paris peace conference.[52] Initially Dube doubted the wisdom of approaching the British government before constitutional means in South Africa were exhausted, but later on he agreed that perhaps more could be achieved in Britain than locally.[53] H.S. Msimang further suggested that they

should broaden their platform and involve blacks from South-West
Africa in the venture since the future of the former German colony was
an important item on the agenda at the peace conference. Although
the idea was considered sympathetically, there was not sufficient time
to act upon it.[54] Otherwise there was little to debate and Congress
decided unanimously to send a deputation to Britain and to the peace
conference in Paris.

To pave the way a petition to the King was drawn up in December
1918 at a special session of Congress. The petition strongly emphasized
black loyalty and participation in the war and the King's own speech
to the SANLC was even quoted back at him. It was argued that their
war-time record entitled them to greater consideration and that the
British government should exert pressure on the Union to ensure that
the position of blacks in South Africa was improved.[55] This petition,
however, was never transmitted to the King; Buxton referred the matter to the South African government which reacted in a predictable
way by declaring that either blacks had no reason to be dissatisfied or
their complaints were exaggerated.[56] This rebuff strengthened the
resolve of Congress and in April 1919 three members — R.V. Selope
Thema, L.T. Mvabasa and H.R. Ngcayiya — sailed from Cape Town
for Britain. Later on they were joined by Sol Plaatje and J.T. Gumede.

In Britain the Colonial Office received the news of the black deputation's mission with distinct misgivings and antagonism. Upon learning
that they sought an interview with the King, J. Reid, one of the senior
officials, commented: 'I don't think that H.M. should be advised to
receive the deputation. Its object would be to arraign the Union Govt.;
it can do no good, and would probably embarrass H.M. and annoy
[white] South Africans generally'.[57] Other officials in the Colonial
Office were hardly more sympathetic. They refused a further request
by the deputation to interview the British Prime Minister and, like
Reid's, their marginal comments revealed their real opinions and attitudes. H. Thornton noted that such an interview would only lead to
'further publicity of the deputation's grievances and that would seem
all the more undesirable', while H. Lambert argued that 'these people
no doubt want a little advertisement and take this opportunity to try
and get it'.[58]

The Aborigines Protection Society, which prided itself on being
'friends of the natives', was no source of encouragement either and
ultimately gave the deputation no real moral support. Their assistance
was restricted to some financial aid and offers to find lodgings for the

deputees.[59] Otherwise the organization remained aloof. Its influential secretary, J.H. Harris, had already indicated in an article written in 1916 that he was not in favour of the 'native races' having any say in the possible consultations at the end of the war.[60] It is therefore not surprising that he regarded the deputation as 'ill-advised'. Moreover, as he revealed in a private letter, he was offended because the delegation had not consulted him before their departure from South Africa.[61]

The deputation was thus confronted either by official intransigence or patronizing hypocrisy. However, through the good offfices of W.P. Schreiner, the South African High Commissioner in London who himself had led a deputation to England in 1909 to protest against the colour bar in the Union constitution, they succeeded in arranging an appointment with L.S. Amery, the Under-Secretary of State for Colonies. During the interview which took place on 8 May 1919 Amery could give the delegation little solace and advised them to work patiently within the existing framework of the Union constitution. Although Amery was not prepared to take the matter any further, he was somewhat upset by what he had learnt. In his personal diary he noted that the deputation 'gave a full and not unfair recital of all the grievances suffered by the natives under Union . . . . I replied sympathetically . . . but it was very clear to me that trouble is coming this way, possibly much sooner than we have generally thought'.[62]

Meanwhile Thema and Mvabaza had left for Paris where they unsuccessfully tried to put their cause to the peace conference. However, they did manage to meet Lloyd George who assured them than when he arrived back in London he would find time for an interview.[63] On their return to London the deputation submitted a detailed memorandum on the discriminatory measures in South Africa to Lord Milner, the British Secretary of State for Colonies. This, however, elicited the stock reply, namely that the British government was not in a position to interfere in South African affairs.[64] Nevertheless, the deputation persisted in its task and Sol Plaatje in particular exerted himself to gain general public support. He addressed numerous meetings and to some extent received a favourable response from church circles and certain factions of the labour movement.[65]

Towards the end of November 1919, despite the opposition from the Colonial Office, the long-delayed interview with Lloyd George took place and the deputation once again gave a wide-ranging account of African disabilities in South Africa. In contrast to other high-ranking officials, Lloyd George was not indifferent. After he had

informed them that he had also had an interview with another South
African deputation — that of the National Party under General Hertzog which called for republican independence for South Africa — he
thanked them for the contribution made by the SANLC and for the
loyalty which blacks had generally shown during the war. Lloyd
George was impressed by the clear way in which they had put their
case and informed the deputation that he had 'listened with some
distress to the story you have told of restrictions which are imposed
upon you in your native land'. The constitutional position prevented
him from taking any firm action, but he continued:

> If South Africa were under the control of the British Parliament, well, I
> should know exactly what to do. I should certainly take all your
> grievances into immediate consideration and examine them very care-
> fully and give due weight to all you have said with the feeling that we
> were dealing with a population which has been very loyal to the flag.

Lloyd George also assured them that their cause should receive serious
and sympathetic consideration from the South African government
and that he would inform General Smuts accordingly.[66] The British
Prime Minister remained true to his word and showed his concern by
sending an official report as well as a private letter. In the official
despatch Lloyd George suggested that it was advisable for Smuts to
meet the deputation himself, but in the private communication he
stated that it was a matter of urgency 'to redress any real grievance
from which they may suffer, and to satisfy any legitimate aspirations'.
For Lloyd George it was clear that 'if they have no effective constitutional mode of expression it is obvious that sooner or later serious
results must ensue'.[67] Smuts's response was predictable. He replied
that the deputation had exaggerated black grievances and harmed their
cause by going to Britain, and that there were sufficient constitutional
means through which black aspirations could be accommodated.[68]
   Lloyd George's sympathetic attitude does not mask the obvious
failure of the deputation. Indeed, its abortive mission to Britain only
serves to underline the realities of white domination and the close links
between South Africa and Britain in this respect. As the historian,
Martin Chanock, has noted:

> Lloyd George's letters, a random outburst from an isolated and erratic
> radical, could not alter the fact that . . . Britain shared a common stance

with South Africa . . . . An uninformed sense of disquiet, even in a
Prime Minister, was negligible when weighed against the community of
interest between the white rulers in Africa.[69]

In retrospect then, the attempts of the SANNC may appear
unrealistic and even naive. This, however, would be too harsh a
judgement. Viewed in their own terms and the overall historical context it is clear that in the more hopeful post-war climate their attempts
amounted to a resolute move by constitutionally-minded men to effect
favourable change through the only avenue they deemed promising
and available. 'The Great War has . . . opened a chance to us . . . let
us not lose the chance', argued L.T. Mvabaza on the eve of their
departure to Britain.[70]

The failure of the deputation nevertheless left the SANNC disillusioned and eroded its earlier trust in the British government. Even
Lloyd George's sympathetic attitude was no consolation. 'Lloyd
George said he did not know the black people were so badly treated in
Africa, but Lloyd George is a white man and cannot be trusted', was
the reaction of J.D. Ngoja, a Cape member of the SANNC.[71] Some
members of Congress, though, sought solace in the fact that during
the volatile post-war period the government, through the Native
Affairs Act of 1920, attempted to regularize 'native policy' and created
a Native Affairs Commission which was intended to advise the
government on matters of policy towards Africans. Although these
developments failed to meet the demands and expectations of Congress — Africans, for example, were not included in the Commission
— there were those members of Congress, like R. Selope Thema, who
considered the establishment of such a body a hopeful sign. He argued
that it vindicated their deputation to England in as far as the South
African government had at least shown a willingness to establish the
principle of consultation and to be informed of African interests.[72]
However, even if one is to accept the very dubious proposition that the
commission was a step forward, it remains a moot point whether these
government initiatives were in any way a result of Congress's mission
to England.

The increased expectations brought about by the war only buttressed
the aspirations of Congress for a limited period. The visit to England,
as Peter Walshe has viewed it in his study of the ANC, represented a
watershed in the history of the organization; its constitutional efforts
frustrated, Congress found it difficult to adopt decisive new

strategies.[73] When it became clear that there would be no meaningful concessions in response to black loyalty and sacrifices, the organization lapsed into a mood of political cynicism which contributed towards its relative stagnation in the twenties. However, of greater importance in its decline were the changed socio-economic conditions in which Congress had to operate towards the end and in the aftermath of the war. These conditions, as we shall note in the following chapter, spawned new forms of consciousness and gave rise to popular militancy on the Rand and elsewhere, and also saw the birth of more populist organizations like the ICU. Although some members of Congress tried to meet the new challenges, the organization on the whole became increasingly inactive and alienated from the masses.

In evaluating the broader political significance of the war it is important to look beyond the fluctuating fortunes of an organization like the SANNC. Congress worked within a circumscribed context and its activities do not reflect the more informal and often hidden impact of the war. One particular event — the sinking of the *SS Mendi* with the loss of 615 African lives on 21 February 1917 — stirred the consciousness of numerous Africans outside the formal structures of black politics and in due course the memory of this event became an enduring element in African political thinking.

To many Africans the disaster dramatically symbolized the stark realities of their positions in South Africa: black sacrifices on behalf of white interests. Through the Mendi Memorial Club, initiated by S.M. Bennet Ncwana, and the annual commemoration of Mendi Day in the larger urban centres, the symbolic significance of the tragedy was kept alive. In addition, the Mendi Memorial Bursary Fund was founded in 1936 to sponsor promising black pupils. A distinct feature of this fund was the perceived need to increase black self-esteem through education and to stimulate an awareness of education as an important weapon in the struggle against white domination. Moreover, the message of the Mendi was woven into the fabric of black political consciousness through evocative war poetry in several African languages, glorifying the 'fallen heroes' who had died for 'freedom'.[74]

As the event became embedded in African oral tradition it was, perhaps predictably, enlarged upon and related in exaggerated, heroic terms. One particular version describes an elaborate death drill just before the *Mendi* disappeared beneath the waves and a stirring address by Rev. Isaac Wauchope Dyoba, extolling the virtues of African unity. Such unlikely accounts of the actual events of that fateful day were in circulation during and shortly after the Second World War, and they are significant precisely because they were inflated and distorted. During the forties the *Mendi* disaster had clearly assumed a mythological dimension, with nationalist overtones, in African group-memory.[75] At the same time the annual commemoration services also became rallying points for raising black political consciousness. On such occasions speakers used the opportunity to contrast the sacrifices made by Africans in two world wars to the government's persistence in following a policy of racial domination — a message which obviously struck a sensitive chord amongst often large audiences. Officials of the Native Affairs Department who attended these meetings condemned what they considered 'hot left' speeches by 'extremists', and by 1947 the United Party government was decidedly uneasy about the increasingly political nature of Mendi services.[76]

However, the advent of the reactionary Nationalist regime in 1948 saved the Smuts government from the embarrassment of adopting a firm stance against blacks commemorating a war-time event which occurred while Africans were serving South Africa and the Empire. The Nationalists, of course, had no such qualms, and furthermore in line with the explicit apartheid thinking of the new order it was considered inappropriate for blacks to be reminded that they had actually assisted whites in a European war. Afrikaner officials of the Bantu Affairs Department argued that the 'unfortunate' involvement of blacks should be best forgotten as it could only stimulate integrationist ideas and provide a platform for 'agitators'. During the fifties the Nationalist government stopped short of prohibiting Mendi Day meetings, but actively discouraged their continuation and the organizers had to contend with official harassment and numerous obstacles in their annual efforts to sustain the spirit of the *Mendi*.[77] Not surprisingly, fewer and fewer Mendi Day services were held in the sixties, and with the passage of time the memory of the *Mendi* also started to fade. Although there was still a limited awareness of the event amongst certain black communities in 1984, it had lost virtually all its symbolic significance.[78] In the increasingly polarized South Africa of today, it is also extremely doubtful whether black political groupings would like to be reminded of, much less care to commemorate, the episode.

War-related events had a decided, if uneven, impact on black political consciousness. While many Africans undoubtedly remained untouched by war events, for others the war brought into sharper focus the hypocrisy of white rulers in South Africa as well as the impotence of Britain to intervene in South African affairs, and for a considerable time the *Mendi* contributed its own symbolic political message. However, political consciousness reflects only one dimension of the war as it relates to Africans and furthermore it cannot be seen in isolation. It is therefore necessary to determine whether the war also had a broader and related impact on the structures of South African society.

Notes

1. Compare P. Karsten, *Soldiers and Society: the effects of military service and war on American life*, p.4.
2. W.O.107/37, History of the SANLC, 1918; *Imvo Zabantsundu*, 17 November 1917 (Letter from Capt. L.E. Hertslet).
3. Transcripts from interviews with R. Mohapeloa, Maseru, 9 May 1980 and P. Mabathoana, Maseru, 22 April 1980.
4. Perry, J. and Perry, C. (eds.), *A Chief is a Chief by the People: the autobiography of Stimela Jason Jingoes*, p.80.
5. D.C. 1136/2/1997, Chief Censor to Acting Secretary of Defence, 23 April 1918.
6. Compare C. van Onselen, *Studies in the Social and Economic History of the Witwatersrand, 1886-1914*, Vol. 1, *New Nineveh*, pp.45-50.
7. The commanding officer of the Cape Auxiliary Horse Transport Company (a Cape 'coloured' unit which served in France as drivers) reported in this respect that some 'white women showed partiality towards the Cape men and no matter how strict the control, found means of communicating with them, as is evidenced by a number of venereal cases'. C.O.551/117/39492, Report on the Cape Auxiliary Horse Transport Company, 13 June 1919.
8. *Native Teachers Journal*, October 1920 (Letter from F.H. Kumalo); U.W.H.89/34, Report on the SANLC, 8 March 1919.
9. Perry and Perry (eds.), *Jingoes*, p.93.
10. U.W.H.89/34, Report on the SANLC, 8 March 1919.
11. *Imvo Zabantsundu*, 18 September 1917 (Letter from Z.F. Zibi translated from Xhosa).
12. J.258/3/127/20, Report on a meeting of the Transvaal Native Congress in Johannesburg, 24 August 1921. See also B.P. Willan, 'The South African Native Labour Contingent, 1916-1918', p.78.
13. C.M.T. 3/930/778/2, D.S. Makoliso to Magistrate Cala, 24 February 1917.

14. *The Church Abroad*, 1917, p.122 (Letter from an African in France).
15. G.G. 549/93/56, General report on the chaplaincy and welfare work of the South African Native Labour Corps, 31 July 1918.
16. Stanford Papers, B.C. 293/Frr/2, E. Mdlombo to Stanford, 3 March 1918.
17. S.3/13/2/3, M.L. Posholi to P. Griffiths, 12 July 1917.
18. Quoted in S.M. Bennet Ncwana, *Souvenir of the Mendi Disaster*, 1942, pp.26-27.
19. S.3/13/2/3, M.L. Posholi to P. Griffiths, 12 July 1917.
20. Perry and Perry (eds.), *Jingoes*, p.87. See also Willan, 'South African Native Labour Contingent, 1916-1918', p.79.
21. Perry and Perry (eds.), *Jingoes*, p.92.
22. O.C. Records, 44/22/81, Report on the SANLC, 12 April 1918.
23. *Cape Times*, 18 April 1921 ('What the Native is thinking').
24. *South Africa*, 8 November 1919 ('Natives' proud record').
25. Stanford Papers, B.C. 293/Frr/5, C.L. Harries to Stanford, 7 June 1920.
26. *Cape Times*, 14 August 1920 ('Parliamentary debates'); O.C. Records 89/125, British War Office to Commanding Officer War Records South Africa, 18 October 1919; G.G. 545/9/93/56, Smuts to Governor-General, 30 April 1921; C.M.T. 3/926/778/2, Secretary Department of Native Affairs to Chief Magistrate Transkei, 20 September 1922; *Izwe Lase Afrika*, 21 February 1942 ('War service medals');
27. J.318/3/754/21, Report on a meeting of the Transvaal Native Congress, 7 September 1921; N.A. 9108/20/363, Secretary of Native Affairs to J. Morie, 18 May 1918; E. Roux, *Time Longer than Rope*, p.113.
28. *The African Defender*, September and October 1938, 17 (Letter from 'An African').
29. N.A. 9108/26/363, E.Q. Madayi to Secretary of Native Affairs, 20 January 1921.
30. N.A. 9108/26/363, S.T. Zondani and E. Ntusi to Magistrate East London, 24 January 1920.
31. C.M.T. 3/925/778/2, A.K. Xabanisa to Chief Magistrate Transkei, 28 December 1919.
32. Roux, *Time Longer than Rope*, p.114.
33. D.D.T. Jabavu, *The Black Problem*, p.17.
34. J. 225/3/527/17, District Commandant Pietersburg to Assistant Commissioner of Police Pretoria, 21 December 1917.
35. N.A. 9108/22/363, Complaints re behaviour of native overseas troops, 18 January 1918.
36. S.A.P. file 6/592/18, Report from Detective P. Mokhatla, 7 March 1918.

37. For a detailed analysis of these movements see R.R. Edgar, 'Garveyism in Africa: Dr Wellington and the American movement in the Transkei', *Ufahamu*, VI, 3 (1976), pp.31-57; R.R. Edgar, 'The Fifth Seal: Enoch Mgijima, the Israelites and the Bulhoek massacre, 1921', unp. Ph.D. thesis, University of California, Los Angeles, 1977, esp. pp.151-181.

38. D.D.T. Jabavu, 'Native unrest in South Africa', pp.250 and 254 vaguely hints at this, but millenarian ideas were primarily transmitted by migrant workers. See Edgar, 'Garveyism in Africa', p.35; Edgar, 'Fifth Seal', p.159.

39. P.M. 1/1/300, Secretary of the Prime Minister to Secretary of the Governor-General, 20 February 1919; P.L. Wickins, *The Industrial and Commercial Workers Union of Africa*, pp.35, 61, 67-68, 76, 147, 163; Willan, 'The South African Native Labour Contingent, 1916-1918', p.83.

40. J. and R. Simons, *Class and Colour in South Africa, 1850-1950*, p.241; G. Pirio, 'The role of Garveyism in the making of the South African working classes and Namibian Nationalism', unp. paper, New York, 1982, pp.6-7.

41. Pirio, 'Role of Garveyism', p.6.

42. See Chapter 6.

43. Perry and Perry (eds.), *Jingoes*, p.93.

44. *Ilanga Lase Natal*, 26 May 1917 ('Under the flag of freedom').

45. *Abantu-Batho*, 14 February 1918 ('Our position').

46. G.N.L.B. 187/1217/14/D110, Report of the annual SANNC conference, 29 March 1918.

47. *Abantu-Batho*, 25 April 1918 ('Notes and comments').

48. *Contact*, 3, 7 April 1960 (Interview with H. Selby Msimang).

49. *Abantu-Batho*, 7 February 1918 ('The future of the German colonies').

50. G.G. 1169/50/759, Petition to King George V, 16 December 1918 (copy). Buxton's address is quoted in this petition.

51. Quoted in Edgar, 'Garveyism in Africa, p.37.

52. Walshe, *African Nationalism*, p.62.

53. *Ilanga Lase Natal*, 17 November 1918 ('Generalities'), 13 December 1918 ('The proposed deputation'), 28 February 1919 ('Lack of unity'), 28 March 1919 ('Off to England').

54. *Contact*, 3, 15 July 1960 (Second interview with H. Selby Msimang).

55. G.G. 1169/50/759, Petition to King George V, 16 December 1918 (copy).

56. G.G. 1169/50/759, F.S. Malan to Buxton, 20 February 1919.

57. C.O. 551/111/15305, Marginal notes by J. Reid, 4 April 1919.

58. C.O. 551/122/35102, Marginal note by H. Thornton,19 June 1919; C.O. 551/122/35007, Marginal note by H. Lambert, 13 June 1919.

59. A.P.S. Papers, S 23 H 2/50, J.H. Harris to Selope Thema, 12 January 1920 (copy).

60. J.H. Harris, 'Native races and peace terms', in *Contemporary Review*, 606, June 1916, pp.752-759.
61. A.P.S. Papers S 23 H 2/50, Harris to M.E. Sadler, 12 February 1920 (copy). See also Smuts Collection CXV/8, Harris to private secretary of the South African High Commissioner, 10 April 1919 (copy). Walshe, *African Nationalism*, p.62, is obviously mistaken in claiming that the APS encouraged Congress to send a deputation to Britain.
62. J. Barnes and D. Nicholson (eds.), *The Leo Amery Diaries, I, 1896-1929*, p.260, 8 May 1919.
63. C.O. 551/114/58532, H. Lambert to South African High Commissioner, 21 November 1919.
64. C.O. 551/112/30799, Deputation to Milner, 22 May 1919 and Milner to Deputation, 4 June 1919.
65. B.P. Willan, *Sol Plaatje: a biography*, pp.247-248.
66. C.O. 537/1197/1486, Transcript of an interview between Lloyd George and the deputation, 21 November 1919.
67. C.O. 537/1197/1486, Lloyd George to Smuts, 3 March and 7 January 1920.
68. C.O. 537/1198/17397, Smuts to Lloyd George, 12 May 1920.
69. M. Chanock, *Unconsummated Union: Britain, Rhodesia and South Africa*, 1900-1945, p.134.
70. J.256/3/527/17, Report of a meeting of the Transvaal Native Congress, 17 December 1918.
71. J.257/3/527/17, Report of a meeting of the Transvaal Native Congress, 8 February 1920.
72. Willan, *Sol Plaatje*, p.296.
73. Walshe, *African Nationalism*, p.65.
74. G.G. 1169/50/771, S.M. Bennett Ncwana to Buxton, 12 March 1919; Willan, 'South African Native Labour Contingent, 1916-1918', p.85; *Abantu-Batho*, 14 January 1918 ('Wail of the native widows'); *Cape Times*, 19 February 1936 ('In memory of the Mendi'); *Inkundla ya Bantu*, 17 March 1944 ('Mendi anniversary').
75. Willan, 'South African Native Labour Contingent, 1916-1918', p.85; *The Star*, 22 February 1952 ('They were brothers').
76. N.A. 9111/36/363, S.A. Rogers to Secretary of Native Affairs, 22 February 1941, Native Commissioner Pretoria to Secretary of Native Affairs, 27 February 1945, G. Mears to S.A. Rogers, 7 March 1947.
77. N.A. 9111/36/363, Memorandum on Mendi Day, 6 March 1959.
78. *City Press*, 19 February 1984 ('Tragedy of the Mendi lingers on'); *Sowetan*, 29 February 1984 ('Death of the Mendi').

CHAPTER 6

The War and Social Change

In the introduction to a recent volume of essays on African class formation, culture and consciousness in South Africa between 1870 and 1930, the editors hinted at the possibility that the first World War might have had a more profound effect on the economy than has been realized.[1] It is hoped that this chapter will shed some more light on the subject. The aim is to establish the correlation between the war and economic developments in three major sectors — mining, manufacturing and agriculture — and to consider the implications of such changes as ensued for the Africans concerned. Obviously the analysis has to review the on-going process of capital accumulation in order to evaluate the precise impact of war, but it is not meant to be a detailed exposition of the process as such. The discussion thus takes the form of a panoramic overview with the emphasis on war-related change. And finally, moving away from explicit socio-economic change, but still staying within the general ambit of war-related social change, the disastrous influenza epidemic which struck South Africa during the last quarter of 1918 is placed in the context of the war.

As far as the mining industry is concerned, the war had a direct and immediate impact on diamond mining. Shortly after the outbreak of hostilities the directors of De Beers decided to suspend all their mining operations on the diamond fields. The mining magnates argued that the uncertain war conditions in Britain and Europe would have a detrimental effect on the international demand for diamonds. Besides cheap labour, the profitability of the industry was dependent on the careful marketing of diamonds and it was therefore essential to avoid flooding the market at a time when the international prospects for luxury items like diamonds appeared decidedly bleak. The possibility of continuing mining operations and stockpiling diamonds to market at a later stage was also considered unfeasible because of the considerable capital investment and high risk involved. Consequently some 5 000 whites and 45 000 blacks were dismissed from the various diamond mines and mining operations were only resumed on a limited scale in July 1916.[2]

To the mining magnates such a policy made sound financial sense, but the summary shutdown caused considerable resentment amongst the unemployed workers. After the closure of the Jagersfontein mine, an indignant white worker asked:

> Is it right that a few men who have obtained their wealth by the labour and sweat of their employees in Jagersfontein, can stop a whole industry and plunge a whole town into the misery of starvation, to save themselves not from ruin but from the temporary loss of their fat dividends and profits?[3]

And, one may very well ask, how much more applicable must these sentiments have been to the black workers who stood on the bottom rung of the labour ladder?

While white workers were offered some financial assistance to tide them over, no such provision was made for African labourers. With a large number of unemployed blacks roaming the streets of Kimberley, a potentially explosive situation developed. Since these Africans were 'threatened with starvation', the city councillors feared that 'there would be serious trouble which the present Police Force was inadequate to deal with'.[4] However, most of the unemployed were speedily repatriated. Many of them were in dire distress; without food and with little money they were forced to return to the poverty-stricken areas which they had left to supplement their meagre resources in the first place. This was particularly the case with the Sotho who had left Basutoland on account of a shortage of food during 1914. Not surprisingly the police on the border between South Africa and Basutoland reported that 'a disquieting feature is the behaviour of the natives who are returning from the diamond fields. Their attitude is mutinous and quite unlike their usual behaviour'.[5] Equally clear is the motivation which prompted a number of labourers returning from Kimberley to Basutoland to plunder a shop in Brandfort and remove the food supplies in it.[6]

Whereas the war caused severe dislocation in the diamond mining industry, it made, in the beginning at least, less of an impact on gold mining. In August 1914 the mine owners entered into an agreement with the Bank of England that all South African gold would be purchased at the standard rate of 85*s* per fine ounce.[7] Gold was not only the bulwark of the South African economy, but was also of increasing importance to the war-strained British economy. The significance of this was not lost on some educated Africans who pointed out: 'The mass of African labour has made it possible to win so much gold from mother earth, that labour has made it possible to apply the great means of exchange to the great national purposes that are now demanded of Britain'. This in turn raised the question whether the efforts of the African working class on the mines would be acknowledged: 'And as that giant native labour has so faithfully served, and is still serving, shall no notice be taken of it, not a word of recognition be made?'[8] This however, was a forlorn, and some might even say a naive hope. Because of the costs involved in extracting gold from the generally low-grade ore on the Rand, ultra-cheap exploitable labour constituted the very basis of profitable production in the industry, and in consequence the mine owners would be unlikely to make any concessions to the black working class unless they were actually forced to do so. As a matter of fact, the only recognition blacks received between 1914 and 1920, and then only after militant action, was a paltry 12.2 per cent increase compared to the 58.5 per cent increase made to white workers during the same period.[9]

Although the outbreak of hostilities did not check the production of gold, subsequent war-related conditions had a profound effect on the industry. The war caused a sharp escalation in the price of mining materials as a result of general wartime inflation and because European production was geared to meet more pressing and immediate war requirements. Between 1914 and 1918 the working costs per ton of ore milled on the Rand rose by 28 per cent and the gross profit per ton plummeted from 8*s*.5*d*. to 3*s*.9*d*.[10] From 1917 onwards these developments, in conjunction with the fixed gold price, led to a serious profitability crisis which necessitated measures to cut back on production costs which included a restructuring of the labour force. However, conditions generated by the war also provided the Chamber of Mines with a launching pad for implementing a policy of cost reduction. Approximately 25 per cent of the skilled and semi-skilled predominantly English-speaking white miners left for active service during the war, and the mine owners were in favour of replacing them with black workers; not only would black labour have been cheaper, but it would also have meant that one section of the black work-force could be played off against the other.[11]

It can be argued though that at least for certain Africans such a policy would have meant some upward mobility, albeit not at the same wage rate which applied to whites. The extent to which this actually happened during the war years as such is, however, a matter of some dispute. In a recent book David Yudelman has claimed that 'the early years of the war were marked by black advances in job opportunities, many of them replacing whites who had gone to war or moving into new jobs created by the shortage of skilled labour.'[12] On African advancement in particular, Yudelman exaggerates. There is no evidence that 'many' of them took the place of white labour at any point during the war period. Although a few Africans may have advanced, the positions of absent white workers were mainly taken by 'poor white' Afrikaners or 'coloureds', and not by Africans.[13] To be fair, Yudelman shows an awareness of this in his further treatment of the subject, but his original statement stands unmodified, thus conveying the misleading impression that a considerable number of Africans, instead of an insignificant fraction of the labour force, moved up the hierarchy as a result of war conditions.

The main opposition to African advancement came from the white Mine Workers' Union (MWU) which protested vigorously against the 'coloureds' who had been moving into 'white' jobs. The bias of the MWU was reinforced during the war years as a result of the influx of 'poor white' Afrikaners. According to R.H. Miller, Inspector of Labour, these Afrikaners were 'if anything, more insistent on the demand [the retention of the colour bar] than the English section, the invariable retort to discussions on this question being that niggers have no right to any class of employment other than as hewers of wood and drawers of water'.[14] This difference cannot, however, be explained solely in terms of greater ingrained racial prejudice on the part of these Afrikaners and must be seen in the context of their structural vulnerability. Once driven off the land and into the harsh industrialized urban environment, the material position of the Afrikaner newcomers was threatened by blacks competing for the same semi-skilled jobs. English-speaking miners, on the contrary, generally occupied higher skilled jobs and were therefore less exposed to the thrust from below.

Nevertheless, these developments led to the so-called *status-quo* agreement of 1918 between the mine owners and the MWU, protecting 19 job categories and 4 020 white workers. Despite this agreement, in the immediate post-war period a persistent drop in profit margins caused the mine owners to resume their attempts to bring blacks into the categories reserved for whites — a policy which eventually contributed to the 1922 strike of white workers. One must be careful, though, not to construe this policy as an automatic gain for black workers. As Duncan Innes has explained recently:

> But while the strategy was *seemingly* directed against only a section of the white labour force, it was *actually* an assault on the whole labour force in the industry, though it affected sections of that labour force differentially. What the mine owners sought to gain . . . was not only the expulsion of a section of white labour from production, but also a more general process of deskilling among white workers as a whole and a particular rise in the level of exploitation of black workers.[15]

Therefore, although some Africans steadily moved into semi-skilled jobs after 1918 as a result of conditions initially generated by the war, this was not necessarily to their benefit, since the labour process itself was thus altered to facilitate a higher rate of exploitation. Since a reduction of the general wage bill was crucial and African semi-skilled (and unskilled) wages did not keep pace with the increased cost of living, there was, in fact, no gain in real terms; on the contrary, the aim of the mine owners was to extract more profit from the labour force.[16]

Returning specifically to the 1914-1918 period, it is necessary to assess the impact of the war on the labour supply to the mines. The total number of black workers stayed constant between 1914 and 1919: 179 837 labourers in 1914 as against 179 530 in 1919. In March 1916 the chairman of the Chamber of Mines, W.H. Davies, could state that 'the industry is in the unusual position of having all the native labour it can employ.' This was due to the fact that many unemployed workers affected by the closing of the diamond mines found their way to the gold mines, while a prevailing drought also forced more blacks to seek work on the mines. These developments offset the slight drop caused by the recruitment of blacks for the labour contingent in France in late 1916 and during 1917.[17] However, in 1918 the situation had changed drastically and the new chairman, E.E. Wallers, declared that 'our supply is probably worse now than it has ever been in the history of the Rand, having regard to the scale of operations'. This sudden change was mainly due to the expansion of the mining industry on the Far East Rand and to increasing competition for labour with a burgeoning manufacturing industry.[18] The war featured indirectly in this shortage of labour to the extent, as we shall note shortly, that it stimulated the growth of manufacturing which contributed to a greater overall demand for labour than before.

The war years and their immediate aftermath were further marked by one of the most sustained periods of worker action in the labour history of South Africa. On the gold mines black workers manifested a high degree of resistance to exploitation and the following strikes, mainly for higher wages, occurred in the industry: in December 1915 at the Van Ryn Deep Mine; in January 1916 at the Government Gold Mines Area; in February 1916 at the Modderfontein Mine; and in July 1918 at the Crown, Robinson Deep and Ferreira Deep mines. In addition there was a widespread boycott of mine concession shops in February 1917, affecting nearly all the mines on the East Rand. These developments foreshadowed the large-scale strike of 1920 which involved 71 000 workers (almost 40 per cent of the black labour force) and affected 21 of the 35 mines on the Witwatersrand. Worker demands were firmly rejected, and it was only after the 1920 strike that labourers were paid a small bonus.[19]

Strained relations between capital and labour were of course not confined to the gold mines. Outside the mining industry considerable labour unrest occurred during 1918-1920: the demands for higher wages in Bloemfontein in February 1919; the large-scale revolt against passes in Johannesburg in March and April 1919; the dock strike in Cape Town in December 1919 which launched Clements Kadalie's ICU; and the agitation for wage increases in Port Elizabeth in January 1920. These upheavals, which were particularly sustained in Johannesburg during 1918-1919 have been well documented by other historians and will not be discussed further here.[20] However, several writers have suggested or tacitly assumed that the war contributed to the rising tide of militancy. Although this assertion is undoubtedly valid, it has not been demonstrated, except for rather vague statements,[21] how hostilities conducted mainly in Europe influenced black workers in a country 10 000 kilometres removed from the main zone of the war. Within the context of this study it is therefore important to establish the links between the war and labour unrest.

In this respect it is essential to note the rapid secondary industrialization which occurred during the war years. There was a brief decline in trade and industry at the outbreak of war, but soon after, remarkable growth took place. From 1915-16 the number of factories and other manufacturing enterprises increased from 3 998 to 6 890 in

1919-1920, an increase of 72 per cent. The main areas of expansion were in the light consumer and processing industries and the metal and building industry.[22] Basically these developments were related to the war in that South Africa was unable to import articles not usually produced locally and local manufacturers were induced to take advantage of the opportunity created by diminishing foreign competition. Moreover, the natural protection which South African industries enjoyed as a result of being thousands of kilometres from Europe and America was increased during the war by the rise in freight, insurance and other import charges as well as the substantially reduced commercial output of the belligerent nations.[23] The industrial upsurge was closely allied to accelerated urbanization. During and immediately after the war, the number of unskilled workers (mainly Africans) employed in urban industries (excluding mines) rose dramatically by 83 per cent: from 61 654 in 1915-16 to 113 037 in 1919-20.[24] The vast majority of these workers were concentrated in the industrial heartland of South Africa, the Witwatersrand area, where they were housed in appalling conditions. The rapid proletarianization clearly had important implications for labour unrest and indirectly the war thus provided the broad socio-economic context for strained industrial relations. This connection did not go unnoticed among officials of the Native Affairs Department. In a memorandum of May 1919, dealing with the position of Africans on the Witwatersrand, it was explicitly emphasized:

> The disorganisation of the commercial world . . . has thrown the British Dominions on their own resources, and one is amazed at the strides that have been made in local manufacturing during the past four years. In short, the war has put the hand of time forward many years . . . and this is perhaps most noticeable in regard to the natives . . . . They have been awakened by the roar and noise of a universal war . . . . Johannesburg has become the centre in which native thought has developed most during the war, and from which native political movements will radiate . . . . It is on the Witwatersrand that the native has had the opportunity of realising what industrial labour strikes mean.[25]

Important as war-time industrialization might have been in accelerating proletarianization it was, of course, not the only contributory factor. Under-development of the reserves — an ongoing process which drove Africans off the land — as well as the effects of droughts in the rural areas also loomed large in this transformation. The necessity of balancing war-related developments against other trends in society is clearly evident.

A further consideration in examining the links between the war and labour unrest is inflation. As a result of war conditions in Britain, the demand for goods exceeded supply and consequently prices increased drastically. Since South Africa had intimate trade links with Britain, this also affected the price structure in the Union. Moreover, banking and credit facilities were considerably extended during wartime in-dustrialization and the unproductive debt almost doubled between 1910 and 1920. The cost of living, according to official statistics, increased by 15,07 per cent between 1914 and 1918, but there are indications that retail prices for the same period rose between 31 per cent and 39 per cent.[26] Although white salaries were generally adjusted accordingly, black wages were either pegged at pre-war levels or only marginally increased.[27] Not surprisingly, the issue of wages became a burning grievance and the focal point for industrial unrest.

In addition to these developments, the sacrifices made by African participants in the war also impinged on the ideological consciousness of blacks during the unrest on the Witwatersrand. Thus a black woman, E. Mallela, declared: 'King George in France said to the natives you are my soldiers. Why should we be arrested and killed under the Union Jack? We have helped. We must be free; why should we be slaves? Think of the blood of our boys in France.'[28] Essentially the same point was made by an anonymous African at more or less the same time: 'Some of our brothers are in France today. Some of us are dying for Botha's Government which do[es] not give us anything.'[29] These were not isolated examples and it may be readily assumed that this awareness must have had an effect in arousing a more general resentment. However, despite the significance of these war-related ideas actually surfacing on the Rand during 1918 and 1919, there is no satisfactory evidence that these were important considerations in spurring either black workers or petty bourgeois elements into revolt.

The links between the war and labour unrest are therefore mainly confined to industrialization, proletarianization and inflation. Of these, the effects of inflation on black wages were directly connected with the primary cause for agitation. But, as one historian has noted, it would be wrong 'to exaggerate the importance of this factor [black wages] at the expense of the wider range of repressive discriminatory mechanisms . . . .' The iniquitous pass system, poor housing and in-adequate educational facilities were all interrelated and integral to the system of labour repression which evoked such sustained resistance.[30] In evaluating the effect of the war on urban discontent, these inherent structural inequalities are obviously of overriding and paramount importance; war-related developments only served to expose and emphasize the exploitable position of African workers.

Specific conditions generated by the war also highlight the nature and ambiguities of African class formation and attitudes in the industrialized environment of the Rand. The growth of the African working class, and the labour unrest during and after the war, reveal the structural insecurity of the petty bourgeois and aspirant petty bourgeois elements. Their material position often differed little from that of the working class, but they enjoyed certain advantages, particularly in educational background, and self-consciously strove to set themselves apart from the rest of society. During the unrest, however, they had to contend with a movement whose membership, according to a contemporary white observer, consisted of persons 'who had developed into the "skebenga" type — young men mostly, not even partially educated'.[31] Once the lumpenproletarian section of society had asserted itself, the position of the petty bourgeoisie became distinctly contradictory. P.L. Bonner has described this situation and the factors involved as follows:

> On the one hand, the cohering of the urban petty and aspirant petty bourgeoisie: on the other, the possibilities of mobilising a broad class alliance comprising the proletariat, lumpenproletariat and petty bourgeoisie. Only the day-to-day flux of the class struggle, and the respective pressures and inducements offered by the main protagonists in the conflict — capital and labour — would determine the eventual position of the petty bourgeoisie. Ultimately certain elements of the petty bourgeoisie identified with the working class, while some remained waiverers and others kept aloof.[32]

It is also necessary to consider whether the changes brought about by the war had an effect on the role and position of black women in society, especially since women in other industrial countries were markedly affected by war-time changes. In Britain, for example, large numbers of women had replaced men who were on active service, and the growing dependence on female labour meant that the traditional view of what constituted men's work and women's spheres of activity no longer held good. Although the nature of the labour undertaken was often harsh and could scarcely be regarded as a step towards emancipation, there were, as Sheila Rowbotham has indicated, significant changes in women's attitudes to work:

> The war broke down many of the assumptions which had persisted throughout the industrial revolution. Young women . . . from the upper middle classes came to assume that they had a right to work. Working-class women who experienced their capacity to do a man's job began to question female subordination at work. The numbers of women in trade unions went up during the war. This meant that for the first time, outside textiles, women workers were organised on a sustained and continuing basis.[33]

In South Africa the entry of women into the expanding manufacturing industry was also hastened by the departure of men on active service, and the number of white women employed by the manufacturing sector on the Rand between 1915-1916 and 1919-1920 increased by 181 per cent from 1 147 to 3 232.[34] Although the war thus had a decided impact on the employment pattern of white females, the same cannot be said for black women. The rate of urbanization of black women was far slower, and the numerical superiority of white females on the Rand as well as prevailing practices in the manufacturing industry ensured that black women were virtually excluded. Employment opportunities for African women were extremely limited. Domestic service provided a number with a fairly regular if meagre income, but many more operated on the fringes of the economically active population, eking out a precarious existence as brewers of beer, laundresses, hawkers, and prostitutes.[35] War-time conditions, particularly soaring inflation, doubtless greatly aggravated the poverty in which many black women found themselves. Perhaps the comment of an anonymous African best describes the general plight: 'The hardships that the natives had to go through for the last two years with war prices will only be known by those who move and speak with the natives as an equal'.[36]

It would be wrong to assume that the relatively slow rate of urbanization of black women — only about 6 per cent were urbanized by 1921 — implies that African women in general played no part in the evolving capitalist system. On the contrary, with the growing war-time demand for industrial (male) labour, the role of women in the reserves became increasingly important. By anchoring the African family (and labour power reproduction) in the reserves and through subsistence production reducing the goods that had to be bought for cash, they became even more vital as 'capitalist appendages', compelled to subsidize the system that lowered the value of African labour power and the level of African wages.[37] Equally, some of these women who had migrated to the cities were also 'unseen' hostages to the system in that they had to subsidize the low wages of African men with cash earnings.

For people in the rural areas, the question of land loomed large during the war years. After the passing of the 1913 Land Act, the Beaumont Commission toured the country in 1916, examining a host of witnesses on the question of a further division of land and precisely defining the areas to be released and added to those scheduled in 1913 under the Land Act.

The commission's recommendations were contained in the Native Affairs Administration Bill of 1917 which was designed to turn the principle of land segregation into reality. Once again black ownership of land was restricted to specific, if somewhat enlarged, areas and a separate administrative system for the scheduled reserves was envisaged. Numerous Africans viewed the new bill with trepidation since the areas demarcated for blacks, although a slight improvement on the 1913 Act, were still completely inadequate. They also objected to the possible enactment of such sensitive legislation while the country was fighting a war in which, through the labour contingent and in other ways, they had made a considerable contribution. If the proposed legislation were to be passed, it would be a very poor return for their loyalty. Already, it was pointed out, some families of those who had joined the contingent had been summarily evicted in the northern Transvaal because they were unable to pay their rent; it would have been an even greater blow for those loyally serving in France to find on their return that in their absence they had been deprived, by law, of the land they had previously occupied.[38]

The bill was, in fact, shelved, though it cannot be said that its withdrawal was primarily the result of African opposition. Black legal action did, it is true, give rise to an appeal court ruling, in June 1917, which determined that the intended legislation would be invalid in the Cape Province. There the land question was bound up, in terms of article 35 of the South Africa Act of 1909, with the African franchise, to which changes could only be effected by a two-thirds majority of both houses of parliament. This decision proved a considerable stumbling-block to the government. Another, perhaps preponderant reason for shelving the bill lay in the hostility of vested white farming interests, particularly in Natal. The farmers objected strongly to the allocation of any additional land to Africans. Although Botha favoured the proposed legislation, he needed the support of the Unionists for the government's war policy and was therefore reluctant to coerce them into accepting a measure which clearly ran counter to their material interests. The war effort took precedence over domestic legislation and the world conflict thus indirectly played a part in the demise of the bill through Botha's deference to the interests of his only parliamentary allies.[39]

While the war was merely of contextual importance in the question of land division, it had a direct impact on agricultural production. It was quickly realized in white farming circles in South Africa that the severe dislocation in European and British agriculture caused by the war offered unique prospects. The war not only stimulated an internal market from which foreign competition was to a considerable degree eliminated, but also opened up a larger export market. 'With the vast armies in the field the consumption of food has increased enormously, and every one of these men has to be fed. It means not only an increase in price, but that we in South Africa have a glorious opportunity of producing more', was the euphoric comment of an agricultural journal in February 1915.[40] Despite a drought in 1916, as well as problems in importing certain farming implements and a sharp rise in freight rates during the war, these were boom years for white farmers. With the exception of three products — wattle bark, which suffered from the closing of the German market; fruit, which was handicapped by competition with meat for cold storage space on the ships; and ostrich feathers, which went out of fashion during the war years — 'practically everything the farmer had to sell realized extremely high prices'.[41] Cattle farmers, and to a slightly lesser extent maize and wool farmers, were the main beneficiaries of the changed conditions brought about by the war. After the initial disruption in trade, the value of South African agriculture and pastoral exports during the war years showed an increase of approximately 62 per cent in real terms.[42] Not surprisingly, most white South African farmers could in 1919 look back upon a four-year period of 'remarkable prosperity due to the war.'[43]

Whereas white farmers were structurally well positioned to take advantage of the opportunities offered by the war, the productive base and competitiveness of black peasants and sharecroppers had already been so undermined that they were unable to derive real benefit from the war boom. The years preceding the First World War were marked by a sustained assault on black producers with underdevelopment culminating in legislative terms in the 1913 Land Act. Colin Bundy has explained this process succinctly:

> The cluster of political and economic forces, evident in the years 1890 to 1913, underlay a series of legislative pressures upon the peasantry. Access to land was made more difficult; taxes, rents, and other fees were raised; the control of various forms of squatting was intensified. During precisely this period, the belated commercialization of white agriculture meant that land value rose and land usage altered: squatter-peasants were evicted or offered stiffer terms. State aid for agriculture, the provision of credit facilities, and especially the development of a modern economic structure in white areas by the spread of the rail network, adversely affected the competitiveness of peasant production. The relations between peasant and market, in the shape of peasant/trader dealings, the peasant's distance from markets, his exaggerated vulnerability to depression, and the spread of debt, further diminished the peasant's ability to generate a surplus.[44]

It is against this background that black farming during the war years must be seen. Although in a few instances peasants and sharecroppers responded to the new market opportunities, particularly as far as maize and tobacco were concerned,[45] the structurally disadvantaged position of the majority of black agriculturalists and pastoralists largely prevented them from participating gainfully in the altered and generally favourable economic circumstances generated by the war.

The conditions brought about by the war also affected class relations in the 'white' countryside. Central in the context of these developments, as in much else in the history of South African political economy, was the 1913 Land Act. The ultimate significance of the act, according to Tim Keegan, was that the 'state could lay down the conditions and delimit the battleground for the struggle between landlords and tenants. It allowed some landlords increasingly to limit peasant independence and to impose even stricter conditions on tenants. But it was an uneven, gradual and sporadic process.'[46] It is certainly true that there was no sudden transformation of this process during the war period. However, the infusion of additional capital into agriculture as a result of the buoyant war conditions, did contribute to an intensification of the struggle between 'progressive' capitalizing farmers on the one hand, and sharecroppers and independent peasants on the other.

Increased agricultural production and capitalization during the war years exacerbated the perennial labour 'problem'. In addition, whereas in the period before 1914 agriculture's main competitor for labour had been the mines, with the rapid growth of secondary industries during the war a second urban based competitor now made its presence felt. Moreover, the war-time expansion of agriculture and greater availability of finance did not necessarily lead to a marked increase in agricultural wage rates, and agriculture was still at a disadvantage in competing with the wages paid by the mines and secondary industry.[47]

There were of course considerable regional differences, but the general response from white capitalizing farmers, in the Transvaal and the northern Orange Free State at least, was a renewed attempt to limit the already tenuous African access to land. The productive base of blacks, whether as sharecroppers or as independent peasant producers, had to be further eroded in order to turn them into dependent wage-earning farm labourers. To this end there were insistent calls that the relevant sections of the 1913 Land Act, aimed at the removal of this type of African producer, should be applied more stringently and consistently. 'One of the causes of the shortage of labour', a farmer from the Free State inveighed,

> is that curse, ploughing on the halves which, although supposed to be illegal, goes on merrily and never a policeman interferes. Some time back a prosecution for this did take place, I think in Bloemfontein, and the occurrence was so unusual that it was mentioned in the papers. As long as the native can scratch over a few acres and run his stock for nothing, he is not likely to work.[48]

And from the eastern Transvaal G.F. Warren claimed:

> There are hundreds of farmers, like myself, who to-day have plenty of land, implements, and, after the recent beautiful rains, ideal weather, but cannot take advantage of it owing to shortage of labour; and yet all around them they know of dozens of farms where natives are squatting and ploughing land on the shares with so-called white farmers, who are content so long as they get a few bags of mealies, which ensures them an idle existence, and who allow dozens of lazy kaffirs to plough up a few acres of ground in the spring.[49]

These 'progressive' farmers were clearly exasperated by the persistence of sharecropping and regarded it as an obstacle inhibiting the growth of capitalist farming. The increased demand for labour as a result of the expanding war-time agriculture served to sharpen this awareness and bolstered their on-going attack on the sharecropping system.

During the war years a number of farmers' organizations approached the state for additional assistance in the quest for labour. In 1917 the South African Maize Growers' Association, for one, impressed upon the Native Affairs Department that the situation could be eased by allowing 'piccanins and native youths to go and work on farms without the written consent of their parents or guardians.' It was considered essential to abolish this requirement, since 'an abundant supply of cheap native labour' was necessary for the 'increase in production of foodstuffs throughout the Union'. The department was very sympathetic to these appeals and the maize farmers were assured that the 'Government is endeavouring in every way to encourage natives to send their young sons out for this form of employment, it being recognised that as regards adult labour the agricultural industry has difficulty in competing with the mines.'[50]

These developments bear testimony to the increased pressure on black agriculturalists to become wage labourers. But the mere fact that the required labour was not forthcoming, and that it was necessary to call for more state intervention, also points to the vigorous efforts on the part of African cultivators to retain a hold on their productive base and to avoid being forced into wage employment. In some instances the resistance was so effective that farmers were unable to obtain wage labourers for any extended period and were compelled to engage labour by the day. Other farmers were bluntly told by black producers: 'We will not work for a white man, as we can work for ourselves'.[51] Even in cases where once independent peasants and semi-independent sharecroppers were reduced to the status of labour tenants, they still resisted attempts to change the conditions of labour into wage employment. This is abundantly clear from the evidence of an irate Transvaal farmer in October 1918:

> A few days ago a native came to look for work, and I offered him £2 per month and enough mealies or meal to keep his family going for the year; but he scoffed at it and told me that his previous employer gave him six acres to plant each year, for which he had to work eight months . . . . The only point he could see was that under one system he was a landholder and under the other a farm labourer.[52]

Furthermore, those who were forced to become wage labourers had a well-developed intelligence network which kept them informed about the conditions on particular farms. This enabled them to avoid those farms where the *sjambok* was the main form of communication bet-ween landlord and labourer. 'Let me remind those baases', J.N. Tatane informed the white farmers, 'if the treatment is harsh the native will not stand for it. He will not only desert his service, but he will go about telling his comrades what kind of baas you are'.[53]

However, despite the resilience displayed by rural Africans in general, the 'final victory of capitalist landlords over the sharecropping peasantry was assured, and the conditions of that victory were being laid all the time'.[54] The spread of capitalist relations in the countryside as a result of the favourable conditions generated by the war accelerated this process and helped to cement the structures which ultimately served to envelop rural Africans in a world neither of their own making nor of their own choosing. This does not, however, imply that the process was inevitable or that the war was necessarily a major turning-point; the capitalization of agriculture was characterized by its uneven and halting advance, and with hindsight the war was only one, if hitherto unrecognized, signpost on the long and slippery road travelled by capitalist agriculture in South Africa.

Besides its impact on the socio-economic structure, the war also played a role in the demographic changes which occurred through the devastating influenza epidemic of the last few months of 1918. In the context of this study we therefore turn to discuss the connection between the war and the epidemic. War-time conditions abroad facilitated the spread of contagious disease; thousands of soldiers were crowded into military camps and then cooped up in the even more confined space of troopships which transported them to all parts of the world. Towards the end of August 1918 the most dangerous in-fluenza virus known to medical science at the time appeared almost simultaneously in three important North Atlantic harbours: Freetown in Sierra Leone, where local inhabitants came into contact with British, South African and Australian troops on their way either to or from the war front in Europe; Brest in France, where large numbers of Allied troops embarked; and Boston, Massachusetts, a key embarka-tion port where large numbers of military and civilian personnel from several countries came into contact with one another. The virus spread from these centres and 'within days thousands were sick and hundreds were dying as the new strain or strains moved outwards from these foci'.[55]

Influenza appeared in South Africa about the middle of September 1918, and numerous whites and blacks died in the ensuing epidemic which lasted until about the end of November. According to the official return of the commission of enquiry, 11 726 whites lost their lives as a result of influenza. The Native Affairs Department estimated that by the end of 1918 80 000 blacks had succumbed, but the official commission which reported in February 1919 calculated that 127 745 blacks had died during the epidemic.[56] There are sound reasons to believe that even this figure is too low, simply because the deaths of many blacks were not officially registered. The ravages of the epidemic must have had a profound psychological and extremely debilitating sociological impact on black communities, but it is only recently that the catastrophic effects of this disaster have attracted the attention of historians.[57]

While general war-time conditions accounted for the rapid spread of the virus, there is an even more specific correlation between its introduction into South Africa and black participation in the war. It was widely suspected by the white public that former members of the SANLC, returning from France, carried the influenza strain into South Africa and were responsible for its further dissemination. In Nationalist circles in particular this idea became firmly entrenched. Significantly Nationalists described the epidemic as the 'kaffer-khaki pes'[58] — a term which graphically reveals the racist and political dimensions of their perceptions of the epidemic.

In the official enquiry the commission also focussed on the SANLC and paid particular attention to two ships, the *Jaroslav*, and the *Veronej*. These ships arrived in Cape Town on 13 and 18 September 1918 and had respectively 1 274 and 1 769 members of the contingent on board — the last groups to leave France. Both called at Sierra Leone, one of the focal points of the world-wide epidemic. The enquiry found, however, that serious cases of influenza had already been noted on 14 and 18 September respectively in Durban and on the Rand; that is, before those aboard these ships had reached their homes. Although the commission took careful note of the destinations to which ex-members left in order to find a possible connection between the outbreak of the epidemic and the dates of arrival of the two ships, no such link could be found. The commission was nevertheless of the opinion that the disease could have been latent amongst some members of the contingent and that this could have contributed to the spread of the epidemic. Consequently they concluded that 'the *Jaroslav* and *Veronej* cannot be incriminated as having originated the epidemic, but they probably assisted in its spread'. As far as the origins of the epidemic in South Africa were concerned, the commission claimed that 'it was impossible to determine the exact manner in which introduction from outside sources operated and it is impossible to fix any route or vehicle'.[59] However, in a recent study by Howard Phillips on the epidemic a distinction is drawn between earlier, milder forms of influenza and the deadly second wave which swept through the country. This leads him to the conclusion that although the commission may have been 'technically corrrect in asserting that the *Jaroslav* and *Veronjev* troops were not the first to bring Spanish 'flu to Cape Town, everything points to their being the ones who introduced the fatal second wave.'[60] It thus appears that there was a closer connection between the introduction of the deadly influenza epidemic and the SANLC than the official commission had revealed.

Finally, in general terms it is clear that the First World War affected the lives of Africans on a broad front — from rapid changes in the socio-economic structure to the way in which many died from a war-related epidemic. War-time developments weighted the scales even more against Africans. Their struggle against white domination within a set of social relations increasingly permeated by capitalism became progressively more difficult, for the changes induced by the war added to their structural vulnerability and highlighted the on-going process of exploitation and resistance.

Notes

1. S Marks and R Rathbone (eds), *Industrialization and Social Change*, p.31.
2. H.A. Chilvers, *The Story of De Beers*, pp.209-213; *Diamond Fields Advertiser*, 29 July 1915 ('Report on the annual meeting of shareholders'); M.N.I. 258/2195/14, Memorandum on the closing of the mines, 15 August 1914.
3. *The Friend*, 14 August 1914 (Letter from 'Anti-capitalist').
4. M.N.I. 282/1587/15, Report of an interview between the deputation from Kimberley and F.S. Malan, 14 August 1914.
5. J. 208/5/314/14, Lt. E. Hardiman to Staff Officer Bloemfontein, 13 August 1914 (copy).

6. *Tsala ea Batho*, 12 September 1914 ('Basuto and the war').
7. M.H. de Kock, *Selected Subjects in the Economic History of South Africa*, p.252.
8. *Ilanga Lase Natal*, 26 March 1915 ('Natives and gold').
9. F.A. Johnstone, *Class, Race and Gold: A study of class relations and racial discrimination in South Africa*, p.100, table 6.
10. D. Innes, *Anglo: Anglo American and the rise of modern South Africa*, p.75-76.
11. Johnstone, *Class, Race and Gold*, pp.95, 104-105, 120. See also M.N.I. 939/1738/19, Chamber of Mines to Acting Prime Minister, 19 May 1919 (copy).
12. D. Yudelman, *The Emergence of Modern South Africa: State, capital, and the incorporation of organized labor on the South African gold fields, 1902-1939*, pp.145-46. See also Johnstone, *Class, Race and Gold*, p.107, for a similar statement.
13. M.N.I. 373/1212/17, Report on Van Ryn Deep strike, 1 February 1917; M.N.I. 939/1738/19, Low Grades Mine Commission of 1919, Minutes of evidence, pp.63-64.
14. M.N.I. 427/2270/18, R.H. Miller to Chief Inspector of Labour, 4 July 1918.
15. Innes, *Anglo*, p.81.
16. Johnstone, *Class, Race and Gold*, pp.120, 180.
17. *Annual Address of the President of the Transvaal Chamber of Mines*, 27 March 1916, p.7, and 26 March 1917, p.17.
18. *Annual Address of the President of the Transvaal Chamber of Mines*, 25 March 1918, p.8.
19. For these developments see U.G. 38/19, *Annual Report of the Secretary for Mines and Industries and the Government Mining Engineer*, 1918, pp.89-90; M.N.I. 514/1633/20, Report on the Native Mine Workers' Strike, 1920; P.L. Bonner, 'The 1920 black mineworkers' strike: a preliminary account' in B. Bozzoli (ed.), *Labour, Township and Protest*, pp.273-97; Johnstone, *Class, Race and Gold*, pp.172-74, 181-84.
20. See for instance, P.L. Bonner, 'The Transvaal Native Congress, 1917-1920: the radicalisation of the black petty bourgeoisie on the Rand' in Marks and Rathbone (eds), *Industrialisation and Social Change*, pp.270-313; P.L. Wickins, *The Industrial and Commercial Workers' Union of Africa*, pp.23-38, 43-44, 52-57; Walshe, *African Nationalism*, pp.70-74, 89; F.A. Johnstone, 'The I.W.A. on the Rand: socialist organising among the black workers on the Rand, 1917-18' in Bozzoli (ed.), *Labour, Township and Protest*, pp.248-72; Johnstone, *Class, Race and Gold*, pp.174-79.
21. For example the statement by Walshe, *African Nationalism*, p.89 that 'a combination of economic development and social unrest, allied to the

Fighting Their Own War

impact of new ideas in the aftermath of World War I, produced an increased level of political awareness within African society . . . .' Somewhat simplistically D.D.T. Jabavu had also observed: 'The war has awakened an otherwise long-dormant race consciousness in the Bantu as witnessed by the spirit of union and growing tendencies for organisation on trade union lines . . . .' (Jabavu, 'Native unrest in South Africa', p.254).

. D.H. Houghton and J. Dagut (eds), *Source Material on the South African Economy, 1860-1970, 2, 1899-1919*, p.209, Industrial Census, 1915-1916, 1919-1920; G. Bloch, 'The development of manufacturing industry in South Africa, 1939-1969' (Unpublished M.A. dissertation, University of Cape Town, 1980), p.76.

23. C.W. Pearsall, 'Some aspects of the development of secondary industry in the Union of South Africa', *The South African Journal of Economics*, 5, 1937, p.414; De Kock, *Economic History of South Africa*, pp.130, 290; B. Bozzoli, *The Political Nature of a Ruling Class: capital and ideology in South Africa*, pp.143-45; Innes, *Anglo*, p.119.

24. Houghton and Dagut (eds), *Source Material*, 2, pp.210, 226, Industrial Census 1915-1916, 1919-1920, National resources of South Africa.

25. S.N.A. 1/4/26, Memorandum relating chiefly to Native political affairs on the Witwatersrand, 14 May 1919.

26. *Cape Times*, 18 January 1918 ('The cost of living'); De Kock, *Economic History*, p.131; Houghton and Dagut (eds), *Source Material, 2*, pp.192, 214, 233, Cost of living, Report of the trade commissioner, National resources of South Africa.

27. Bonner, 'The Transvaal Native Congress, 1917-1920',p.273. *Rand Daily Mail*, 4 April 1919 ('Natives and the unrest').

28. J. 256/3/527/17, Report of a meeting of the Native Women's League, 7 July 1918.

29. J. 256/3/527/17, Report of a meeting of the Industrial Workers of Africa, 28 May 1918.

30. Bonner, 'The Transvaal Native Congress, 1917-1920', pp.274.

31. *Rand Daily Mail*, 20 July 1918 ('Why the agitators failed').

32. Bonner, 'The Transvaal Native Congress, 1917-1920', pp.278, 289.

33. S. Rowbotham, *Hidden from History: Rediscovering women from the 17th century to the present*, pp.111-12.

34. H. Pollak, 'Women in the Witwatersrand industries', unpublished M.A. dissertation, University of the Witwatersrand, 1932, p.6.

35. A.M. Mariotti, 'The incorporation of African women into wage employment in South Africa, 1920-1970', unpublished Ph.D. thesis, University of Connecticut, 1980, p.85; Bonner, 'The Transvaal Native Congress, 1917-1920', p.278.

36. *Ilanga Lase Natal*, 1 March 1918 (Letter from a 'Johannesburg Native').

37. Mariotti, 'Wage employment', pp.86, 260.
38. *Abantu-Batho*, 22 November 1917 ('The Native Bill'); *Ilanga Lase Natal*, 28 November 1917 ('South African Native National Congress'); U.G. 32-18, *Minutes of Evidence of the Eastern Transvaal Natives Land Committee*, p.113, evidence of S.M. Makgatho.
39. M. Lacey, *Working for Boroko: the origins of a coercive labour system in South Africa*, pp.29, 86-90; A.G. Smurthwaite, 'The policy of the Smuts Government towards Africans, 1919-1924', unpublished M.A. thesis, University of South Africa, 1975, pp.11-14; Garson, 'South Africa and World War I', p.81.
40. *The Agricultural Journal of South Africa*, February 1915, pp.170-171 (Editorial).
41. U.G. 25-17, *Annual Report of the Department of Agriculture for the year ended 31 March 1916*, pp.25-26; U.G. 40-19, *Annual Report of the Department of Agriculture for the year ended 31 March 1919*, p.27.
42. Compare De Kock, *Economic History*, p.175; U.G. 40-19, *Annual Report Agriculture*, p.27.
43. *The Agricultural Journal of South Africa*, July 1919, p.8 (Editorial).
44. C. Bundy, *The Rise and Fall of the South African Peasantry*, p.240.
45. T. Matsetela, 'The life story of Nkgomo Mma-Pooe: Aspects of sharecropping and proletarianisation in the northern Orange Free State, 1890-1930' in Marks and Rathbone (eds), *Industrialisation and Social Change*, p.225; W. Beinart, *The Political Economy of Pondoland*, p.90. See also R. Edgar, 'Lesotho and the First World War', p.101, for increased production of various products in Lesotho during the war.
46. T. Keegan, 'The sharecropping economy, African class formation and the 1913 Natives' Land Act in the highveld maize belt' in Marks and Rathbone (eds), *Industrialisation and Social Change*, p.205.
47. Compare A.M.D. Humphrey, 'South African agriculture in a period of transition, 1913-1924', unpublished Honours dissertation, University of the Witwatersrand, 1978, p.55-56.
48. *Farmer's Weekly*, 18 December 1918, p.1671 (Letter from 'Snowball').
49. *Farmer's Weekly*, 2 October 1918, p.502 (Letter from G.F. Warren).
50. *The Agricultural Journal of South Africa*, November 1917, pp.197-99, correspondence between South African Maize Growers' Association and Native Affairs Department, October 1917.
51. *Farmer's Weekly*, 10 July 1918, p.2047 (Editorial); *Farmer's Weekly*, 2 October 1918, p.503 (Letter from G.F. Warren).
52. *Farmer's Weekly*, 16 October 1918, p. 730 (Letter from 'The Quare Fellow').
53. *Farmer's Weekly*, 6 November 1918, p.1031 (Letter from J.N. Tatane).
54. Keegan, 'Sharecropping economy', p.204.
55. A.W. Crosby, 'The pandemic of 1918' in J.E. Osborn (ed.), *Influenza in*

America, 1918-1976, p.8.

56. U.G. 7-19, *Report of the Department of Native Affairs for the Years 1913 to 1918,* p.29; U.G. 15-19, *Report of the Influenza Epidemic Commission, 1919,* pp.10, 23, Appendix C.

57. Howard Phillips completed a Ph.D. in 1984 at the University of Cape Town on the epidemic.

58. Communication from Howard Phillips, 28 September 1981.

59. U.G. 15-19, *Epidemic Commission,* pp.7-9, 19-22, Appendix B.

60. H. Phillips, 'The impact of the Spanish flu epidemic of 1918 on Cape Town', unpublished paper, South African Historical Society, 1985, pp.6-7.

Conclusion

Although critics may argue that the period of the First World War is a 'Eurocentric time capsule, artificially introduced into the African context',[1] it is hoped that this study has demonstrated that in many different and sometimes unexpected ways the war was very much a reality for numerous South African blacks.

From the very outset Africans responded to the European conflagration and showed a keen awareness of the implications of the conflict. The black elite, as represented in part by Congress, argued, though not unanimously, that they should suspend their protest campaign against discrimination and support the war effort in the hope that such a policy would, at the conclusion of hostilities, be rewarded. Not surprisingly, this approach was encouraged by the government. It can be claimed that Congress, in aligning itself so closely with ruling class interests, sacrificed the opportunity of mounting a meaningful challenge at a time when the state was comparatively vulnerable. Congress certainly did not adopt a confrontationist stance, demanding tangible concessions in return for support of the war effort, and on the whole also failed to provide effective and decisive leadership for an increasingly volatile black working class. However, it must be borne in mind that the historian has the benefit of hindsight; at the time Congress sincerely believed that 'loyalty' during the war would provide blacks with at least some leverage, and in the aftermath of the war a deputation was sent to Britain in an effort to capitalize on this policy.

Congress nevertheless reflected only one strand of African political consciousness during the war. Outside the structures of formal black politics some workers and peasants saw the war as an opportunity to voice their discontent forcefully and even to strike at the system of domination. In one case, the peasant uprising of late 1914 in the Matatiele district, consciousness was translated into collective action

South African blacks were not alone in reacting to the war in the way they did. Indeed, viewed from a wider perspective, there were marked similarities between the responses of black South Africans and those of Africans in the rest of the continent. While the educated elite in colonial Africa generally declared their loyalty to the imperial powers, some of the other classes regarded the war as an opportune time to come out in revolt as is evident from uprisings in Nyasaland (Malawi), Mozambique, and British and French West Africa.[2] And as the Afrikaner rebellion of 1914 in South Africa illustrates, this strategy was not confined to black people. Despite divergent motives, disaffected Boers and certain blacks nevertheless shared a common perception of the war as offering an opportunity for resistance.

As far as recruitment and the nature of military service are concerned, there were also some parallels between the experiences of South African blacks and their counterparts elsewhere on the continent. Many black recruits from the Union were, like Africans in the British, French, German and Portuguese colonies, deceived, cajoled, coerced or forcefully compelled to serve. Unlike the German askaris or the British King's African Rifles who were armed, black South Africans served as general labourers and transport drivers in South West Africa, and along with thousands of blacks from Britain's African colonies, did duty in East Africa as carriers and porters. Indeed, in these debilitating, disease-ridden territories they literally carried the Allied forces into battle. The SANLC, however, had the dubious distinction of being the only sub-Saharan African force from the British Empire to be used in Europe where they helped to haul and load the armies to victory.[3] Perhaps the outstanding feature of the SANLC's service in France was the way in which the South African authorities sought to prevent members from getting ideas above their socio-political station in the domestic order. However, Africans resisted this policy and forced the government into an impasse so that, given its refusal to abandon the compound system, it was obliged to recall the contingent

It is a popular, though not universally accepted theme in Anglo-American and European studies of war and society that the social forces generated by the war often work to the benefit of subordinate classes. With industries geared towards greater war production, the bargaining power of such classes increases and ultimately their overall position in the labour market is strengthened. In the long run, this development, it is claimed, tends to flatten the social pyramid with increasing upward mobility for the underclasses. The common endeavours of war-time society also to some extent forge a common sense of purpose and in the process perceptions of class lines can be blurred. A second strand in this proposition deals with the effects of military service itself. It is argued that as the intensity of sustained conflict calls for greater manpower, there is a 'greater participation on the part of larger underprivileged groups in society who tend correspondingly to benefit, or at least develop a new self-consciousness.'[4]

Whatever this theory's validity in highly industrialized Britain, America and Europe, trends in southern Africa tend to contradict it. In an area where race overlay class and where the pressures of war were less intense and pervasive the subordinate groups in society did not find that war-time developments improved their position. Nevertheless, S.E. Katzenellenbogen, one of the few historians who has commented on the impact of the First World War on southern Africa, has suggested that 'generally all social groups benefitted economically from the war. Wages were driven up by the greater shortage of labour . . . .'[5] This assertion can be dismissed; the economic position of black South Africans actually declined during 1914-1918 as a result of war-time inflation. Nor did those blacks who served in the military benefit materially or politically from their participation. Admittedly, some returned with a heightened political awareness, but they did not exert a significant and decisive influence on post-war African political developments. Political consciousness was not necessarily translated into political action, and moreover, the way in which African military participation was limited and narrowly circumscribed tended to weaken the potential of ex-servicemen to serve as catalysts for change. Ultimately, then, military service was not a crucial variant in determining political behaviour.

In this respect there is also a noticeable parallel with trends in other African colonies. Although the political role of veterans in all the colonies is yet to be analyzed systematically, the available evidence suggests that it is easy to overestimate their importance in post-war movements.[6] There is a contrast here with the post-war impact of black Americans who served in Europe in a non-combatant as well as combatant capacity. The long-term role of these veterans in politics still remains somewhat hazy, but immediately after the war they were very much involved in the unrest that swept through America. While the general underlying causes of the riots in *inter alia* Charleston, South Carolina, Washington D.C., New York City and Chicago were socio-economic, political and psychological, it was the return of black veterans that seems to have triggered off bloody clashes during

America's 'red summer' of 1919. In particular the lynching of black ex-soldiers by white racists, who believed that the veterans had come back with 'wrong ideas' about their social status after having served in Europe, sparked off retaliations by some veterans and widespread anger and counter attacks by the black community in general.[7] Thus Afro-American veterans, driven by specific circumstances and living in a rather different kind of society, featured more prominently in immediate post-war developments than ex-servicemen on the African continent.

Obviously a key question in determining the impact of war is whether the war itself actually initiated new trends or reinforced existing ones. For South Africa it would be claiming too much to aver that the war was responsible for a completely original departure, but in certain respects the pace of change was accelerated. Besides the intensification of agricultural capitalization, important changes occurred in the fields of manufacturing and commerce. 'While imperial capital's influence declined', as Bozzoli has recently shown, 'that of national capital rose; while the elements that constituted imperial capital were shaken by the war, those of national capital seized the opportunity to grow and become firmer . . . .'[8] Closely allied to the growth of local capital was the extension of social and political control over urban Africans in the post-war period — formally embodied in the 1923 Natives (Urban Areas) Act especially. This legislation, as Peter Kallaway has interpreted it, was 'the basis of a much tougher political creed, namely the foundation of a stable urban African community in the towns of South Africa, which would, because of its stake in the status quo, form a bulwark against labour unrest and political agitators.'[9] In the short term Africans were thus not only affected by war-induced changes like rampant inflation, but structural war-related developments also had detrimental long-term implications. Isang Pilane, the Kgatla chief, certainly spoke for many blacks in southern Africa when he declared in 1923: 'We see that the Great War has left poverty and distress behind it.'[10] Africans, however, were neither powerless nor passive victims of the new environment; the changed conditions also forged new ideological constructs as illustrated by working class militancy on the Rand in particular, and the emergence of the populist I.C.U. which gradually eclipsed an increasingly inactive A.N.C.

Though South African blacks were thus drawn into the 'white man's war' and affected by its wider ramifications, essentially they had to fight their own war within a war. Indeed, as S.M. Makgatho testified before the Eastern Transvaal Native Land Commission in connection with the 1917 Native Administrative Bill: 'You see, this bill is in itself war against us, as we have to fight against certain things.'[11] In general terms the war against domination during this period was fought by those who explored the opportunities for revolt or constitutional change, by those who refused to serve in the military, by those who were enrolled but resisted the discriminatory measures of the South African authorities, by those in the increasingly industrialized and capitalist urban environment who came out on strike, and by those who tried to stave off and cope with the implications of the growth of agricultural capitalism. In short, on different levels Africans fought for their livelihood, for the recognition of their dignity and for their rightful place in South African society. That war is still being fought.

Notes

1. The phrase quoted is from R. Rathbone, 'World War I and Africa: Introduction' in *Journal of African History*, XIX, 1, 1978, p.9.
2. Rathbone, 'World War I and Africa: Introduction', p.5; A. Osun- tokun, 'West African armed revolts during the First World War' in *Tarikh*, 5, 3, August 1979, pp.6-17.
3. Compare D. Killingray and J. Matthews, 'Beasts of Burden: British West African carriers in the First World War' in *Canadian Journal of African Studies*, 13, 1-2, 1979, pp.7-23; M.E. Page, 'Fighting for their world: Black men in a white men's war', unpublished paper, A.S.A. Conference, Washington D.C., November 1982, p.9.
4. See for instance, A. Marwick, *War and Social Change*, pp.12-13; W.L. Young, *Minorities and the Military: a cross-national study in world perspective*, p.257. This view has been criticized by, amongst others, P.Abrams, 'The failure of social reform' in *Past and Present*, 26, 1963, pp.23-44; C.H. Enloe, *Ethnic Soldiers: state security in divided societies*, p.73.
5. S.E. Katzenellenbogen, 'Southern Africa and the War of 1914-1918', p.115.
6. See for instance L.J. Greenstein, 'The impact of military service in World War I on Africans: the Nandi of Kenya' in *Journal of Modern African Studies*, 16, 1978, pp.495-507; Killingray, 'The colonial army in the Gold Coast', pp.375-415. J.Matthews, 'World War I and the rise

of African nationalism: Nigerian veterans as catalysts of change' in *Journal of Modern African Studies*, 20, 3, September 1982, pp.493-502, tends to argue the opposite, but his work is not free from methodological problems.

7. A.Barbeau and F. Henri, *The Unknown Soldiers: Black American troops in World War I*, p.178; R.W Mullen, *Blacks in America's Wars*, p.50.

8. B. Bozzoli, *The Political Nature of a Ruling Class*, p.172.

9. P. Kallaway, 'F.S. Malan, the Cape liberal tradition and South African politics' in *Journal of African History*, XV, 1, 1974, p.124.

10. C.O. 417/694/2314, Address to High Commissioner, undated but received 9 August 1923.

11. U.G. 32-18, *Minutes of Evidence of the Eastern Transvaal Natives Land Committee*, p.113.

Sources

A. ARCHIVAL SOURCES

I. SOUTH AFRICA

1. TRANSVAAL AND CENTRAL ARCHIVES DEPOT, PRETORIA

Accessions

A. 20, Colonel W.H.M. Bamford.
A. 75, T. Boydell.
A. 120, L.B. Cross.
A. 58, L. Esselen.
A. 32, J.B.M. Hertzog.
A. 34, General J.C.G. Kemp.
A. 69, H. Oost.
A. 90, Commandant N. Orpen.
A. 787, Dr. G.S. Preller.
A. 1, General J.C. Smuts.

Archives of the Magistrate Bethal (BL)
Vols.: 4-9, 24-26.

Archives of the Government Native Labour Bureau (G.N.L.B.)
Vols.: 1-4, 19-91, 173-210, 312.

Archives of the Governor-General (G.G.)
Vols.: 92, 120, 458-629, 721, 854, 1094-97, 1162-70, 1271-82, 1432, 1275-82, 1731.

Archives of the Secretary for the Department of Justice (J.)
Vols.: 37, 54, 106, 117, 122, 126, 137, 141, 161, 162, 165, 177-212, 248, 260, 269-302, 318, 330, 334, 357, 361, 371, 383, 386, 390, 412.

Archives of the Secretary for the Department of Mines and Industries (M.N.I.)
Vols.: 206, 224-395, 409-92, 512, 510-27, 628, 939.

Archives of the Secretary for the Department of Native Affairs (N.A.)
Vols.: 2, 65, 82, 97, 99-201, 205, 207, 213, 215-37, 246, 259-70, 301-09, 315, 527, 9106-14.

Archives of the Secretary for the Department of the Prime Minister (P.M.)
Vols.: 1-50, 53, 61, 129, 137-40, 143-56, 165-70, 208-28, 243-45, 247, 258, 271-72, 274-75, 280-85, 300-302, 312-14, 318, 333-36, 361, 372-92, 407, 476-84, 487-88, 533.

Archives of the Rebellion Losses Commission (K 1)
Vols.: 3-16, 18-60.

Archives of the South African Police (S.A.P.)*
Files: 35/7-35/18, 6/245/1/14-6/245/999/20, 6/271, 6/646-6/967, 15/18/47, 1/250, 1363/18/18.

2. SOUTH AFRICAN DEFENCE FORCE DOCUMENTATION CENTRE, PRETORIA.

Archives of the Adjutant-General (A.G.)
Vols.: 3, 5, 10, 13, 14, 16, 25, 36, 42, 79-82, 108, 152-66, 172, 173, 178, 183-89, 194, 204-05.

Archives of the Chief Staff Officer (C.S.O.)
Vols.: 1-2, 12-20, 27-28, 34, 38, 50, 57, 62, 65, 70, 83.

Archives of the Commandant-General (C.G.)
Vols.: 3, 4, 8, 12, 36, 43, 45.

Archives of the Secretary for the Department of Defence (D.C.)
Vols.: 22-35, 43-47, 63, 65, 90, 110-12, 121, 128, 136, 141, 147, 156, 164, 167-89, 229, 232, 249, 250, 253, 256-78, 288-348, 354-65, 377, 393, 405-29, 446, 450, 465, 474-90, 520-25, 530, 564, 582, 595, 600-26, 636, 643, 651, 657-68, 690-703, 711-20, 732, 738, 742, 748, 756, 759-798, 804, 810, 826, 833, 844-64, 880-922, 960-1197, 1201, 1218, 1220, 1230, 1236-98, 1303-66, 1410-53, 1930, 3030.

*This group was unsorted at the time it was consulted and material could only be traced by file number.

Archives of the Officer Commanding Records (O.C. Records)
Vols.: 2-28, 37-109, 125-135, 227, 290-318.

Archives of the Provost Marshal, K. Series (P.M.L.)
Vols.: 32-33, 46-51, 60, 76-87, 99-105, 115, 121, 124, 127-136.

South African Native Labour Contingent Attestation Forms (SANLC)
Vols.: 1-21.

Union War Histories Group (U.W.H.)
Vols.: 65, 89, 158-159.

W.W. I 1914/1918 Group (W.W. I 1914/1918)
Vols.: 1-6, South African Native Labour Contingent

*W.W. I German South West Africa Group, 1914/1918 (W.W. I
G.S.W.A. 1914/1918)*
Vols.: 5, 14, 20, 23, 30, 31, 35-43, 77, 79, 84, 110, 117-121, 136.

W.W. I Imperial Service Details, 1914/1918 (W.W. I I.S.D.)
Vols.: 3-6, 19-36.

3. CAPE ARCHIVES DEPOT, CAPE TOWN

Accessions
A. 608, H.E.S. Fremantle.
A. 583, F.S. Malan;

Archives of the Magistrate East London (1/ELN)
Vols.: 3, 70-71.

Archives of the Magistrate Ladysmith (1/LSM)
Vols.: 7-9.

Archives of the Magistrate Tabankulu (1/TBU)
Vols.: 25, 89.

Archives of the Chief Magistrate Transkei (C.M.T.)
Vols.: 3/790, 3/925-3/937, 3/942.

Archives of the Magistrate Umtata (1/UTA)
Vols.: 6-7

4. NATAL ARCHIVES DEPOT, PIETERMARITZBURG

Accessions
H.E. Colenso.
Natal Wesleyan Mission.
Zulu Society Papers.

Archives of the Chief Native Commissioner (C.N.C.)
Vols.: 187-93, 244-48, 286, 298, 310-15, 330, 342.

Archives of the Secretary for Native Affairs, Natal (S.N.A.)
Vols.: 1/4-1/27.

5. ALBANY MUSEUM, GRAHAMSTOWN

D.L. Smit Papers.

6. RHODES UNIVERSITY, CORY LIBRARY, GRAHAMSTOWN

Lovedale Collection
Methodist Church Collection.
W.B. Rubusana Collection.

7. KILLIE CAMPBELL LIBRARY, DURBAN

J. Hertslet Papers.
J.S. Marwick Papers.
G.H. Nicholls Papers.

8. SOUTH AFRICAN PUBLIC LIBRARY, CAPE TOWN

J.X. Merriman Papers.
W.P. Schreiner Papers

9. UNIVERSITY OF CAPE TOWN, JAGGER LIBRARY, CAPE TOWN

W.E. Stanford Papers.

10. UNIVERSITY OF SOUTH AFRICA, SANLAM LIBRARY, PRETORIA

S.T. Plaatje Papers/S.T. Molema Papers.

11. UNIVERSITY OF THE WITWATERSRAND, LIBRARY, JOHANNESBURG

J. Howard Pim Papers.

II. LESOTHO

1. LESOTHO NATIONAL ARCHIVES, MASERU

Archives of the Secretary to the Government (S.)
Vols.: S/3/13/1/1-S/3/13/6/1.

III. BRITAIN

1. PUBLIC RECORD OFFICE, KEW, LONDON

Colonial Office Records (C.O.)
Vol. series: 521, 532, 537, 547, 551, 573, 581, 616.

Cabinet Papers (CAB.)
Vol. series: 5, 23, 37, 42.

Ministry of Munitions (MUN.)
Vol. series: 4, 5.

Board of Trade Records (T)
Vol. series: 9

War Office Records (W.O.)
Vol. series: 95, 106, 107, 158, 163.

2. HOUSE OF LORDS RECORD OFFICE, WESTMINISTER, LONDON

A. *Bonar Law Papers.*

3. IMPERIAL WAR MUSEUM, LONDON

Maj.-Gen. E. Northey Papers.
Archival Film on the SANLC, 1917.

4. UNIVERSITY OF LONDON, SCHOOL OF ORIENTAL AND AFRICAN STUDIES, LONDON

H.S. Msimang, unpublished 'Autobiography'.

5. UNIVERSITY OF LONDON, KING'S COLLEGE, LIDDELL HART CENTRE, LONDON

Brig.-Gen. G. Aston Papers.

6. OXFORD UNIVERSITY, BODLEIAN LIBRARY, OXFORD

L. Harcourt Papers.
A. Milner Papers.

7. OXFORD UNIVERSITY, RHODES HOUSE, OXFORD

Aborigines Protection Society Papers (A.P.S.)

8. CAMBRIDGE UNIVERSITY, CHURCHILL COLLEGE, CAMBRIDGE

M. Hankey Papers.

9. WILTSHIRE COUNTY RECORD OFFICE, COUNTY HALL, TROWBRIDGE, WILTSHIRE

W.H. Long Papers.

10. NEWTIMBER PLACE, HASSOCKS, SUSSEX*

S.C. Buxton Papers.

B. OFFICIAL GOVERNMENT PUBLICATIONS

I. SOUTH AFRICA

Official History: Union of South Africa and the Great War
Pretoria, 1924.

S.C.   1-15, *Report of the Select Committee on the Rebellion.*
S.C.   3-15, *Union of South Africa, Senate, Report of the Government's Special Commissioner.*
S.C.   1-19, *Report of the Commissioner appointed to enquire into and report upon the causes which led up to the partial cessation of the municipal sanitary services at Johannesburg, 6-8 June 1918.*
U.G. 37-14, *Report of the Native Grievances Inquiry 1913-1914.*
U.G. 10-15, *Report on the Outbreak of the Rebellion and the policy of the Government with regard to its suppression.*
U.G. 13-16, *Report of Commission of Enquiry into the treatment of Prisoners of War by the German Protectorate Authorities during the late hostilities.*
U.G. 14-16, *Report on the work done by the Inspection Staff on War Expenditure in connection with the Rebellion and the German South West African campaign up to the end of October 1915.*
U.G. 19-16, *Report of the Native Land Commission.*
U.G. 22-16, *Report of the Native Land Commission: Minutes of Evidence.*
U.G. 24-16, *Report of the Board of the South African Railways and Harbours.*
U.G. 40-16, *Report of the Rebellion Losses Commission.*
U.G. 42-16, *Judicial Commission of Inquiry into the Causes and Circumstances relating to the recent Rebellion in South Africa: Minutes of Evidence.*

*I am indebted to Mrs G. Clay for permission to consult these documents.

U.G. 46-16, *Report of the Judicial Commission of Inquiry into the Causes and Circumstances relating to the Recent Rebellion in South Africa.*

U.G. 25-17, *Annual Report of the Department of Agriculture for the year ended 31 March 1916.*

U.G. 32-18, *Minutes of Evidence of the Eastern Transvaal Natives Land Committee.*

U.G. 7-19, *Report of the Department of Native Affairs for the years 1913 to 1918.*

U.G. 15-19, *Report of the Influenza Epidemic Commission, 1919.*

U.G. 38-19, *Annual Report of the Secretary for Mines and Industries and the Government Mining Engineer, 1918.*

U.G. 40-19, *Annual Report of the Department of Agriculture for the year ended 31 March 1919.*

U.G. 45-19, *Interim Rapport van de Lage Graad Mijnen Kommissie, 1919.*

U.G. 34-20, *Final Report of the Low Grade Mines Commission, 1919.*

U.G. 34-22, *Report of the Department of Native Affairs for the years 1913 to 1918.*

U.G. 39-25, *Report of the Native Churches Commission.*

Union of South Africa. House of Assembly Debates, 1911, 1912, 1914-1915.

Union of South Africa. Union Statistics for Fifty Years, Jubilee Issue, 1960.

Acts of the Union of South Africa, 1912.

II. BRITAIN

Parliamentary Debates (House of Commons), 1916.

C. OTHER OFFICIAL PUBLICATIONS

Annual Address of the President of the Transvaal Chamber of Mines, 1915.

Annual Address of the President of the Transvaal Chamber of Mines, 1916.

Annual Address of the President of the Transvaal Chamber of Mines,
1917.
Annual Address of the President of the Transvaal Chamber of Mines,
1918.
Annual Address of the President of the Transvaal Chamber of Mines,
1919.
Annual Report of the Witwatersrand Native Labour Association,
1914.
Annual Report of the Witwatersrand Native Labour Association,
1915.
Annual Report of the Witwatersrand Native Labour Association,
1916.
Annual Report of the Witwatersrand Native Labour Association,
1918.
Annual Report of the Witwatersrand Native Labour Association,
1919.
Juta's Daily Reporter: Decisions of the Cape Provincial Division of the
Supreme Court of South Africa, 1918.

D. SOURCE PUBLICATIONS

Barnes, J. and Nicholson, D. (eds.) *The Leo Amery Diaries, I,*
1896-1929, London, 1980.
Hancock, W.K. and Van der Poel, J. (eds.), *Selections from the Smuts*
Papers, III, 1910-1919; IV, 1918-1919; V, 1919-1934, Cambridge,
1966 and 1973.
Houghton, D.H. and Dagut, J. (eds.), *Source Material on the South*
African Economy, 1860-1970: 2, 1899-1919, Cape Town, 1972.
Karis, R. and Carter, G.M. (eds.), *From Protest to Challenge: A*
documentary history of African politics in South Africa, 1882-1964, I,
Protest and Hope, 1882-1934; 4, Political Profiles, 1882-1964, Stanford, 1972 and 1977.
Lewsen, P., *Selections from the Correspondence of John X Merriman,*
1905-1924, Van Riebeeck Society, 50, Cape Town, 1969.
Meinertzhagen, R., *Army Diary, 1899-1926*, London, 1960.

E. NEWSPAPERS AND PERIODICALS

Abantu-Batho, 1917-1919, 1923.

African Times and Orient Review, 1917.
African World, 1914-1916.
Agricultural Journal of South Africa, 1914-1920.
Alice Times, 1916-1918.
A.P.O., 1914-1915, 1919.
Cape Times, 1914-1921, 1936.
Cape Times Annual, 1919.
Church Times, 1914-1916.
City Press, 1984.
Contact, 1960.
Daily Chronicle, 1916.
De Burger, 1916-1918.
De Volkstem, 1914-1919.
Diamond Fields Advertiser, 1914-1918.
East London Daily Dispatch, 1914-1917.
Farmer's Weekly, 1914-1920.
Het Volksblad, 1916.
Ilanga Lase Natal, 1914-1920.
Imvo Zabantsundu, 1914-1920.
Inkundla ya Bantu, 1944.
Izwe la Kiti, 1914-1915.
Izwe Lase Afrika, 1941-1942.
Natal Advertiser, 1916-1917.
Natal Mercury, 1914-1919.
Native Teachers Journal, 1920.
Ons Vaderland, 1915-1916.
Pretoria News, 1916-1917.
Rand Daily Mail, 1914-1920.
Round Table, 1914-1918.
South Africa, 1916-1919.
Sowetan, 1984.
Sunday Express, 1938.
Sunday Times, 1914-1918.
Territorial News, 1914-1918.
The African Defender, 1938.
The African World, 1914, 1916.
The Bantu World, 1946.
The Christian Express, 1914-1920.
The Church Abroad, 1917.
The Friend, 1914, 1916.

The Imperialist, 1914-1918.
The South African Review, 1918.
The Star, 1914, 1916-1919, 1952, 1967.
The Times, 1916.
Transvaal Leader, 1914-1915.
Tsala ea Batho, 1914-1915.
Zululand Times, 1916-1917.

F. BOOKS, JOURNAL ARTICLES, PAMPHLETS, UNPUBLISHED THESES AND PAPERS.

Abrams, P., 'The failure of social reform' in *Past and Present*, 26, 1963.

Adler, F.B., Lorch, A.E. and Curson, H.H., *The South African Field Artillery in German East Africa and Palestine, 1915-1919*, Pretoria, 1958.

Allport, G.W., *The Nature of Prejudice*, New York, 1958.

Allport, G.W. and Postman, L., *The Psychology of Rumour*, New York, 1947.

Andrew, C.M. and Kanya-Forstener, A.S., 'France, Africa and the First World War' in *Journal of African History*, XIX, 1, 1978.

A.P.S. Pamphlet, *British Africans in Europe and the Work of the Welfare Committee*, London, 1917.

Ballinger, M., *From Union to Apartheid*, Cape Town, 1969.

Barbeau, A.E. and Henri, F., *The Unknown Soldiers: Black American Troops in World War I*, New York, 1974.

Beaton, A.J., 'Railway construction during the campaign of 1914-1915 in German South West Africa' in *Transactions of the South African Society of Civil Engineers*, July 1916.

Beinart, W., *The Political Economy of Pondoland 1860-1930*, Cambridge and Johannesburg, 1982.

Beinart, W. and Bundy, C., 'State intervention and rural resistance in the Transkei, 1900-1915' in M.A. Klein (ed.), *Peasants in Africa, Historical and Contemporary Perspectives*, London, 1980.

Bevan, E., *Brothers All: The war and the race question*, London, 1915.

Bisset, W.M., 'Unexplored aspects of South Africa's First World War history' in *Militaria*, 6/3, 1976.

Blignaut, C.J.J., 'Die reënval van die Pietersburg-plato', Unpublished

M.A. dissertaion, University of Pretoria, 1952.

Bloch, G., 'The development of the manufacturing industry in South Africa, 1939-1969', unpublished M.A. dissertation, University of Cape Town, 1980.

Boell, L., *Die Operationen in Ostafrika: Weltkrieg, 1914-1918*, Hamburg, 1951.

Bond, B. and Roy, I. (eds.). *War and Society, I* and *II*, London, 1975 and 1977.

Bonner, P.L., 'The 1920 black mineworkers' strike: a preliminary account' in Bozzoli, B. (ed.), *Labour, Townships and Protest: Studies in the social history of the Witwatersrand*, Johannesburg, 1979.

Bonner, P.L., 'The Transvaal Native congress, 1917-1920: The radicalisation of the black petty bourgeoisie on the Rand' in Marks, S. and Rathbone, R. (eds.), *Industrialisation and social change in South Africa: African class formation, culture and consciousness*, London, 1982.

Bouch, R.J., 'The railways and the war effort, 1914-1915' in *Militaria*, 4/3, 1972.

Bottomley, J., 'The South African Rebellion of 1914: the influence of industrialisation, poverty and poor whiteism', African Studies Institute, University of the Witwatersrand, Seminar Paper, June 1982.

Bozzoli, B., *The Political Nature of a Ruling Class: Capital and ideology in South Africa, 1890-1933*, London, 1981.

Bozzoli, B. (ed.), *Town and Countryside in the Transvaal: Capitalist penetration and popular response*, Johannesburg, 1983.

Bozzoli, B., 'Class, community and ideology in the evolution of South Africa society', African Studies Institute, University of the Witwatersrand, Seminar Paper, May 1985.

Bradford, H., 'Mass movements and the petty bourgeoisie: the social origins of I.C.U. leadership, 1924-1929' in *Journal of African History*, 25, 1984.

Brown, I.C., *Understanding Race Relations*, New York, 1973.

Brownlee, W.T., *Reminiscences of a Transkeian*, Pietermaritzburg, 1975.

Buchan, J., *History of the South African Forces in France*, London, 1921.

Buchanan, A.R., *Black Americans in World War II*, Santa Barbara, 1977.

Buell, R.L., *The Native Problem in Africa. I and II*, New York, 1928.

Bundy, C., *The Rise and Fall of the South African Peasantry*, London, 1979.

Bundy, C., 'Dissidents, detectives, and the dipping revolt: social control and collaboration in East Griqualand in 1914', Centre for Southern African Studies, University of York, Seminar Paper, 1982.

Buxton, S.C., *General Louis Botha*, London, 1924.

Callaway, G., 'Umlungu: or the European in South Africa' in *East and West*, February, 1917.

Chanock, M., *Unconsummated Union: Britain, Rhodesia, and South Africa, 1900-1945*, Manchester, 1977.

Chilvers, H.A., *The Story of De Beers*, London, 1939.

Coetzee, D.J.J., 'Die onafhanklikheidstrewe van die Nasionale Party' in Marais, A.H. and Geyser, O. (eds.), *Die Geskiedenis van die Nasionale Party 1910-1924, I: Agtergrond stigting en konsolidasie*, Cape Town, 1975.

Collyer, J.J., *The Campaign in German South West Africa, 1914-1915*, Pretoria, 1937.

Crosby, A.W. jr., 'The Pandemic of 1918' in J.E. Osborn, *Influenza in America, 1918-1976*, New York, 1977.

Crowder, M., 'The impact of two world wars on Africa' in *History Today*, 34, January 1984.

Crowe, J.H.B., *General Smuts' Campaign in East Africa*, London, 1918.

Dalby, D. and Harrison Church, R.J. (eds.), *Drought in Africa*, London, 1977.

Davenport, T.R.H., *The Beginnings of Urban Segregation in South Africa: The Natives (Urban Areas) Act of 1923 and its background* Rhodes University, Occasional Papers, 15, Grahamstown, 1971.

De Kock, M.H., *Selected Subjects in the Economic History of South Africa*, Cape Town, 1924.

Desmore, A.J.B., *With the 2nd Cape Corps thro' Central Africa*, Cape Town, 1920.

De Villiers, J., 'Die Kaapse Regiment, 1806-1817' in *South African Historial Journal*, 7, 1975.

De Wet, J.M., *'n Lewenskets van Jopie Fourie*, Cape Town, 1946.

Dieterlen, H., *Bahlankana ba Fora* ('The Sons of France'), Morija, 1918.

Difford, I.D., *The Story of the 1st Battalion Cape Corps, 1915-1919*, Cape Town, 1920.

Donajgrodzki, A.P. (ed.), *Social Control in Nineteenth Century Britain*, London, 1977.

Donaldson, K. (ed.), *South African Who's Who, 1919-1920*, Cape Town, 1921.

Downes, W.D., *With the Nigerians in German East Africa*, London, 1919.

Doxey, G.V., *The Industrial Colour Bar in South Africa*, Cape Town, 1961.

Duff, H., 'White men's war in black men's countries' in *The National Review*, LXXXIV, February, 1925.

Duminy, A. and Ballard, C. (eds.), *The Anglo-Zulu War, New Perspectives*, Pietermaritzburg, 1981.

Edgar, R.R., 'Garveyism in Africa: Dr Wellington and the American movement in the Transkei' in *Ufahamu*, VI, 3, 1976.

Edgar, R.R., 'The fifth seal: Enoch Mgijima, the Israelites and the Bulhoek Massacre, 1921', unpublished Ph.D. dissertation, University of California, Los Angeles, 1977.

Edgar, R.R., 'Lesotho and the First World War: Recruiting, resistance and the South African Native Labour Contingent' in *Mohlomi, Journal of Southern African Historical Studies*, III, IV, V, 1981.

Ellinwood, D.C. and Pradhan, S.D. (eds.), *India and World War I*, Columbia, 1978.

Enloe, C.H., *Ethnic Soldiers: state security in a divided society*, New York, 1980.

Evans, M.S., *Black and White in South East Africa*, London, 1911.

Flemmer, M., 'Sir William H. Beaumont and the Natives Land Commission, 1913-1916' unpublished M.A. dissertation, University of Natal, 1976.

Foot, M.R.D. (ed.), *War and Society*, London, 1973.

Frankel, P.H., *Pretoria's Praetorians: civil-military relations in South Africa*, Cambridge, 1984.

Gardner, B., *German East: The story of the First World War in East Africa*, London, 1963.

Garson, N.G., Party politics and the plural society: South Africa, 1910-1929' in *Collected Seminar Papers on the Societies of Southern Africa in the 19th and 20th Centuries*, 10, 1970, Institute of Commonwealth Studies, University of London, London, 1970.

Garson, N.G., 'South Africa and World War I' in *The Journal of Imperial and Commonwealth History*, VIII, 1, 1979.

Greenstein, L.J., 'Military service and the Nandi of Kenya' in *Journal of Modern African Studies*, 16, 3, 1978.

Grundlingh, A.M., 'Die rebellie van 1914: 'n historiografiese verkenning' in *Kleio*, XI, 1 and 2, 1979.

Grundy, K.W., *Soldiers without politics: blacks in the South African armed forces*, Berkeley, 1983.

Hancock, W.K., *Smuts: I, The Sanguine Years, 1870-1919*, Cambridge, 1962.

Hancock, W.K., *Smuts: II, The Fields of Force, 1919-1950*, Cambridge, 1968.

Harris, J.H., 'Native races and peace terms' in *Contemporary Review*, 606, June 1916.

Hellman, E., 'Non-Europeans in the army' in *Race Relations*, X, 2, 1943.

Henri, F., *Bitter Victory: A History of Black Soldiers in World War I*, New York, 1970.

Henriksen, T.H., *Mocambique: A History*, London, 1978.

Hernton, C.C., *Sex and Racism*, New York, 1969.

Hobsbawn, E.J., 'From social history to the history of society' in F. Gilbert and S.R. Graubard (eds.), *Historical Studies Today*, New York, 1972.

Hodges, G.W.T., 'African manpower statistics for the British forces in East Africa' in *Journal of African History*, XIX, 1, 1978.

Holbrook, W.P., 'The impact of the Second World War on the Gold Coast, 1939-1945', unpublished Ph.D. dissertation, Princeton University, 1978.

Hopkins, H., *The Strange Death of Private White: A Victorian scandal that made history*, London, 1977.

Hordern, C., *Military Operations in East Africa, 1914-1916*, London, 1941.

Horwitz, S., 'The non-European war record in South Africa' in E. Hellman and L. Abrahams (eds.), *Handbook on Race Relations in South Africa*, London, 1949.

Howard, M., *War and the Liberal Conscience*, Oxford, 1978.

Howard, M., *War in European History*, Oxford, 1976.

Humphrey, A.M.D., 'South African agriculture in a period of transition, 1913-1924', unpublished Honours dissertation, University of the Witwatersrand, 1978.

Innes, D., *Anglo: Anglo American and the rise of Modern South Africa*, Johannesburg, 1984.

Jabavu, D.D.T., *The Black Problem*, Lovedale, 1920.

Jabavu, D.D.T., 'Native unrest in South Africa' in *International Review of Missions*, 1922.

Jeffreys. M.D.W., 'The "Mendi" and After' in *Africana Notes and News*, 15, 5, March 1963.

Johnstone, H., *The Black Man's Part in the War*, London, 1917.

Johnstone, F.A., *Class, Race and Gold: A study of class relations and racial discrimination in South Africa*, London, 1976.

Kagan, N., 'African settlements in the Johannesburg area, 1903-1923', unpublished M.A. dissertation, University of the Witwatersrand, 1978.

Kallaway, P., 'F.S. Malan, the Cape liberal tradition and South African politics' in *Journal of African History*, XV, 1, 1974.

Kaplan, D.E., 'The South African State: the origins of a racially exclusive democracy' in *The Insurgent Sociologist*, X, 2, Fall 1980.

Karsten, P., *Soldiers and Society: the effect of military service and war on American life*, Westport, 1978.

Katzenellenbogen, S.E., 'Southern Africa and the War of 1914-1918' in Foot, M.R.D. (ed.), *War and Society*, London, 1973.

Keable, R., 'African priests in France' in *The East and West*, January 1918.

Keable, R., *Standing By: War time reflections in France and Flanders*, London, 1919.

Keegan, T., 'Lapsed whites and moral panic: an aspect of the South African ideological crisis', unpublished seminar, University of Cape Town, 1979.

Keegan, T., 'The sharecropping economy, African class formation and the 1913 Natives Land Act in the highveld maize belt' in Marks, S. and Rathbone, R. (eds.), *Industrialisation and Social Change*, London, 1982.

Keiser, R.D., 'The South African Governor-General, 1910-1919', unpublished D.Phil. dissertation, University of Oxford, 1975.

Keith, A.B., *War Government of the British Dominions*, London, 1921.

Kiernan, V.G., 'Colonial Africa and its Armies' in Bond, B. and Roy, I. (eds.), *War and Society, II*, London, 1977.

Killingray, D., 'Repercussions of World War I in the Gold Coast' in

Journal of African History, XIX, 1, 1978.

Killingray, D., 'War and society in British colonial Africa: Themes and Prospects' in Ray, P.I., Shinnie, P. and Williams, D. (eds.), *Into the 80s: The proceedings of the Eleventh Annual Conference of the Canadian Association of African Studies*, Calgary, 1981.

Killingray, D., 'The colonial army in the Gold Coast: Official policy and local response, 1890-1947', unpublished Ph.D. dissertation, University of London, 1982.

Killingray, D. and Matthews, J., 'Beasts of burden: British West African carriers in the First World War' in *Canadian Journal of African Studies*, 13, 1-2, 1979.

Lacey, M., *Working for Boroko: the origins of a coercive labour system in South Africa*, Johannesburg, 1981.

Louis, W.R., *Great Britain and Germany's Lost Colonies*, Oxford, 1969.

Lucas, C. (ed.), *The Empire at War, IV, Africa*, London, 1924.

Marais, A.H., 'Die 'derde rebellie' in *Acta Diurna Historica*, 1, 4, December 1972.

Mariotti, A.M., 'The incorporation of African women into wage employment in South Africa, 1920-1970', unpublished Ph.D. dissertation, University of Connecticut, 1980.

Marks, S. and Rathbone, R. (eds.), *Industrialisation and social change in South Africa: African class formation and consciousness 1870-1930*, London, 1982.

Marks, S., *Reluctant Rebellion: The 1906-1908 disturbances in Natal*, London, 1970.

Marwick, A., *War and Social Change in the Twentieth Century: A comparative study of Britain, France, Germany, Russia and the United States*. London, 1974.

Marwick, A., *Women at War, 1914-1918*, London, 1977.

Matloff, M., 'The nature and scope of military history' in Weigley, R.F. (ed.), *New Dimensions in Military History*, New York, 1975.

Matthews, J.K., 'World War I and the rise of African nationalism: Nigerian veterans as catalysts of change' in *Journal of Modern African Studies*, 20, 3, September 1982.

Mayer, P., 'The origin and decline of two rural resistance ideologies' in P. Mayer (ed.), *Black Villagers in an Industrial Society: Anthropological perspectives on labour migration in South Africa*, Cape Town, 1980.

Mayer, S.L. and Koenig, W.J., *The Two World Wars: A guide to manuscript collections in the United Kingdom*, London, 1976.

McLaughlin, P., *Ragtime Soldiers: The Rhodesian experience in the First World War*, Bulawayo, 1980.

Miller, C., *Battle for the Bundu: The First World War in East Africa*, London, 1974.

Milward, A.S., *The Economic Effects of the World Wars on Britain*, London, 1970.

Molema, S.M., *The Bantu: Past and Present*, Edinburgh, 1920.

Moroney, S., 'Mine worker protest on the Witwatersrand, 1901-1912' in E. Webster (ed.), *Essays in Southern African Labour History*, Johannesburg, 1978.

Mullen, R.W., *Blacks in America's Wars*, New York, 1973.

Nasson, W.R., 'Doing down their masters: Africans, Boers, and treason in the Cape Colony, 1899-1902' in *Journal of Imperial and Commonwealth History*, 12, 1, 1983.

Nasson, W.R., 'Moving Lord Kitchener: black military transport and supply work in the South African War, 1899-1902, with particular reference to the Cape Colony' in *Journal of Southern African Studies*, 11, 1, October 1984.

Nattrass, J., *The South African Economy: Its growth and change*, Cape Town, 1981.

Ncwana, Bennet S.M., *Souvenir of the Mendi Disaster*, Cape Town, 1940.

Nelson, K.L., 'Black horror on the Rhine: Race as a factor in post-World War I diplomacy' in *Journal of Modern History*, 42, 4, December 1970.

Nettleship, M.A., Givens, R.D. and Nettleship, A. (eds.), *War, its Causes and Correlates*, The Hague, 1975.

Ngubo, A., 'The development of African political protest in South Africa, 1882-1910: an analytical approach', unpublished Ph.D. dissertation, University of California, 1973.

Nzula, A.T., and others, *Forced Labour in Colonial Africa*, London, 1979.

Odendaal, A., *Vukani Bantu! The Beginnings of Black Protest Politics in South Africa to 1912*, Cape Town, 1984.

Ogot, B.A. (ed.), *War and Society in Africa*, London, 1972.

Oost, H., *Wie is die Skuldiges?*, Johannesburg, 1958.

Osuntokun, A., *Nigeria in the First World War*, London, 1979.

Osuntokun, A., 'West African armed revolts during the First World

War' in *Tarikh*, 5, 3, August 1979.

Osur, A.M., *Blacks in the Army Air Forces during World War II: The problem of race relations*, New York, 1977.

Page, M.E., 'Malawians in the Great War and after, 1914-1925', unpublished Ph.D. dissertation, Michigan State University, 1977.

Page, M.E., 'Fighting for their world: black men in a white man's war', unpublishd paper, African Studies Association Conference, Washington, D.C., 1982.

Park, R.E., 'The social function of war' in Bramson, L. and Goethals, G.E. (eds.), *War: Studies from Psychology, Sociology and Anthropology*, New York, 1964.

Pearsall, C.W., 'Some aspects of the development of secondary industry in the Union of South Africa' in *The South African Journal of Economics*, 5, 1937.

Peregrino, F.Z.S., *His Majesty's Black Labourers: a treatise on the camp life of the S.A.N.L.C.*, Cape Town, 1917.

Perry, J. and Perry, C. (eds.), *A Chief is a Chief by the People: The Autobiography of Stimela Jason Jingoes*, Oxford, 1975.

Phillips, H., 'The impact of the Spanish 'flu epidemic of 1918 on Cape Town', seminar paper, South African Historical Society Conference, Cape Town, 1985.

Pirio, G.A., 'The role of Garveyism in the making of Southern African working classes and Namibian nationalism', seminar paper, conference on 'South Africa in the Comparative Study of Class, Race and Nationalism', New York, 1982.

Plaatje, S.T., *Native Life in South Africa*, London, 2nd Edition, 1917.

Pollak, H., 'Women in the Witwatersrand industries', unpublished M.A. dissertation, University of the Witwatersrand, 1932.

Potgieter, A.J., 'Die swartes aan die Witwatersrand, 1900-1933', unpublished D.Litt. dissertation, Rand Afrikaans University, 1978.

Qualter, T.H., *Propaganda and Psychological Warfare*, New York, 1965.

Rathbone, R., 'World War I and Africa: Introduction' in *Journal of African History*, XIX, 1, 1978.

Rayner, W.S. and O'Shaughnessy, W.W., *How Botha and Smuts conquered German South West*, London, 1916.

Reinders, R.C., 'Racialism on the Left: E.D. Morel and the "Black Horror on the Rhine' in *International Review of Social History*, 13, 1968.

Robinson, J.P.K., *With Botha's Army*, London, 1916.

Roux, E., *Time Longer than Rope: A history of the black man's struggle for freedom in South Africa*, Madison, 1972.

Rowbotham, S., *Hidden from History: rediscovering women from the 17th century to the present*, New York, 1974.

Saunders, C., 'F.Z.S. Peregrino and the South African Spectator in *Quarterly Bulletin of the South African Public Library*, XXXII, 3, March 1978.

Schleh, E.P.A., 'Post-service careers of African World War Two veterans: British East and West Africa with particular reference to Ghana and Uganda', unpublished Ph.D. dissertation, Yale University, 1968.

Scholtz, G.D., *Die Rebellie, 1914-15*, Johannesburg, 1942.

Scully, W.C., 'The colour problem in South Africa' in *The Edinburgh Review or Critical Journal*, July 1919.

Shepherd, R.H.W., *Lovedale, South Africa: the story of a century*, Lovedale, 1941.

Shepperson, G.A., 'External factors in the development of African nationalism, with particular reference to British Central Africa' in *Phylon*, XXII, 3, 1961.

Shepperson, G.A., 'Nyasaland and the Millenium' in Thrupp, S. (ed.), *Millenial Dreams in Action*, The Hague, 1962.

Shepperson, G.A., 'The comparative study of millenarian movements in Thrupp, S. (ed.), *Millenial Dreams in Action*, The Hague, 1962.

Shepperson, G.A. and Price, T., *Independent Africa: John Chilembwe and the Origins, Settings and Significance of the Nyasaland Native Rising of 1915*, Edinburgh, 1958.

Shiroya, O.J.E., 'The impact of World War II on Kenya: The role of ex-servicemen in Kenyan nationalism', unpublished Ph.D. dissertation, Michigan State University, 1968.

Silburn, P.A., *The Colonies and Imperial Defence*, London, 1909.

Simons, H.J. and Simons, R.E., *Class and Colour in South Africa, 1850-1950*, Harmondsworth, 1969.

Skota, T.D.M., *African Yearly Register*, Johannesburg, 1931.

Smurthwaite, A.G., 'The policy of the Smuts government towards Africans 1919-1924', unpublished M.A. dissertation, University of South Africa, 1975.

Spiers, E.M., *The Army and Society*, London, 1980.

Spies, S.B., *Methods of Barbarism? Roberts and Kitchener and*

Civilians in the Boer Republics, January 1900-May 1902, Cape Town and Pretoria, 1977.

Spies, S.B., 'The outbreak of the First World War and the Botha government' in *South African Historical Journal*, 1, 1969.

Stedman Jones, G., 'Class expression versus social control? A critique of recent trends in the social history of "leisure"' in *History Workshop*, 4, Autumn, 1977.

Stember, E., *Sexual Racism*, New York, 1976.

Sloley, H., 'The African Native Labour Contingent and the Welfare Committee' in *Journal of African Society*, XVII, 1918.

Stuart, J., *A History of the Zulu Rebellion, 1906*, London, 1913.

Stuart-Stephens, D., 'Our million black army' in *The English Review*, October 1916.

Switzer, L. and Switzer, D. (eds.), *The Black Press in South Africa and Lesotho*, Chicago, 1978.

Tate, M., 'The war aims of World War I and World War II and their relation to the darker peoples of the world' in *Journal of Negro Education*, 12, 19, 1943.

Tatz, C.M., *Shadow and Substance in South Africa*, Pietermaritzburg, 1962.

Thompson, L.M., *The Unification of South Africa, 1902-1910*, Oxford, 1960.

Ticktin, D., 'The war issue and the collapse of the South African Labour Party, 1914-15' in *South African Historical Journal*, 1, 1969.

Trapido, S., 'White conflict and non-white participation in the politics of the Cape of Good Hope, 1853-1910', unpublished D.Phil. dissertation, University of London, 1970.

Trew, H.F., *Botha Treks*, London, 1936.

Tylden, G., *The Armed Forces of South Africa with an Appendix on the Commandos*, Johannesburg, 1954.

Van der Horst, S.T., *Native Labour in South Africa*, Cape Town, 1942.

Van der Schyff, P.F., 'Die rebellie wat nooit plaasgevind het nie' in *Die Huisgenoot*, 21 Junie 1968.

Van Onselen, C., *Chibaro: African Mine Labour in Southern Rhodesia, 1900-1933*, London, 1976.

Van Onselen, C., *Studies in the Social and Economic History of the Witwatersrand, 1886-1914: Vol. I. New Babylon, Vol. 2, New Nineveh*, London and Johannesburg, 1982.

Von Lettow-Vorbeck, P.E., *My Reminiscences of East Africa*, London, 1920.

Von Lettow-Vorbeck, P.E., *East African Campaigns*, New York, 1957.

Walshe, P., *The Rise of African Nationalism in South Africa: The African National Congress, 1912-1952*, London, 1970.

Warwick, P., *Black People and the South African War, 1899-1902*, Cambridge and Johannesburg, 1983.

Warwick, P. and Spies, S.B. (eds.), *The South African War, 1899-1902*, London, 1980.

Webster, E., 'Background to the supply and control of labour in the gold mines' in E. Webster (ed.), *Essays in Southern Africa Labour History*, Johannesburg, 1978.

Whittal, W., *With Botha and Smuts in Africa*, London, 1917.

Wickins, P.L., *The Industrial and Commercial Workers' Union of Africa*, Cape Town, 1978.

Willan, B.P., 'The Anti-Slavery and Aborigines Protection Society and the South African Natives' Land Act of 1913' in *Journal of African History*, XX, 1, 1979.

Willan, B.P., 'The role of Solomon T. Plaatje (1876-1932) in South African society', D.Phil. dissertation, University of London, 1979.

Willan, B.P., *Sol Plaatje: a biography*, Johannesburg, 1984.

Willan, B.P., 'The South African Native Labour Contingent, 1916-1918' in *Journal of African History*, XIX, 1, 1978.

Wilson, F., 'Farming, 1866-1966' in Wilson, M. and Thompson, L.M. (eds.), *The Oxford History of South Africa, 1870-1966, II*, London, 1969.

Wilson, F., *Labour in South African Gold Mines, 1911-1969*, Cambridge, 1972.

Winter, J.M. (ed.), *War and Economic Development*, Cambridge, 1975.

Wynn, N.A., *The Afro-American and the Second World War*, London, 1976.

Young, A.D.T., 'British policy towards the Union of South Africa, 1919-1929', unpublished D.Phil. dissertation, Bristol University, 1974.

Young, W.L., *Minorities and the Military: A cross-national study in world perspective*, Westport, 1982.

Yudelman, D., *The Emergence of Modern South Africa: State, capital and the incorporation of organised labour on the South African gold fields, 1902-1939*, Cape Town, 1984.

G. COMMUNICATIONS AND ORAL INTERVIEWS

1. Letter from Dr. Howard Phillips, Department of History, University of Cape Town, 28 September 1981 in connection with the influenza epidemic of 1918.
2. Transcripts of oral interviews with P. Mabatoana (17 and 22 April 1980) and R. Mohapeloa (7 May 1980) at Maseru. (I am indebted to Dr. R.R. Edgar, Howard University, Washington, D.C. for copies of these interviews.)
3. Oral History Project, African Studies Institute, University of the Witwatersrand.
   Transcripts of interviews with: K.S. Modipa (17 October 1979), P.M. Masike (24 February 1980), T. Manoto (26 February 1980), K. Maine (17 September 1980), M. Moloko (20 November 1979) and S. Phala (6 September 1979). (I am indebted to Prof. Charles van Onselen, Director of the Institute, for drawing my attention to these interviews.)

Index

Mahabane, Z.R., 114
Maine, K., 25
Makgatho, S.M., 11, 133, 171
Makohliso, D.S., 64, 125
Malan, F.S., 10, 14, 26
Maritz, S.G., 14
Masabalala, S.M., 131
Matatiele (rebellion, 1914), 19-20, 167
Mdlombo, E., 125
Mendi, 93-96, 139-141
Merriman, J.X., 30, 45, 96
military labour, *see* labour
military service, *see* Africans, South
    African Native Labour Contingent
Militiades, 110
millenarianism, 18, 130-131, 134
mines, *see* Chamber of Mines, diamond
    mines, gold mines
Mine Workers' Union, 148
missionaries, 49
Modiakgotla, D., 131
Mohapeloa, R., 123
Mokwena, M., 125
Mopedi, 24
Mozambique, 59, 60
Msimang, H.S., 134
Mtemba, J., 77
Mvabaza, L.T., 133, 135, 136, 138

Nasson, W.R., 3, 108
Natal, 11, 17-19, 48
National Party, 10, 22, 27, 29, 44-45, 46,
    112, 137
Native Affairs Act (1920), 138
Native Affairs Administration Bill (1917),
    73, 155, 171
Native Labour Contingent, *see* South
    African Native Labour Contingent
Native Land Act, *see* Land Act (1913)
Native Urban Areas Act (1923), 170
Ncwana, S.M. Bennet, 131, 139
Ngcayiya, H.R., 135
Ngoja, J.D., 138
'Ninevites', 79
Nkabindi, S., 18
Northern Transvaal, 75-76, 79, 130
Nourse mines, 15
Nyombolo, B., 131

Nzulu, A., 13

Paget, E., 92
Peregrino, F.Z.S., 61, 63
Phala, S., 79
Phillips, H., 162
Pilane, I., 170
Plaatje, S., 24, 61, 63, 73, 86, 135, 136
political consciousness, *see* Africans,
    South African Native National Con-
    gress, South African Native Labour
    Contingent
Pondoland, 71
Posholi, M.L. 125
Pritchard, S.M., 57, 59, 97, 102, 127
proletarianization, 151
propaganda, 14, 62-63, 71, 97

Rabie, J.J., 27, 28
Ralitane, L., 15
Roets, N.J.R., 28
Roux, E., 129
Rubusana, W., 39

Schreiner, T.L., 38
Sekhukhune II, 70
sex, racism of, 47
Silburn, P.A., 38
Sloley, H., 42, 98
Smit, D.L., 65
Smuts, General J.C., 11, 38, 40, 59, 137
social control, concept of, 101
Solomon, 65-66
South African Defence Force Act (1912),
    37, 38, 39
South African Native Labour Contingent -
    black chaplains of, 104-105, 109
    black elite in, 76-78
    and compound system, 74, 105-109,
        112-114, 168
    control and discipline of, 99-109
    criminals in, 78-79
    decision to disband, 114
    decision to raise, 41-44
    educational classes for, 109
    health of, 98
    and influenza epidemic, 161
    and *Mendi*, 93-96